Ecclesia Aethiopica

Ecclesia Aethiopica

Unveiling the Rich Tapestry of the Ethiopian Orthodox Tewahedo Church

Solomon Sahle

Solomon Sahle
Ecclesia Aethiopica
All rights reserved
Copyright © 2024 by Solomon Sahle

Published by Spines
ISBN: 979-8-89383-904-3

Contents

Foreword

By Solomon Sahle

In my hands rests a manuscript that is more than just a collection of words; it is a portal to a world rich in history, faith, and cultural vibrancy. Ecclesia Aethiopica: Unveiling the Rich Tapestry of the Ethiopian Orthodox Church is not merely a book, but an invitation to embark on a spiritual and intellectual journey into the heart of one of the world's oldest Christian traditions.

As a deacon at Ethiopian Orthodox Church for the past thirty years and a passionate advocate for interfaith understanding, I have long been fascinated by the Ethiopian Orthodox Tewahedo Church. Its unique blend of ancient traditions, vibrant liturgical practices, and deep-rooted social engagement offers a compelling model for how faith can shape and enrich a nation's identity. This book, meticulously researched and beautifully written, provides a comprehensive and insightful exploration of this remarkable institution.

Through its pages, we journey through the Church's long and storied history, witnessing its pivotal role in shaping Ethiopia's political, cultural, and spiritual landscape. We delve into the depths of its theological teachings, uncovering the unique doctrines and beliefs that distinguish Ethiopian Orthodoxy from other Christian traditions. We are immersed in the beauty and mystery of its liturgical practices, the vibrant tapestry of its festivals, and the enduring power of its oral traditions.

But this book is not merely a historical or theological treatise. It is also a celebration of Ethiopian culture, a testament to the Church's profound influence on art, music, literature, and social customs. It is a story of resilience and adaptation, as the Church navigates the challenges of the modern world while remaining steadfast in its commitment to its faith and its people.

As you embark on this journey through the pages of Ecclesia Aethiopica, I invite you to open your hearts and minds to the richness and diversity of the Ethiopian Orthodox Tewahedo Church. May this book inspire you to deepen your understanding of this ancient faith, to appreciate its unique contributions to global Christianity, and to embrace the beauty of its enduring legacy.

Chapter 1

Introduction

Purpose of the Book: Objectives and goals of the book.

"Ecclesia Aethiopica: Unveiling the Rich Tapestry of the Ethiopian Orthodox Church" is not merely a book; it is an invitation to embark on a captivating journey through time, faith, and culture. It seeks to illuminate the multifaceted dimensions of the Ethiopian Orthodox Tewahedo Church, a venerable institution that has played a pivotal role in shaping Ethiopia's history, identity, and spiritual landscape. This book is not just for scholars or theologians; it is for anyone curious about the world's diverse religious traditions, the interplay of faith and culture, and the enduring power of ancient wisdom in the modern world.

The primary objective of this book is to provide a comprehensive and accessible exploration of the Ethiopian Orthodox Tewahedo Church. It aims to delve deep into the Church's historical roots, tracing its origins from the early days of Christianity to its current status as a global faith community. By examining key historical events, influential figures, and theological developments, the book seeks to shed light on the Church's evolution and its enduring impact on Ethiopian society.

Beyond its historical narrative, the book aims to illuminate the unique doctrines and beliefs that distinguish Ethiopian Orthodoxy. It will explore the Church's theological foundations, its interpretations of scripture, and its distinctive liturgical practices. By delving into these theological depths, the book seeks to foster a deeper understanding of the Church's spiritual essence and its contribution to the broader Christian tradition.

Furthermore, the book aims to capture the vibrant cultural tapestry woven by the Ethiopian Orthodox Church. It will explore the Church's role in shaping Ethiopian art, music, literature, and social customs. By examining the interplay of faith and culture, the book seeks to reveal the profound ways in which the Church has influenced and been influenced by the Ethiopian people.

In addition to its scholarly objectives, the book aims to be a source of inspiration and reflection for readers of all backgrounds. It seeks to foster empathy and understanding by sharing the stories of individuals whose lives have been touched by the Ethiopian Orthodox faith. Through personal narratives, historical anecdotes, and theological insights, the book aims to create a connection between the reader and the rich spiritual heritage of Ethiopia.

The book also aims to address contemporary challenges and opportunities facing the Ethiopian Orthodox Church. It will explore the Church's responses to modernization, globalization, and internal divisions. By examining these issues, the book seeks to provide a balanced and nuanced perspective on the Church's role in the 21st century.

Ultimately, the goal of "Ecclesia Aethiopica" is to unveil the rich tapestry of the Ethiopian Orthodox Church in all its complexity and beauty. It seeks to educate, inspire, and foster dialogue, inviting readers to explore the depths of this ancient faith and its enduring legacy. Whether you are a scholar, a student, a person of faith, or simply a curious reader, this book offers a unique opportunity to discover the hidden treasures of Ethiopian Orthodoxy and its profound impact on the world.

Target audience and expected outcomes

"Ecclesia Aethiopica: Unveiling the Rich Tapestry of the Ethiopian Orthodox Church" is tailored to a diverse audience, each with unique interests and expectations. By understanding the target readers and their desired outcomes, the book aims to cater to their specific needs and provide a fulfilling reading experience.

1. Scholars and Students: For scholars and students of religious studies, theology, history, and African studies, this book serves as an invaluable resource. It offers a meticulously researched and comprehensive overview of the Ethiopian Orthodox Tewahedo Church, delving into its historical development, theological nuances, and cultural significance. The book's detailed analysis of doctrines, rituals, and traditions, supported by extensive references and citations, makes it a valuable reference tool for academic research and coursework.

- **Expected Outcomes:** Scholars and students can expect to gain a deeper understanding of the Church's unique place in Christian history, its distinct theological perspectives, and its profound impact on Ethiopian society. The book can serve as a catalyst for further research, sparking new inquiries and contributing to the growing body of knowledge on Ethiopian Orthodoxy.

2. Cultural Enthusiasts: For those fascinated by Ethiopia's rich cultural heritage, this book offers a captivating exploration of the Church's role in shaping and preserving Ethiopian traditions. It delves into the intricate connections between faith and culture, examining how the Church has influenced art, music, literature, and social customs. The book's vivid descriptions and engaging narratives bring Ethiopian culture to life, allowing readers to immerse themselves in its vibrant tapestry.

- **Expected Outcomes:** Cultural enthusiasts can expect to gain a deeper appreciation for the richness and diversity of Ethiopian culture, recognizing the Church's pivotal role in its preservation and evolution. The book can inspire further exploration of Ethiopian arts, crafts, music, and traditions, fostering a greater understanding and appreciation of this unique cultural heritage.

3. Faith Practitioners: For members of the Ethiopian Orthodox Tewahedo Church, both in Ethiopia and the diaspora, this book serves as a source of spiritual nourishment and a means of deepening their faith. It provides a comprehensive overview of the Church's doctrines, rituals, and traditions, offering insights into their historical context and theological significance. The book's emphasis on personal narratives and spiritual reflections can resonate with believers, strengthening their connection to their faith and community.

- **Expected Outcomes:** Faith practitioners can expect to gain a deeper understanding of their own religious heritage, enriching their spiritual practice and fostering a stronger sense of belonging to the Ethiopian Orthodox community. The book can also serve as a valuable resource for religious education, providing a comprehensive and accessible guide to the Church's teachings and practices.

4. General Readers: For general readers with an interest in history, religion, or cultural studies, this book offers a captivating and informative introduction to the Ethiopian Orthodox Tewahedo Church. Its accessible language, engaging narratives, and vivid descriptions make it a pleasure to read, even for those with no prior knowledge of Ethiopian Orthodoxy. The book's balanced and objective approach, presenting multiple perspectives and encouraging critical thinking, makes it a valuable resource for anyone seeking to broaden their understanding of the world's diverse religious traditions.

- **Expected Outcomes:** General readers can expect to gain a newfound appreciation for the richness and complexity of Ethiopian Orthodoxy, recognizing its historical significance, cultural impact, and spiritual depth. The book can spark curiosity and inspire further exploration of Ethiopia's unique heritage, fostering cross-cultural understanding and appreciation.

By catering to these diverse audiences and their specific

needs, "Ecclesia Aethiopica" aims to achieve several key outcomes:

- Education: To educate readers about the history, theology, and cultural significance of the Ethiopian Orthodox Tewahedo Church, providing a comprehensive and accessible resource for scholars, students, and general readers alike.
- Inspiration: To inspire readers with the rich spiritual heritage of Ethiopia, fostering a deeper appreciation for the Church's traditions, rituals, and artistic expressions.
- Dialogue: To promote dialogue and understanding between different faith communities, highlighting the unique contributions of Ethiopian Orthodoxy to the broader Christian tradition.
- Preservation: To contribute to the preservation and promotion of Ethiopian cultural heritage, ensuring that the Church's rich traditions and practices are passed on to future generations.
- Empowerment: To empower members of the Ethiopian Orthodox community, both in Ethiopia and the diaspora, by providing them with a deeper understanding of their faith and its relevance in the modern world.

Through its comprehensive exploration, engaging narrative, and balanced perspective, "Ecclesia Aethiopica" aspires to be more than just a book; it aims to be a bridge between cultures, a source of inspiration, and a catalyst for dialogue and understanding.

Scope and Structure

Explanation of the book's layout.

To ensure a seamless and enriching reading experience, "Ecclesia Aethiopica: Unveiling the Rich Tapestry of the Ethiopian Orthodox Church" is meticulously structured, guiding you through the intricate layers of this ancient faith. Each chapter serves as a stepping stone, building upon the previous one to create a comprehensive and nuanced understanding of the Ethiopian Orthodox Tewahedo Church.

1. **Chapter I: Introduction:** Our journey commences with an introduction that sets the stage, offering a glimpse into Ethiopia's rich historical and cultural tapestry. We'll explore the significance of the Ethiopian Orthodox Church in the nation's life, outlining the key themes that will unfold in the chapters to come. Consider this your invitation to a captivating exploration of faith, history, and culture.

2. **Chapter II: Historical Foundations:** In this chapter, we'll delve into the historical roots of the Church, tracing its origins from the early days of Christianity to its evolution over the centuries. We'll encounter key figures who shaped its destiny and witness the Church's profound impact on Ethiopia's political and cultural landscape.

3. **Chapter III: Doctrines and Beliefs:** Here, we'll unlock the spiritual heart of Ethiopian Orthodoxy, exploring its core doctrines and beliefs. We'll delve into its unique theological perspectives, understanding of the Holy Trinity, Christology, and the role of the Holy Spirit. We'll also examine the Church's sacraments, sacred scriptures, and its relationship with other Christian denominations.

4. **Chapter IV: Liturgy and Worship:** Prepare to be immersed in the rich liturgical traditions of the Ethiopian Orthodox Church. We'll witness the Divine Liturgy, explore the liturgical calendar and festivals, and uncover the significance of icons, religious art, and sacraments in worship. We'll also delve into the Church's unique musical traditions, where prayer, chanting, and traditional instruments intertwine to create a symphony of devotion.

5. **Chapter V: Scriptural Canon:** In this chapter, we'll examine the Ethiopian Orthodox Bible, its unique books, and the importance of the Ge'ez

language in liturgical and scriptural practices. We'll explore the Church's interpretive traditions, its approach to biblical translation, and the role of scripture in religious education.

6. **Chapter VI: Monasticism and Spirituality:** Journey with us into the heart of Ethiopian monasticism, where ancient traditions of prayer, fasting, and spiritual discipline continue to thrive. We'll explore the daily lives of monks and nuns, their contributions to Ethiopian society, and their role in preserving the Church's teachings and traditions.

7. **Chapter VII: Church and State:** This chapter delves into the complex relationship between the Ethiopian Orthodox Church and the state throughout history. We'll examine the Church's influence on political decisions, its role in cultural policy, and the dynamics between Church leaders and state officials. We'll also address the challenges and opportunities presented by the separation and integration of Church and state.

8. **Chapter VIII: Cultural Dimensions:** Prepare to be dazzled by the vibrant cultural tapestry woven by the Ethiopian Orthodox Church. We'll explore its influence on Ethiopian art, music, literature, and social customs. We'll also examine the Church's role in shaping cultural practices, such as traditional clothing, symbols, and festivals.

9. **Chapter IX: Challenges and Adaptations:** In this chapter, we'll confront the contemporary challenges facing the Ethiopian Orthodox Church, including social, political, and technological pressures. We'll explore the Church's responses to these challenges, its efforts to adapt to modernization and globalization, and its strategies for maintaining its relevance in the 21st century.

10. **Chapter X: Global Diaspora:** Our journey takes us beyond Ethiopia's borders to explore the Ethiopian Orthodox diaspora communities around the world. We'll delve into their history, cultural preservation efforts, and their relationship with the mother Church in Ethiopia. We'll also examine the challenges and opportunities faced by diaspora communities, their contributions to global Christianity, and their role in promoting Ethiopian culture and identity.

11. **Chapter XI: Interfaith Relations:** This chapter explores the Ethiopian Orthodox Church's interactions with other Christian denominations and other faiths. We'll examine historical dialogues, collaborative efforts, and the Church's participation in ecumenical movements. We'll also address challenges and conflicts in interfaith relations and their impact on the Church's doctrines and practices.

12. **Chapter XII: Future Perspectives:** As our journey concludes, we'll reflect on the future

prospects of the Ethiopian Orthodox Tewahedo Church. We'll analyze current trends, anticipate future challenges, and identify opportunities for growth and development. We'll also discuss the Church's evolving role in modern Ethiopian society and its potential for global influence.

By following this carefully crafted structure, "Ecclesia Aethiopica" ensures a coherent and engaging narrative that unveils the rich tapestry of the Ethiopian Orthodox Church in all its complexity and beauty. Each chapter builds upon the previous one, providing a comprehensive and nuanced understanding of this ancient faith and its enduring legacy.

Overview of main themes covered

In the following chapters, we will embark on a captivating exploration of the Ethiopian Orthodox Tewahedo Church, delving into its multifaceted dimensions and uncovering the rich tapestry that makes it a unique and enduring institution. Our journey will encompass a wide range of themes, each shedding light on a different facet of this ancient faith.

We will trace the historical roots of the Church, from its legendary beginnings to its establishment as the state religion of Aksum. We will witness the pivotal moments that shaped its evolution, from the rise of monasticism to the challenges of modernization and globalization. Through this historical lens, we will gain a deeper understanding of the Church's resilience, adaptability, and enduring influence on Ethiopian society.

At the heart of our exploration lies the spiritual essence of Ethiopian Orthodoxy. We will delve into the Church's core doctrines and beliefs, examining its unique theological perspectives and its interpretations of scripture. We will uncover the mysteries of its liturgical practices, the symbolism of its art and architecture, and the profound significance of its sacraments. Through this spiritual lens, we will gain a deeper appreciation for the Church's rich traditions and its enduring appeal to millions of believers.

Our journey will also take us beyond the walls of churches and monasteries, exploring the Church's profound impact on Ethiopian culture. We will witness how faith and culture intertwine, shaping art, music, literature, and social customs. We will discover the vibrant tapestry of Ethiopian traditions, from the colorful festivals to the intricate rituals of daily life, and we will see how the Church has played a central role in preserving and enriching this cultural heritage.

As we venture into the modern era, we will confront the challenges and opportunities facing the Ethiopian Orthodox Church in the 21st century. We will examine the impact of modernization, globalization, and internal divisions on the Church's traditions and practices. We will also explore the Church's responses to these challenges, its efforts to adapt and evolve while remaining true to its core values.

Our exploration will not be confined to Ethiopia's borders. We will journey with the Ethiopian diaspora, tracing their history, cultural preservation efforts, and their relationship with the mother Church. We will witness the challenges and triumphs of diaspora communities as they strive to maintain their faith and identity in new lands.

Finally, we will broaden our perspective to examine the Ethiopian Orthodox Church's interactions with other Christian denominations and other faiths. We will explore historical dialogues, collaborative efforts, and the Church's participation in ecumenical movements. We will also address the challenges and conflicts that have arisen in interfaith relations and their impact on the Church's doctrines and practices.

As our journey concludes, we will reflect on the future prospects of the Ethiopian Orthodox Tewahedo Church. We will analyze current trends, anticipate future challenges, and identify opportunities for growth and development. We will also discuss the church's evolving role in modern Ethiopian society and its potential for global influence.

Through this comprehensive exploration, "Ecclesia Aethiopica" seeks to unveil the rich tapestry of the Ethiopian Orthodox Church in all its complexity and beauty. It is an invitation to discover the enduring power of faith, the richness of cultural heritage, and the resilience of the human spirit.

Historical Context of Ethiopia

Overview of Ethiopia's ancient history:

In the annals of human civilization, few nations boast a history as rich and captivating as Ethiopia. Nestled in the Horn of Africa, this ancient land has been a cradle of culture, a crossroads of civilizations, and a bastion of faith for millennia. Its historical tapestry is woven with threads of ancient kingdoms, powerful empires, and a unique cultural identity that has endured through the ages.

Ethiopia's history traces back to the dawn of humanity, with archaeological evidence suggesting the presence of early hominids in the region millions of years ago. The discovery of "Lucy" a remarkably well-preserved Australopithecus afarensis skeleton dating back over 3 million years, solidified Ethiopia's place as a significant site in the study of human origins.

As the centuries unfolded, Ethiopia witnessed the rise and fall of various kingdoms and empires. The Kingdom of Aksum, which flourished from the 1st to the 8th centuries AD, stands as a testament to Ethiopia's early prominence. Aksum's strategic location along trade routes connecting the Roman Empire, India, and the Far East fueled its economic and cultural growth. The kingdom's adoption of Christianity in the 4th century, under the reign of King Ezana, marked a pivotal moment in Ethiopian history, establishing a religious tradition that continues to shape the nation's identity to this day.

The Aksumite Empire left behind a legacy of impressive architectural feats, including towering obelisks and intricately carved stelae, which serve as enduring symbols of Ethiopia's ancient grandeur. The kingdom's influence extended beyond its borders, with its maritime trade routes reaching as far as India and Ceylon. Aksum's decline in the 8th century, attributed to various factors including economic shifts and the rise of Islam in the region, marked the end of an era but did not diminish Ethiopia's historical significance.

Following the decline of Aksum, Ethiopia entered a period of political fragmentation and regional kingdoms. The Zagwe dynasty, which rose to power in the 12th century, ushered in a new era of artistic and architectural achievements. The rock-hewn churches of Lalibela, carved out of solid volcanic rock, stand as a testament to the Zagwe's devotion to Christianity and their remarkable engineering skills. These monolithic churches, often referred to as the "New Jerusalem," continue to be a site of pilgrimage and spiritual significance for Ethiopian Orthodox Christians.

The Solomonic dynasty, which claimed descent from the biblical King Solomon and the Queen of Sheba, ascended to power in the 13th century and ruled Ethiopia for over 700 years. This dynasty solidified Ethiopia's Christian identity and expanded its territorial reach. The Solomonic kings, such as Emperor Zara Yaqob and Emperor Lebna Dengel, played crucial roles in defending Ethiopia against external threats and fostering cultural and religious development.

The 16th century brought significant challenges to Ethiopia, with the rise of the Ottoman Empire and the expansion of Islam in the region. The Ethiopian-Adal War, a protracted conflict between Christian Ethiopia and the Muslim Adal Sultanate, tested the resilience of the Ethiopian state and its people. Despite facing formidable adversaries, Ethiopia emerged from this conflict with its independence intact, a testament to the unwavering faith and determination of its people.

The 19th century marked a period of modernization and consolidation under Emperor Tewodros II and Emperor Menelik II. These visionary leaders sought to centralize power, modernize the military, and resist European colonial ambitions. Menelik II's decisive victory over Italian forces at the Battle of Adwa in 1896 secured Ethiopia's independence and made it a symbol of African resistance against colonialism.

The 20th century brought both triumphs and tribulations to Ethiopia. The Italian occupation during World War II and the subsequent overthrow of Emperor Haile Selassie in 1974 ushered in a period of political instability and social upheaval. The Derg regime, a Marxist-Leninist military junta, ruled Ethiopia with an iron fist, implementing radical reforms and suppressing dissent. The Ethiopian Civil War, which raged for over a decade, resulted in widespread suffering and loss of life.

In 1991, the Ethiopian People's Revolutionary Democratic Front (EPRDF) overthrew the Derg regime and established a new government. The EPRDF, led by Meles Zenawi, implemented economic reforms and initiated a process of political liberalization. However, the EPRDF's rule was not without controversy, with accusations of human rights abuses and political repression.

In recent years, Ethiopia has experienced a period of significant political change and social unrest. The resignation of Prime Minister Hailemariam Desalegn in 2018 and the subsequent appointment of Abiy Ahmed as Prime Minister marked a turning point in Ethiopian politics. Abiy Ahmed's ambitious reform agenda, which included releasing political prisoners, opening up the political space, and making peace with Eritrea, earned him international acclaim and the Nobel Peace Prize. However, his reforms also unleashed long-suppressed ethnic tensions, leading to conflict and displacement in several regions of the country.

Key historical events shaping Ethiopian identity

Ethiopia's identity has been shaped by a series of pivotal historical events that have left an enduring mark on its cultural, religious, and political landscape. These events, spanning centuries, have forged a unique national character that is both resilient and deeply rooted in tradition.

1. **Early Christianization (4th Century):** The adoption of Christianity in the 4th century, under King Ezana of Aksum, was a watershed moment in Ethiopian history. It not only established Ethiopia as one of the first Christian nations but also laid the foundation for the Ethiopian Orthodox Tewahedo Church, which became deeply intertwined with the country's cultural and social fabric. This early embrace of Christianity set Ethiopia apart from its neighbors and contributed to its distinct identity.

2. **The Rise of Islam and Ethiopian Isolation (7th Century):** The rise of Islam in the 7th century and the subsequent expansion of Muslim empires in the region led to Ethiopia's relative isolation. This isolation, while posing challenges, also allowed the Ethiopian Orthodox Church to develop its unique traditions and practices, further solidifying its role as a central pillar of Ethiopian identity.

3. **The Solomonic Dynasty (13th Century):**
   The establishment of the Solomonic dynasty, which claimed descent from the biblical King Solomon and the Queen of Sheba, reinforced Ethiopia's connection to ancient biblical traditions. This dynasty played a crucial role in consolidating power, expanding the empire, and promoting Christianity throughout the land.

4. **The Ethiopian-Adal War (16th Century):**
   The Ethiopian-Adal War was a fierce conflict between Christian Ethiopia and the Muslim Adal Sultanate. Ethiopia's victory in this war, despite being outnumbered and outgunned, solidified its reputation as a resilient and independent nation. This victory also had a profound impact on Ethiopian national identity, reinforcing the importance of faith and resistance against external threats.

5. **The Battle of Adwa (1896):** Emperor Menelik II's decisive victory over Italian forces at the Battle of Adwa in 1896 was a defining moment in African history. It marked one of the few instances where an African nation successfully resisted European colonialism. This victory not only preserved Ethiopia's independence but also made it a symbol of hope and resistance for the entire continent.

6. **Italian Occupation and Resistance (1935-1941):** The Italian occupation of Ethiopia during

World War II was a dark chapter in the nation's history. However, the Ethiopian resistance movement, led by Emperor Haile Selassie, ultimately succeeded in liberating the country with the help of British forces. This period of occupation and resistance further strengthened Ethiopian national identity and resolve.

7. **The Derg Regime and Civil War (1974-1991):** The overthrow of Emperor Haile Selassie in 1974 and the subsequent Derg regime, marked by political repression and civil war, were tumultuous times for Ethiopia. The resilience of the Ethiopian people during this period, their ability to endure hardship and ultimately overthrow the regime, is a testament to their strength and determination.

8. **The Rise of Abiy Ahmed and Political Reforms (2018-Present):** The appointment of Abiy Ahmed as Prime Minister in 2018 ushered in a new era of hope and change in Ethiopia. His ambitious reform agenda, including peace with Eritrea and political liberalization, earned him international recognition. However, the challenges and conflicts that have arisen during his tenure highlight the complexities of Ethiopia's political landscape and the ongoing struggle to forge a united national identity.

These key historical events, while not exhaustive, provide a glimpse into the forces that have shaped Ethiopian identity. They reveal a nation that has faced adversity with resilience, embraced its unique cultural and religious heritage, and continuously strived for progress and unity. The Ethiopian Orthodox Tewahedo Church, as a central institution throughout much of this history, has played a pivotal role in shaping and preserving this identity, making it an integral part of the nation's story.

Cultural Background

Significance of culture in Ethiopia:

In the heart of Ethiopia, culture is not merely a collection of traditions and customs; it is the lifeblood that courses through the veins of the nation, shaping its identity, values, and worldview. The significance of culture in Ethiopia is profound and multifaceted, permeating every aspect of life, from the spiritual to the mundane. It is a tapestry woven with threads of ancient traditions, diverse ethnic groups, and a deep-rooted sense of community.

At its core, Ethiopian culture is a celebration of diversity. The nation is home to over 80 distinct ethnic groups, each with its own language, customs, and traditions. This rich mosaic of cultures has created a vibrant and dynamic society, where different communities coexist and contribute to the nation's unique identity. The Amhara, Oromo, Tigray, Somali, and countless other ethnic groups have all played a role in shaping Ethiopia's cultural landscape, enriching it with their unique perspectives and contributions.

One of the most striking aspects of Ethiopian culture is its deep connection to the land. The rugged mountains, fertile valleys, and vast plains of Ethiopia have not only provided sustenance for its people but have also inspired their art, music, and folklore. The land is revered as a source of life and a sacred connection to ancestors. This reverence for nature is reflected in traditional agricultural practices, religious rituals, and even in the design of Ethiopian homes and villages.

Religion plays a central role in Ethiopian culture, with the Ethiopian Orthodox Tewahedo Church being the dominant faith. The Church's teachings, rituals, and traditions have permeated every aspect of Ethiopian life, from birth to death. Religious festivals, such as Timkat and Meskel, are celebrated with great fervor and are integral to the cultural calendar. The Church's influence extends beyond the spiritual realm, shaping social norms, ethical values, and even artistic expressions.

Ethiopian culture is also characterized by a strong sense of community and social cohesion. Family ties are paramount, and communal values are deeply ingrained in the social fabric. Traditional social structures, such as the "Idir" and "Ekub," provide support networks for individuals and families, fostering a sense of belonging and mutual responsibility. These communal values are reflected in various aspects of life, from the sharing of meals to the collective celebration of festivals.

The arts are a vibrant expression of Ethiopian culture, showcasing the creativity and ingenuity of its people. Traditional music, with its unique scales and rhythms, is an integral part of religious ceremonies, social gatherings, and everyday life. Ethiopian dance, characterized by its graceful movements and intricate footwork, is a visual feast that tells stories of history, mythology, and everyday life. Traditional crafts, such as weaving, pottery, and metalwork, are not only functional but also artistic expressions of cultural identity.

Ethiopian cuisine is a culinary adventure, reflecting the diversity of the land and its people. Injera, a spongy sourdough flatbread, is a staple food that is eaten with various stews and curries. Coffee, believed to have originated in Ethiopia, is a national treasure and an integral part of social rituals. The Ethiopian coffee ceremony, elaborate ritual involving the roasting, grinding, and brewing of coffee, is a cherished tradition that brings people together and fosters social bonds.

Language is another important aspect of Ethiopian culture. Amharic, the official language, is spoken by a majority of the population, but there are also numerous other languages spoken by different ethnic groups. This linguistic diversity is a testament to the richness and complexity of Ethiopian culture.

In recent years, Ethiopia has experienced rapid modernization and globalization, which have brought both challenges and opportunities. While some traditional practices and values are being challenged by modern influences, there is also a growing awareness of the importance of preserving cultural heritage. Efforts are underway to document and promote traditional arts, crafts, and music, ensuring that they are passed on to future generations.

The Ethiopian diaspora, scattered across the globe, plays a crucial role in preserving and promoting Ethiopian culture. Diaspora communities have established cultural centers, organized festivals, and published literature, all aimed at keeping their cultural heritage alive. They also serve as ambassadors of Ethiopian culture, introducing it to new audiences and fostering cross-cultural understanding.

The significance of culture in Ethiopia cannot be overstated. It is the glue that binds the nation together, providing a sense of identity, belonging, and continuity. It is a source of pride and inspiration, a testament to the resilience and creativity of the Ethiopian people. As Ethiopia continues to evolve and adapt to the challenges of the modern world, its culture remains a beacon of hope and a source of strength, reminding its people of their rich heritage and their potential for a bright future.

Cultural Background

Ethiopia's cultural milestones are not merely events frozen in time; they are living testaments to the nation's enduring spirit and its ability to adapt and thrive amidst changing tides. These milestones, etched in the annals of history, have shaped the nation's identity, values, and aspirations, leaving an enduring legacy that continues to inspire and guide its people.

The Aksumite Obelisks (4th Century): The towering obelisks of Aksum, some reaching over 100 feet in height, are not only architectural marvels but also symbols of Ethiopia's ancient ingenuity and cultural sophistication. These intricately carved stone structures, believed to mark royal tombs, stand as silent witnesses to the Aksumite Empire's power and influence. They are a testament to the advanced engineering and artistic skills of the time, and their preservation serves as a reminder of Ethiopia's rich historical heritage.

The Rock-Hewn Churches of Lalibela (12th Century): The rock-hewn churches of Lalibela, carved out of solid volcanic rock, are a testament to the Zagwe dynasty's devotion to Christianity and their remarkable architectural vision. These eleven monolithic churches, each with its unique design and intricate carvings, are a UNESCO World Heritage site and a pilgrimage destination for Ethiopian Orthodox Christians. They represent a fusion of faith, artistry, and engineering, and their enduring presence is a source of national pride.

The Kebra Nagast (14th Century): The Kebra Nagast, or "Glory of Kings," is a literary masterpiece that intertwines history, mythology, and religious beliefs. It narrates the legendary story of the Queen of Sheba's visit to King Solomon and the birth of their son, Menelik I, who is believed to have brought the Ark of the Covenant to Ethiopia. This epic tale has played a crucial role in shaping Ethiopian national identity, reinforcing the belief in the divine origins of the Solomonic dynasty and Ethiopia's special place in biblical history.

The Zemene Mesafint (Era of the Princes) (18th-19th Centuries): The Zemene Mesafint, a period of political fragmentation and regional rivalries, was a time of cultural and intellectual ferment. Despite the political instability, this era witnessed a flourishing of literature, poetry, and religious scholarship. The Zemene Mesafint also saw the emergence of regional cultural centers, each with its unique artistic and literary traditions, contributing to the diversity and richness of Ethiopian culture.

The Battle of Adwa and Its Cultural Impact (1896): The Battle of Adwa, a resounding victory over Italian colonial forces, had a profound cultural impact on Ethiopia. It not only solidified Ethiopia's independence but also instilled a sense of national pride and unity. The battle became a symbol of African resistance against colonialism and inspired artistic expressions, including poetry, music, and visual arts, that celebrated Ethiopian heroism and resilience.

The Ethiopian Coffee Ceremony (Ancient Tradition): The Ethiopian coffee ceremony is a cherished cultural tradition that has been passed down through generations. It is a ritualistic process involving the roasting, grinding, and brewing of coffee, accompanied by the burning of incense and the sharing of stories and conversation. This ceremony is not merely about consuming coffee; it is a social event that fosters community bonds, promotes hospitality, and provides a space for relaxation and reflection.

The Gurage Cluster and Its Cultural Significance (Ongoing): The Gurage cluster, a group of culturally and linguistically related communities in southern Ethiopia, is known for its unique cultural practices and traditions. The Gurage people have a rich heritage of music, dance, and craftsmanship, and their agricultural practices, such as the cultivation of enset (false banana), are deeply rooted in their cultural identity. The Gurage cluster's cultural significance lies in its ability to preserve and celebrate its distinct traditions while contributing to the broader tapestry of Ethiopian culture.

The Ethiopian Diaspora and Its Cultural Contributions (Ongoing): The Ethiopian diaspora, scattered across the globe, plays a vital role in preserving and promoting Ethiopian culture. Diaspora communities have established cultural centers, organized festivals, and published literature, all aimed at keeping their cultural heritage alive. They also serve as ambassadors of Ethiopian culture, introducing it to new audiences and fostering cross-cultural understanding. The diaspora's contributions to Ethiopian culture are multifaceted, ranging from the preservation of traditional music and dance to the promotion of Ethiopian cuisine and fashion.

These cultural milestones, spanning centuries and encompassing diverse aspects of Ethiopian life, collectively paint a portrait of a nation that cherishes its heritage, celebrates its diversity, and embraces its unique identity. They are not merely historical events but living traditions that continue to shape and enrich Ethiopian culture, making it a vibrant and dynamic force in the world.

Ethiopian Orthodox Church Overview

Brief history of the church's founding:

The Ethiopian Orthodox Tewahedo Church, a beacon of ancient Christianity, traces its origins to the earliest days of the faith. Its foundation is steeped in legend and historical accounts, intertwining with the rich tapestry of Ethiopian history and culture. While the exact details of its founding are shrouded in some mystery, the narrative that emerges is one of divine providence, missionary zeal, and the unwavering faith of a nation.

According to Ethiopian tradition, the seeds of Christianity were first sown in the land by none other than the Apostles themselves. It is believed that St. Matthew and St. Bartholomew, two of Jesus's twelve disciples, ventured into Ethiopia to spread the Gospel. While historical evidence for their presence is limited, this tradition underscores the deep-rooted belief in Ethiopia's early connection to Christianity.

The more concrete establishment of the Church is attributed to St. Frumentius, a Syrian Christian who, in the 4th century AD, found himself shipwrecked on the Ethiopian coast. Frumentius, a devout and learned man, was taken to the royal court of Aksum, where he gained the favor of the king and queen. He began to share his Christian faith with the royal family and the court, eventually baptizing King Ezana and Queen Sofya. This pivotal event marked the official adoption of Christianity as the state religion of Aksum, laying the foundation for the Ethiopian Orthodox Church.

Frumentius's missionary efforts did not end there. He traveled to Alexandria, Egypt, where he was consecrated as the first bishop of Aksum by St. Athanasius, the Patriarch of Alexandria. Upon his return to Ethiopia, Frumentius, now known as Abba Selama (Father of Peace), continued to spread the Gospel, establishing churches, ordaining clergy, and translating the Bible into Ge'ez, the ancient Ethiopian language. His tireless efforts earned him the title of

"Apostle of Ethiopia," and he is revered as a saint by the Ethiopian Orthodox Church.

The Aksumite Empire, with its newly established Christian faith, became a center of religious and cultural activity. Churches and monasteries were built, and a vibrant Christian community flourished. The Church's influence extended beyond the spiritual realm, shaping the empire's laws, customs, and social structures. The Aksumite kings, as patrons of the Church, played a crucial role in its growth and development, providing resources and protection.

The Ethiopian Orthodox Church's connection to the Patriarchate of Alexandria remained strong for centuries. The Abuna, or head of the Church, was traditionally appointed by the Patriarch of Alexandria, and the two churches maintained close ties in matters of doctrine and liturgy. This connection to the broader Christian world enriched the Ethiopian Church's traditions and practices, while also allowing it to develop its unique identity.

The Church's growth was not without challenges. It faced periods of persecution, internal strife, and external threats. However, it persevered, adapting to changing circumstances while maintaining its core beliefs and traditions. The Church's resilience is a testament to the unwavering faith of its followers and its deep roots in Ethiopian society.

The Ethiopian Orthodox Tewahedo Church, as it is formally known, is not merely a religious institution; it is a living embodiment of Ethiopian history, culture, and spirituality. Its founding, steeped in legend and historical accounts, is a testament to the enduring power of faith and the transformative impact of missionary zeal. The Church's journey from its humble beginnings in Aksum to its current status as a global faith community is a story of resilience, adaptation, and unwavering devotion. As we delve deeper into the rich tapestry of Ethiopian Orthodoxy, we will uncover the unique doctrines, rituals, and traditions that have shaped this ancient faith and continue to inspire millions around the world.

Current status and influence in Ethiopia.

In contemporary Ethiopia, the Ethiopian Orthodox Tewahedo Church remains a dominant force, deeply interwoven into the fabric of society and wielding significant influence on both the spiritual and secular spheres. Its legacy as one of the world's oldest Christian institutions continues to shape the nation's identity, values, and daily life.

Spiritual Center: The Church serves as the spiritual center for more than 50% of the Ethiopian population, making it the largest religious institution in the country. Its followers, known for their devoutness and adherence to ancient traditions, find solace, guidance, and community within the Church's embrace. The Church's teachings, rituals, and festivals are integral to the lives of millions, providing a sense of continuity and connection to their spiritual heritage.

Cultural Guardian: Beyond its spiritual role, the Church is a guardian of Ethiopian culture and heritage. Its monasteries and churches house invaluable religious artifacts, manuscripts, and works of art, preserving the nation's rich history and traditions. The Church's liturgical language, Ge'ez, is a testament to Ethiopia's ancient linguistic heritage, and its unique calendar and festivals are deeply ingrained in the cultural fabric of the nation.

Social Influence: The Church's influence extends to the social sphere, where it plays a vital role in education, healthcare, and social welfare. It operates schools, hospitals, and orphanages, providing essential services to communities across the country. The Church also actively participates in social and political discourse, advocating for peace, justice, and the well-being of the Ethiopian people. Its leaders often serve as mediators in conflicts and as voices of moral authority.

Political Engagement: While the Church maintains its independence from the state, it is not immune to political influence. Throughout history, the Ethiopian Orthodox Church has had a complex relationship with the ruling powers, sometimes acting as a partner and advisor, and at other times as a critic and challenger. In recent years, the Church has been vocal on issues such as human rights, ethnic tensions, and the need for national unity. Its leaders have called for peaceful dialogue and reconciliation, playing a crucial role in promoting stability and social cohesion.

Challenges and Adaptations: The Ethiopian Orthodox Tewahedo Church faces numerous challenges in the modern era. The rise of secularism, the influence of globalization, and the pressures of modernization have all tested the Church's ability to maintain its traditions and relevance. Internal divisions and theological debates have also posed challenges to its unity. However, the Church has demonstrated remarkable resilience and adaptability. It has embraced technology, using social media and online platforms to reach new audiences and engage with contemporary issues. It has also initiated reforms and dialogues aimed at addressing internal challenges and promoting unity.

Global Presence: The Ethiopian Orthodox Church's influence extends beyond Ethiopia's borders. With a growing diaspora community in North America, Europe, and other parts of the world, the Church has become a global faith community. Diaspora churches serve as cultural and spiritual centers for Ethiopian communities abroad, preserving their traditions and providing a sense of belonging. The Church also participates in international religious dialogues and ecumenical initiatives, contributing to the broader Christian discourse.

Future Prospects: The Ethiopian Orthodox Tewahedo Church stands at a crossroads, navigating the complexities of the modern world while striving to preserve its ancient traditions. Its future will depend on its ability to adapt to changing circumstances, address internal challenges, and engage with the broader society. The Church's commitment to social justice, its role as a cultural guardian, and its spiritual guidance will continue to be vital for the well-being of Ethiopia and its people. As a symbol of faith, resilience, and cultural identity, the Ethiopian Orthodox Tewahedo Church remains a beacon of hope and inspiration for millions, both within Ethiopia and around the world.

Importance of the Church:

Role of the Ethiopian Orthodox Church in society:

The Ethiopian Orthodox Tewahedo Church is not merely a religious institution; it is a cornerstone of Ethiopian society, a pillar that has supported and shaped the nation's identity, values, and way of life for centuries. Its role extends far beyond the spiritual realm, permeating every aspect of Ethiopian society—from the family unit to the national stage.

Spiritual Guidance and Moral Compass: At its core, the Church serves as the spiritual guide and moral compass for millions of Ethiopians. Its teachings, rooted in ancient Christian traditions, provide a framework for ethical living, emphasizing values such as compassion, humility, and love for one's neighbor. The Church's rituals and sacraments mark significant life events, from birth to death, offering solace, guidance, and a sense of community. Through its teachings and practices, the Church instills a deep sense of faith and devotion in its followers, shaping their worldview and guiding their actions.

Preserver of Cultural Heritage: The Church is not only a spiritual guide but also a guardian of Ethiopia's rich cultural heritage. Its monasteries and churches are repositories of ancient manuscripts, religious artifacts, and works of art, preserving the nation's history and traditions for future generations. The Church's liturgical language, Ge'ez, is a testament to Ethiopia's ancient linguistic heritage, and its unique calendar and festivals are deeply ingrained in the cultural fabric of the nation. The Church's commitment to preserving these traditions ensures that Ethiopia's cultural identity remains vibrant and resilient in the face of modernization and globalization.

Educational and Social Services: The Ethiopian Orthodox Church has long been a champion of education and social welfare. It operates schools, hospitals, and orphanages, providing essential services to communities across the country. The Church's educational institutions have played a crucial role in preserving literacy and knowledge, while its healthcare initiatives have provided much-needed medical care to underserved populations. The Church's commitment to social welfare extends to supporting the poor, the elderly, and the marginalized, embodying the Christian values of compassion and charity.

Community Building and Social Cohesion: The church serves as a vital hub for community building and social cohesion. Its churches and monasteries are not only places of worship but also gathering places for social interaction, cultural exchange, and mutual support. The church's festivals and celebrations bring people together from all walks of life, fostering a sense of unity and shared identity. The Church's emphasis on communal values, such as hospitality, generosity, and respect for elders, strengthens the social fabric of Ethiopian society.

Advocate for Peace and Justice: The Ethiopian Orthodox Church has a long history of advocating for peace, justice, and human rights. Its leaders have often spoken out against injustice, oppression, and violence, calling for reconciliation and dialogue. The Church has played a crucial role in mediating conflicts, promoting peace initiatives, and advocating for the rights of the marginalized. Its moral authority and influence have made it a powerful voice for social justice and a force for positive change in Ethiopia.

Environmental Stewardship: In recent years, the Church has also emerged as a leader in environmental stewardship. Recognizing the interconnectedness of faith and the environment, the Church has launched initiatives to promote sustainable agriculture, conserve natural resources, and raise awareness about environmental issues. Its teachings on the sanctity of creation and the responsibility of humans to care for the earth have resonated with many Ethiopians, inspiring them to take action to protect their environment.

The Ethiopian Orthodox Tewahedo Church's role in society is multifaceted and far-reaching. It is a spiritual guide, a cultural guardian, an educator, a social service provider, an advocate for peace and justice, and a champion of environmental stewardship. Its influence permeates every aspect of Ethiopian life, shaping the nation's values, traditions, and aspirations. As Ethiopia continues to navigate the challenges of the modern world, the Church's role as a unifying force and a source of moral guidance remains as vital as ever.

Impact on national and religious identity

The Ethiopian Orthodox Tewahedo Church's impact on national and religious identity is so profound that it is difficult to imagine Ethiopia without it. The Church has been the custodian of the nation's spiritual heritage, cultural traditions, and historical narratives for centuries, weaving itself into the very fabric of Ethiopian identity.

National Identity: The Church has played a pivotal role in shaping Ethiopia's national identity, providing a unifying force that transcends ethnic and linguistic diversity. Its teachings, rituals, and festivals have fostered a shared sense of belonging and common purpose among Ethiopians of various backgrounds. The Church's historical narratives, often intertwined with national myths and legends, have instilled a sense of pride and continuity, connecting present-day Ethiopians to their ancient roots.

The Church's role in resisting foreign invasions and preserving Ethiopia's independence has further solidified its place in the national consciousness. The Battle of Adwa, a resounding victory against Italian colonial forces, is a source of immense national pride, and the Church's contribution to this victory is widely acknowledged. The Church's symbols, such as the cross and the Lion of Judah, have become national emblems, representing Ethiopia's resilience, faith, and unique identity.

Religious Identity: For millions of Ethiopians, the church is not merely a religious institution but the very foundation of their religious identity. Its doctrines, rituals, and traditions shape their beliefs, values, and worldview. The church's emphasis on communal worship, fasting, and pilgrimage fosters a strong sense of religious community and belonging. The faithful find solace, guidance, and spiritual nourishment within the Church's embrace, and their religious identity is deeply intertwined with their cultural and national identity.

The Church's unique theological perspectives, such as its adherence to Miaphysitism and its veneration of saints and angels, distinguish Ethiopian Orthodoxy from other Christian traditions. These distinctive beliefs and practices have contributed to a strong sense of religious identity among Ethiopian Orthodox Christians, setting them apart from other Christian communities and reinforcing their connection to their ancient faith.

Language and Literature: The Church's use of Ge'ez, an ancient Ethiopian language, in its liturgy and scriptures has had a profound impact on Ethiopian language and literature. Ge'ez, considered a sacred language, has been instrumental in preserving Ethiopia's literary heritage, including religious texts, historical chronicles, and royal edicts. The Church's scribes and scholars have played a crucial role in transmitting knowledge and preserving cultural memory through the ages.

Art and Architecture: The Ethiopian Orthodox Church has also left an indelible mark on Ethiopian art and architecture. Its churches and monasteries, adorned with intricate carvings, vibrant murals, and exquisite icons, are not only places of worship but also artistic treasures. The Church's unique architectural style, characterized by its circular design and conical roofs, is a testament to its rich cultural heritage and its adaptation to the Ethiopian landscape.

Music and Dance: The Church's musical traditions, with their distinctive scales, rhythms, and instruments, are an integral part of Ethiopian cultural expression. Religious chants, hymns, and dances are performed during liturgical services and festivals, creating a vibrant and spiritually uplifting atmosphere. The Church's musical heritage has also influenced secular music and dance, contributing to the richness and diversity of Ethiopian artistic traditions.

Social Values and Ethics: The Church's teachings on morality, ethics, and social responsibility have shaped the values and norms of Ethiopian society. Its emphasis on compassion, humility, generosity, and respect for elders has fostered a strong sense of community and social cohesion. The Church's condemnation of social ills, such as injustice, corruption, and violence, has also contributed to a moral discourse that continues to shape public opinion and policy debates.

In conclusion, the Ethiopian Orthodox Tewahedo Church's impact on national and religious identity is both profound and pervasive. It has shaped the nation's history, culture, and spiritual landscape, providing a unifying force that transcends ethnic and linguistic diversity. Its teachings, rituals, and traditions have fostered a strong sense of religious identity and belonging among its followers. The Church's contributions to language, literature, art, architecture, music, and social values have enriched Ethiopian culture and continue to inspire and guide its people. As Ethiopia navigates the challenges of the modern world, the Church's role as a custodian of national and religious identity remains as vital as ever.

In this opening chapter, we have laid the groundwork for our exploration of the Ethiopian Orthodox Tewahedo Church, a faith deeply intertwined with the history, culture, and identity of Ethiopia. We have journeyed through the annals of time, witnessing the rise and fall of ancient kingdoms, the unwavering spirit of a nation that resisted colonialism, and the enduring legacy of a faith that has shaped the lives of millions.

We have seen how the Church, from its legendary beginnings to its current status as a global faith community, has been a beacon of spiritual guidance, a guardian of cultural heritage, and a champion of social justice. We have glimpsed the profound impact it has had on national and religious identity, shaping Ethiopia's values, traditions, and aspirations.

As we move forward, we will delve deeper into the heart of Ethiopian Orthodoxy, exploring its unique doctrines, vibrant liturgical traditions, and rich monastic heritage. We will uncover the treasures of its scriptural canon, the complexities of its relationship with the state, and the dynamic interplay between faith and culture. We will also confront the challenges and opportunities facing the church in the modern world, examining its responses to modernization, globalization, and internal divisions.

Our journey will take us beyond Ethiopia's borders, exploring the vibrant diaspora communities that have carried the flame of Ethiopian Orthodoxy to new lands. We will witness their struggles, triumphs, and contributions to global Christianity. We will also engage in dialogue with other faiths, exploring the Ethiopian Orthodox Church's interactions with other Christian denominations and its role in interfaith relations.

Finally, we will cast our gaze towards the future, reflecting on the Church's prospects in the 21st century. We will analyze current trends, anticipate future challenges, and identify opportunities for growth and development. We will also consider the Church's evolving role in modern Ethiopian society and its potential for global influence.

This is an invitation to join us on this captivating journey of discovery. Whether you are a scholar seeking in-depth knowledge, a cultural enthusiast eager to explore Ethiopia's rich heritage, a devout believer seeking spiritual nourishment, or simply a curious reader, Ecclesia Aethiopica promises to be a rewarding and enlightening experience. Together, let us unveil the rich tapestry of the Ethiopian Orthodox Tewahedo Church and discover the enduring power of faith, the beauty of cultural diversity, and the resilience of the human spirit.

Chapter 2

Historical Foundations

Early Christianization of Ethiopia

The story of Christianity in Ethiopia is a tale as old as the faith itself, a narrative woven into the very fabric of the nation's history. It is a story of divine providence, missionary zeal, and the unwavering faith of a people who embraced Christianity with open arms and made it their own.

Ethiopia's journey towards Christianity began in the 1st century AD, according to Ethiopian tradition, with the baptism of the Ethiopian eunuch by Philip the Apostle, as recounted in the Acts of the Apostles. This event, while not definitively confirmed by historical records, symbolizes the early seeds of Christianity that were sown in the fertile soil of Ethiopia.

The formal introduction of Christianity to Ethiopia, however, is attributed to the remarkable story of St. Frumentius, a Syrian Christian who, in the 4th century AD, found himself shipwrecked on the Ethiopian coast. Frumentius, a man of deep faith and learning, was taken to the royal court of Aksum, where he quickly gained the favor of King Ezana and Queen Sofya. Recognizing the spiritual hunger of the Ethiopian people, Frumentius began to share the teachings of Christ, planting the seeds of a faith that would soon blossom into a national religion.

Frumentius's missionary efforts bore fruit when he baptized King Ezana and Queen Sofya, a pivotal event that marked the official adoption of Christianity as the state religion of Aksum. This momentous decision not only transformed the spiritual landscape of Ethiopia but also laid the foundation for the Ethiopian Orthodox Tewahedo Church, an institution that would become deeply intertwined with the nation's identity and destiny.

Following his success in Aksum, Frumentius embarked on a journey to Alexandria, Egypt, the seat of early Christian learning and authority. There, he was consecrated as the first bishop of Aksum by St. Athanasius, the Patriarch of Alexandria. This act solidified the Ethiopian Church's connection to the broader Christian world, establishing a link that would endure for centuries.

Upon his return to Ethiopia, Frumentius, now known as Abba Selama (Father of Peace), continued his missionary work with renewed vigor. He established churches, ordained clergy, and translated the Bible into Ge'ez, the ancient Ethiopian language. His tireless efforts earned him the title of "Apostle of Ethiopia," and he is revered as a saint by the Ethiopian Orthodox Church to this day.

The Aksumite Empire, under the guidance of its Christian monarchs, became a center of religious and cultural activity. Churches and monasteries were built, and a vibrant Christian community flourished. The Church's influence extended beyond the spiritual realm, shaping the empire's laws, customs, and social structures. The Aksumite kings, as patrons of the Church, played a crucial role in its growth and development, providing resources and protection.

The early Christianization of Ethiopia was not without its challenges. The church faced opposition from traditional religious practices and occasional persecution. However, it persevered, adapting to local customs and incorporating elements of indigenous beliefs, creating a unique blend of Christianity that resonated with the Ethiopian people.

The Ethiopian Orthodox Tewahedo Church's early history is a testament to the power of faith, the dedication of missionaries, and the receptivity of a nation eager to embrace a new spiritual path. It is a story of resilience, adaptation, and the enduring legacy of a faith that has shaped Ethiopia's identity for over 1600 years.

Role of early evangelists like St. Frumentius

The pivotal figure in Ethiopia's early Christianization was undoubtedly St. Frumentius, a man whose life and actions were guided by divine providence and an unwavering commitment to spreading the Gospel. His arrival in Aksum, though born of a shipwreck, was a turning point in Ethiopian history, setting in motion a chain of events that would forever alter the nation's spiritual landscape.

Frumentius, a young Syrian Christian, found himself at the Aksumite court, where his intelligence, piety, and charisma quickly earned him the trust and respect of King Ezana and Queen Sofya. Recognizing an opportunity to share his faith, Frumentius began to instruct the royal family and members of the court in the teachings of Christianity. His eloquence and passion resonated with the Ethiopians, who were drawn to the message of love, compassion, and salvation that Frumentius preached.

The turning point came when Frumentius baptized King Ezana and Queen Sofya, a momentous event that marked the official adoption of Christianity as the state religion of Aksum. This decision had far-reaching consequences, not only for the Aksumite Empire but for the entire course of Ethiopian history. It laid the foundation for the Ethiopian Orthodox Tewahedo Church, which would become deeply intertwined with the nation's identity and destiny.

Frumentius's role as an evangelist did not end with the conversion of the royal family. He understood that for Christianity to take root in Ethiopia, it needed a solid foundation and a dedicated leadership. He journeyed to Alexandria, Egypt, the center of early Christian learning and authority, where he was consecrated as the first bishop of Aksum by St. Athanasius, the Patriarch of Alexandria. This act not only legitimized Frumentius's authority but also established a vital link between the Ethiopian Church and the broader Christian world.

Upon his return to Ethiopia, Frumentius, now known as Abba Selama, embarked on a mission to establish the infrastructure of the Church. He ordained priests and deacons, built churches, and translated the Bible into Ge'ez, the ancient Ethiopian language. His efforts were not limited to the elite; he reached out to the common people, preaching the Gospel in their language and adapting Christian teachings to their cultural context.

Frumentius's approach to evangelism was characterized by sensitivity, respect, and cultural adaptation. He understood that Christianity could not be imposed on the Ethiopian people but had to be integrated into their existing beliefs and practices. He incorporated elements of indigenous traditions into Christian rituals and ceremonies, creating a unique blend of faith that resonated with the Ethiopian people.

Frumentius's legacy as the "Apostle of Ethiopia" is not merely based on his role in establishing the Church but also on his enduring impact on Ethiopian society. He is credited with introducing literacy, education, and social reforms that transformed the Aksumite Empire. His teachings on compassion, justice, and equality resonated with the Ethiopian people, shaping their values and worldview.

The story of St. Frumentius is a testament to the power of individual action, the importance of cultural sensitivity in evangelism, and the enduring impact of a faith that transcends borders and cultures. His legacy continues to inspire generations of Ethiopians, reminding them of the transformative power of Christianity and its role in shaping their nation's destiny.

Development through the Ages

Evolution of the Church from its inception to the present:

In the heart of Africa, where the Nile River begins its majestic journey and ancient civilizations once thrived, lies a land steeped in history, faith, and cultural richness. Ethiopia, a nation with a legacy that stretches back millennia, is home to one of the world's oldest Christian traditions: the Ethiopian Orthodox Tewahedo Church. This venerable institution, with its roots tracing back to the earliest days of Christianity, has been a cornerstone of Ethiopian society, shaping its identity, values, and way of life for centuries.

Our journey through the annals of Ethiopian Orthodoxy begins in the 4th century AD, a time when the Aksumite Empire, a powerful kingdom in northern Ethiopia, embraced Christianity as its official religion. This pivotal moment, marked by the conversion of King Ezana and the tireless efforts of St. Frumentius, the "Apostle of Ethiopia," laid the foundation for a faith that would become deeply intertwined with the nation's destiny.

The Aksumite period was a time of flourishing for the Church, as it established its roots, built magnificent churches and monasteries, and developed its unique liturgical traditions and theological interpretations. The Church's influence permeated all aspects of Aksumite society, shaping its laws, customs, and cultural expressions.

However, the decline of the Aksumite Empire in the 8th century ushered in a period of relative isolation for the Church. Yet, this isolation proved to be a catalyst for further development, as the Church honed its unique identity, enriching its liturgical practices and theological understanding. It also played a crucial role in preserving literacy, education, and cultural heritage during a time of political fragmentation.

The 12th century marked a renaissance for the Ethiopian Orthodox Church with the rise of the Zagwe dynasty. This era, often referred to as the "Golden Age," witnessed a flourishing of religious art, architecture, and literature. The magnificent rock-hewn churches of Lalibela, carved out of solid volcanic rock, stand as enduring testaments to the Zagwe's devotion and architectural ingenuity.

The subsequent Solomonic dynasty, claiming descent from the biblical King Solomon and the Queen of Sheba, further solidified the Church's position. This era saw the expansion of the Church's influence, the establishment of new monasteries, and the production of theological treatises that deepened its doctrinal understanding. The Church also played a crucial role in resisting external threats, such as the Crusades and the expansion of Islam, further strengthening its bond with the Ethiopian people.

The 17th and 18th centuries, known as the Gondarine period, were marked by theological debates and internal divisions within the Church. These debates, often centered on Christological interpretations, led to the emergence of different theological schools and monastic orders. While these divisions posed challenges, they also fostered intellectual inquiry and theological discourse, enriching the Church's intellectual tradition.

The Zemene Mesafint, or "Era of the Princes," which spanned the 18th and 19th centuries, was a time of political fragmentation and regional rivalries. This led to a decentralization of the Church's authority, with regional lords and princes exerting greater control over ecclesiastical affairs. However, this period also witnessed a flourishing of regional cultural and religious expressions, as different regions developed their unique liturgical traditions and artistic styles.

The modern era, beginning in the 19th century, brought significant challenges to the Ethiopian Orthodox Church. The rise of European colonialism, the Italian occupation, and the subsequent political upheavals tested the Church's resilience and adaptability. The Church faced internal divisions, theological debates, and the pressures of modernization. However, it also witnessed a renewed emphasis on education, social services, and engagement with the wider world.

The overthrow of the Derg regime in 1991 marked a new chapter in the Church's history. The Church regained its autonomy and embarked on a process of renewal and reform. It has expanded its educational and social service programs, engaged in interfaith dialogue, and played a crucial role in promoting peace and reconciliation in Ethiopia. The Church has also embraced technology, using social media and online platforms to reach new audiences and spread its message.

The Ethiopian Orthodox Tewahedo Church's journey through the ages is a testament to its enduring strength, adaptability, and deep roots in Ethiopian society. It has weathered storms of political upheaval, theological debates, and social change, emerging as a resilient and influential institution. As it continues to navigate the complexities of the modern world, the Church remains committed to its core values of faith, tradition, and service to the Ethiopian people.

In the chapters that follow, we will delve deeper into the heart of Ethiopian Orthodoxy, exploring its unique doctrines, vibrant liturgical traditions, and rich monastic heritage. We will uncover the treasures of its scriptural canon, the complexities of its relationship with the state, and the dynamic interplay between faith and culture. We will also confront the challenges and opportunities facing the Church in the modern world, examining its responses to modernization, globalization, and internal divisions. Our journey will take us beyond Ethiopia's borders, exploring the vibrant diaspora communities that have carried the flame of Ethiopian Orthodoxy to new lands. We will witness their struggles, triumphs, and contributions to global Christianity. We will also engage in dialogue with other faiths, exploring the Ethiopian Orthodox Church's interactions with other Christian denominations and its role in interfaith relations. Finally, we will cast our gaze towards the future, reflecting on the Church's prospects in the 21st century. We will analyze current trends, anticipate future challenges, and identify opportunities for growth and development. We will also consider the Church's evolving role in modern Ethiopian society and its potential for global influence.

Role in Ethiopian History

The Ethiopian Orthodox Tewahedo Church has been a formidable force in shaping the nation's political and cultural landscape, weaving its threads into the very fabric of Ethiopian identity. Its influence, both subtle and overt, has resonated through the corridors of power, the artistic expressions of the people, and the collective consciousness of the nation.

Political Influence:

The Church's political influence has waxed and waned throughout history, but its presence has always been felt in the halls of power. In the early days of the Aksumite Empire, the Church and state were closely intertwined, with monarchs often acting as patrons and protectors of the faith. This symbiotic relationship continued through the centuries, with the Church often serving as a source of counsel and legitimacy for rulers.

During the Zemene Mesafint, a period of political fragmentation, the Church's influence became more decentralized, with regional lords and princes vying for control over ecclesiastical affairs. This era saw the Church navigating complex political alliances and rivalries, often acting as a mediator and peacemaker.

In the modern era, the Church has continued to play a significant role in Ethiopian politics. During the Italian occupation, the Church served as a rallying point for resistance, with its leaders inspiring the faithful to fight for their freedom. In more recent times, the Church has been vocal on issues such as human rights, social justice, and national unity, often acting as a moral compass and a voice for the voiceless.

Cultural Influence:

The Church's cultural influence is perhaps even more pervasive than its political influence. It has shaped Ethiopian art, music, literature, and social customs, leaving an indelible mark on the nation's cultural identity.

Ethiopian art is replete with religious themes and motifs, from the intricate carvings and vibrant murals adorning churches and monasteries to the exquisite icons and illuminated manuscripts that have been treasured for centuries. The church's liturgical music, with its unique scales, rhythms, and instruments, is an integral part of Ethiopian cultural expression, and its influence can be heard in secular music as well.

The Church's calendar, with its numerous feasts and fasts, shapes the rhythm of Ethiopian life. Religious festivals, such as Timkat and Meskel, are celebrated with great fervor and are integral to the cultural fabric of the nation. The Church's teachings on morality, ethics, and social responsibility have also shaped Ethiopian values and norms, fostering a strong sense of community and social cohesion.

Integration into National Identity:

The Ethiopian Orthodox Tewahedo Church is not merely an institution; it is an integral part of Ethiopian identity. Its history, traditions, and teachings are deeply ingrained in the national consciousness, shaping the way Ethiopians view themselves, their relationship with the divine, and their place in the world.

The Church's role in preserving Ethiopia's independence and cultural heritage has made it a symbol of national pride and resilience. Its teachings on unity, compassion, and social justice have fostered a sense of shared identity and purpose among Ethiopians of diverse backgrounds. The Church's rituals and festivals, celebrated with great enthusiasm and devotion, are a testament to the enduring power of faith and tradition in Ethiopian society.

The Church's integration into national identity is also evident in the way it has shaped the Ethiopian worldview. The Church's teachings on the interconnectedness of all creation, the importance of community, and the value of spiritual contemplation have all contributed to a unique Ethiopian ethos that values harmony, balance, and respect for the natural world.

In conclusion, the Ethiopian Orthodox Tewahedo Church's influence on Ethiopian politics and culture is undeniable. It has been a driving force in shaping the nation's identity, values, and aspirations. Its legacy is not merely confined to the spiritual realm but extends to the political, cultural, and social spheres. As Ethiopia continues to evolve and face new challenges, the Church's role as a guardian of tradition, a voice for justice, and a source of spiritual guidance remains as vital as ever.

Key Figures and Milestones

Prominent leaders and saints:

The Ethiopian Orthodox Tewahedo Church's rich history is illuminated by a constellation of remarkable figures, both leaders and saints, whose lives and deeds have left an enduring legacy on the faith and the nation. Their unwavering devotion, spiritual wisdom, and tireless efforts have shaped the Church's trajectory and continue to inspire generations of believers.

Abba Selama (St. Frumentius): As the "Apostle of Ethiopia," Abba Selama's pivotal role in establishing the Church cannot be overstated. His missionary zeal, diplomatic skills, and deep understanding of Ethiopian culture were instrumental in the conversion of King Ezana and the subsequent adoption of Christianity as the state religion of Aksum. His legacy as a bridge-builder between cultures and a champion of faith continues to inspire Ethiopians today.

The Nine Saints (6th Century): These nine Syrian monks, fleeing persecution in their homeland, sought refuge in Ethiopia and played a crucial role in the Church's development. They established monasteries, translated religious texts, and introduced new liturgical practices, enriching the Ethiopian Orthodox tradition with their knowledge and spiritual fervor. Their monastic communities became centers of learning and piety, nurturing generations of scholars and saints.

Emperor Gebre Meskel Lalibela (12th Century): This visionary king is renowned for his extraordinary feat of commissioning the construction of the rock-hewn churches of Lalibela. These monolithic churches, carved out of solid rock, are a testament to Lalibela's unwavering faith and his desire to create a "New Jerusalem" in Ethiopia. His architectural vision and spiritual devotion continue to inspire awe and wonder, drawing pilgrims from around the world.

Saint Yared (6th Century): A musical genius and devout Christian, Saint Yared is credited with composing the Zema, the liturgical chants that are an integral part of Ethiopian Orthodox worship. His compositions, characterized by their unique scales, rhythms, and spiritual depth, have enriched the Church's musical tradition and continue to inspire devotion among the faithful.

Emperor Zara Yaqob (15th Century): A devout and scholarly king, Zara Yaqob is remembered for his theological contributions and his efforts to strengthen the Church's authority. He convened the Council of Debre Mitmaq, which addressed theological disputes and reaffirmed the Church's adherence to Miaphysite Christology. He also authored religious treatises and hymns, leaving a lasting legacy as a theologian and a patron of the arts.

Abune Tewophilos (20th Century): Abune Tewophilos, the first Ethiopian-born Patriarch of the Ethiopian Orthodox Church, played a crucial role in modernizing the Church and expanding its reach. He established theological schools, initiated social service programs, and advocated for the Church's autonomy during a time of political upheaval. His leadership and vision helped the Church navigate the challenges of the 20th century and maintain its relevance in a changing world.

Abune Paulos (20th-21st Centuries): Abune Paulos, the fifth Patriarch of the Ethiopian Orthodox Church, was a respected leader known for his commitment to interfaith dialogue and peacebuilding. He played a key role in mediating conflicts within Ethiopia and between Ethiopia and Eritrea. His efforts to promote understanding and cooperation between different faiths earned him international recognition and respect.

These are just a few of the many prominent leaders and saints who have shaped the Ethiopian Orthodox Tewahedo Church throughout its long and illustrious history. Their lives and deeds serve as a testament to the enduring power of faith, the importance of spiritual leadership, and the Church's unwavering commitment to serving the Ethiopian people. Their legacy continues to inspire and guide the Church as it navigates the challenges and opportunities of the 21st century.

Significant events in church history

The Ethiopian Orthodox Tewahedo Church's history is punctuated by significant events that have shaped its trajectory, solidified its identity, and tested its resilience. These events, spanning centuries, reflect the Church's deep integration into Ethiopian society and its enduring influence on the nation's spiritual, cultural, and political landscape.

1. **Council of Debre Mitmaq (1450):** This pivotal council, convened by Emperor Zara Yaqob, addressed theological disputes and reaffirmed the Church's adherence to Miaphysite Christology, a doctrine that emphasizes the unified nature of Christ's divinity and humanity. The council's decisions solidified the Church's theological identity and set it apart from other Christian traditions.

2. **Establishment of Gondar as the Ecclesiastical Capital (17th Century):** The establishment of Gondar as the capital of the Ethiopian Empire in the 17th century also marked

a significant shift for the Church. Gondar became a center of religious learning and authority, with the construction of numerous churches and monasteries. This period saw a flourishing of theological scholarship and artistic expression, further enriching the Church's traditions.

3. **The Era of the Princes (Zemene Mesafint) (18th-19th Centuries):** This era of political fragmentation and regional rivalries had a profound impact on the Church. The decentralization of power led to increased autonomy for regional churches and monasteries, fostering a diversity of liturgical practices and theological interpretations. While this period presented challenges to the Church's central authority, it also enriched its cultural and spiritual diversity.

4. **Resistance to Italian Occupation (1935-1941):** The Italian occupation of Ethiopia was a dark chapter in the nation's history, but it also witnessed the Church's unwavering resilience and its role in rallying the people against foreign aggression. The Church's leaders, including Abune Petros, who was martyred by the Italians, became symbols of national resistance and spiritual strength.

5. **Establishment of the Theological College of the Holy Trinity (1961):** The establishment

of the Theological College of the Holy Trinity in Addis Ababa marked a significant step in the Church's modernization efforts. The college provided formal theological education to clergy and laity, fostering a new generation of scholars and leaders who would guide the Church through the challenges of the 20th century.

6. **The Ethiopian Revolution and Its Aftermath (1974):** The Ethiopian Revolution, which overthrew Emperor Haile Selassie and ushered in a period of political instability, had a profound impact on the Church. The Church's properties were nationalized, and its relationship with the state became strained. However, the Church also played a crucial role in providing spiritual guidance and support to the people during this tumultuous period.

7. **Expansion of the Diaspora and Global Reach (20th-21st Centuries):** The 20th and 21st centuries witnessed a significant expansion of the Ethiopian Orthodox diaspora, with communities establishing themselves in North America, Europe, and other parts of the world. This diaspora has played a crucial role in preserving Ethiopian Orthodox traditions, establishing new churches and cultural centers, and contributing to the Church's global reach and influence.

These significant events, while not exhaustive, offer a glimpse into the dynamic and multifaceted history of the Ethiopian Orthodox Tewahedo Church. They highlight the Church's resilience in the face of adversity, its adaptability to changing circumstances, and its enduring influence on Ethiopian society and culture. As we delve deeper into the Church's history, doctrines, and practices, we will uncover the rich tapestry that makes it a unique and enduring institution.

Integration of Monastic Traditions: Influence of the Nine Saints.

The Ethiopian Orthodox Tewahedo Church's monastic tradition, a cornerstone of its spiritual heritage, owes a profound debt to the Nine Saints, a group of Syrian monks who sought refuge in Ethiopia in the 6th century. These nine holy men, fleeing persecution in their homeland, brought with them a wealth of knowledge, spiritual discipline, and monastic practices that would leave an enduring mark on Ethiopian Orthodoxy.

The Nine Saints, also known as the Sadqan, are revered as pivotal figures in the Church's history. Their arrival in Ethiopia coincided with a period of spiritual and intellectual ferment, and their presence catalyzed a monastic revival that would shape the course of Ethiopian Christianity for centuries to come.

The Nine Saints hailed from various parts of the Byzantine Empire, each bringing unique skills and expertise. Some were renowned for their theological knowledge, others for their mastery of liturgical arts, and still others for their ascetic practices. Together, they formed a formidable force for spiritual renewal, establishing monasteries, translating religious texts, and introducing new liturgical practices.

Their influence was not limited to the monastic sphere. The Nine Saints also engaged with the Ethiopian court and society, advising rulers, educating the clergy, and spreading the Gospel to the common people. Their teachings on monasticism, asceticism, and spiritual discipline resonated with the Ethiopian people, who were drawn to their piety and wisdom.

One of the most significant contributions of the Nine Saints was the establishment of monastic communities throughout Ethiopia. These monasteries became centers of learning, prayer, and spiritual practice, attracting devout men and women who sought to dedicate their lives to God. The monastic communities played a crucial role in preserving and transmitting the Church's teachings, traditions, and cultural heritage.

The Nine Saints also introduced new liturgical practices and translated religious texts into Ge'ez, the ancient Ethiopian language. This not only enriched the Church's liturgical tradition but also made Christian teachings more accessible to the Ethiopian people. Their translations of the Bible, patristic writings, and monastic rules laid the foundation for a rich theological and literary tradition that continues to thrive today.

The Nine Saints' emphasis on asceticism and spiritual discipline had a profound impact on Ethiopian monasticism. They introduced practices such as fasting, prayer, and solitary contemplation, which became integral to the monastic way of life. Their teachings on humility, obedience, and detachment from worldly concerns inspired generations of monks and nuns, who sought to emulate their piety and devotion.

The Nine Saints' legacy extends beyond their individual contributions. They are credited with establishing a monastic tradition that has been a cornerstone of Ethiopian Orthodoxy for over 1,500 years. Their monasteries have served as centers of learning, spiritual guidance, and social service, playing a vital role in the preservation of Ethiopian culture and identity.

The Nine Saints' influence is also evident in the Church's liturgical practices, theological interpretations, and artistic expressions. Their hymns, prayers, and theological treatises continue to be studied and recited by the faithful, and their artistic legacy can be seen in the intricate carvings and vibrant murals that adorn Ethiopian churches and monasteries.

In conclusion, the Nine Saints' arrival in Ethiopia in the 6th century marked a turning point in the history of the Ethiopian Orthodox Tewahedo Church. Their contributions to monasticism, liturgy, theology, and education have left an enduring legacy that continues to shape the Church's identity and practices. Their unwavering faith, spiritual wisdom, and dedication to serving God and humanity serve as an inspiration to all who seek to deepen their spiritual lives and contribute to the betterment of society.

Development of monastic life

The development of monastic life within the Ethiopian Orthodox Tewahedo Church is a captivating narrative of unwavering faith, spiritual devotion, and communal resilience. From its humble beginnings in the 6th century to its flourishing presence in the modern era, monasticism has been a cornerstone of Ethiopian Orthodoxy, shaping its spiritual landscape and contributing to its enduring legacy.

The seeds of monasticism were sown in Ethiopia with the arrival of the Nine Saints, who brought with them the rich monastic traditions of Syria and Egypt. These holy men, seeking refuge from persecution, found fertile ground in Ethiopia, where their teachings on asceticism, prayer, and communal living resonated with the spiritual aspirations of the people.

The Nine Saints established monasteries in various parts of Ethiopia, each becoming a beacon of spiritual light and a center of learning. These monastic communities, often located in remote and secluded areas, provided a sanctuary for those seeking to deepen their faith and dedicate their lives to God. The monks and nuns who inhabited these monasteries embraced a life of prayer, fasting, and manual labor, adhering to strict rules and regulations that governed their daily lives.

The monastic movement quickly gained momentum, attracting men and women from all walks of life. Some were drawn by the allure of a life dedicated to spiritual pursuits, while others sought refuge from the turmoil of the world. The monasteries provided a haven for the weary, the downtrodden, and the spiritually hungry, offering them a path towards salvation and enlightenment.

As the monastic movement grew, so did its influence on Ethiopian society. Monasteries became centers of learning, preserving and transmitting knowledge through the copying and illumination of manuscripts. They also served as hospitals, orphanages, and shelters for the poor and needy, embodying the Christian values of compassion and charity.

The monastic tradition in Ethiopia was not monolithic but rather a diverse tapestry of different orders and practices. Some monasteries followed the strict ascetic rules of the Desert Fathers, while others adopted a more moderate approach. Some emphasized communal living and shared labor, while others encouraged solitary contemplation and hermitage. This diversity of monastic expressions enriched the spiritual landscape of Ethiopia, providing a variety of paths for those seeking to deepen their faith.

Over the centuries, Ethiopian monasticism faced numerous challenges, including political upheavals, economic hardships, and external threats. However, it proved to be remarkably resilient, adapting to changing circumstances while maintaining its core values and traditions. The monasteries' ability to adapt and evolve ensured their survival and continued relevance in Ethiopian society.

In the modern era, Ethiopian monasticism continues to thrive, with hundreds of monasteries scattered across the country. These monasteries, while adhering to ancient traditions, have also embraced modernity, incorporating new technologies and engaging with contemporary social issues. They continue to play a vital role in Ethiopian society, providing spiritual guidance, education, and social services.

The development of monastic life in Ethiopia is a testament to the enduring power of faith, the resilience of spiritual communities, and the transformative impact of monastic ideals. It is a story of individuals who, through their unwavering devotion and commitment to a life of prayer and service, have enriched the spiritual landscape of Ethiopia and left a lasting legacy for generations to come.

Impact of External Relations

Interactions with other Christian denominations.

The Ethiopian Orthodox Tewahedo Church, while geographically isolated for much of its history, has not existed in a vacuum. Its interactions with other Christian denominations have been complex and multifaceted, marked by periods of both collaboration and conflict. These interactions have shaped the Church's theological understanding, liturgical practices, and its place in the broader Christian world.

Early Interactions:

In its formative years, the Ethiopian Orthodox Church maintained close ties with the Coptic Orthodox Church of Alexandria. This relationship was cemented by the consecration of St. Frumentius as the first bishop of Aksum by the Patriarch of Alexandria. For centuries, the Ethiopian Church relied on the Coptic Church for the appointment of its Abuna, or Patriarch, and the two churches shared a common theological and liturgical heritage.

Medieval Encounters:

During the medieval period, the Ethiopian Orthodox Church encountered European Christianity through various channels, including diplomatic missions, trade relations, and the Crusades. These encounters exposed the Church to different theological perspectives and liturgical practices, leading to both intellectual exchange and occasional friction. The Ethiopian Church's adherence to Miaphysite Christology, which differed from the Chalcedonian Christology of Western churches, sometimes led to misunderstandings and disagreements.

Modern Era Interactions:

The modern era brought new challenges and opportunities for inter-denominational relations. The arrival of European missionaries in the 19th century, representing various Protestant denominations, introduced new theological ideas and sparked debates within the Ethiopian Orthodox Church. While some Ethiopians embraced these new ideas, others remained steadfast in their traditional beliefs, leading to internal divisions and tensions.

Ecumenical Movement:

In the 20th century, the Ethiopian Orthodox Church became increasingly involved in the ecumenical movement, seeking dialogue and cooperation with other Christian denominations. It joined the World Council of Churches in 1948 and has participated in various interfaith initiatives. These ecumenical engagements have fostered greater understanding and cooperation between the Ethiopian Orthodox Church and other Christian traditions, while also allowing the Church to share its unique theological perspectives and rich spiritual heritage with the wider world.

Contemporary Relations:

Today, the Ethiopian Orthodox Tewahedo Church maintains relationships with various Christian denominations, both in Ethiopia and abroad. It engages in theological dialogues, participates in joint projects, and collaborates on social and humanitarian initiatives. While theological differences remain, there is a growing recognition of the importance of interfaith dialogue and cooperation in addressing common challenges and promoting peace and understanding.

The Ethiopian Orthodox Church's interactions with other Christian denominations have been a complex and evolving journey. These interactions have shaped the Church's theological understanding, liturgical practices, and its place in the broader Christian world. While challenges and disagreements have arisen at times, the Church has also demonstrated a willingness to engage in dialogue, learn from other traditions, and share its unique spiritual heritage with the world. As the Church continues to navigate the complexities of the modern world, its relationships with other Christian denominations will undoubtedly play a crucial role in shaping its future.

Historical conflicts and resolutions

The Ethiopian Orthodox Tewahedo Church, throughout its long and storied history, has not been immune to conflicts, both internal and external. These conflicts, often rooted in theological disagreements, political rivalries, or external pressures, have tested the Church's resilience and its ability to adapt and evolve. However, they have also served as catalysts for change, prompting the Church to re-examine its doctrines, practices, and relationship with the state and society.

Internal Conflicts:

Internal conflicts within the Ethiopian Orthodox Church have often revolved around theological interpretations, monastic reforms, and questions of authority. One of the most significant internal conflicts occurred during the Gondarine period (17th-18th centuries), when debates over the nature of Christ and the role of the Holy Spirit led to the emergence of different theological schools and monastic orders. These debates, while sometimes heated, also fostered intellectual inquiry and theological discourse, enriching the Church's intellectual tradition.

Another source of internal conflict has been the issue of monastic reform. Throughout history, various monastic leaders have sought to purify and revitalize monastic life, often leading to tensions between reformers and tradition-alists. These reform movements, while sometimes causing divisions, have also played a crucial role in maintaining the Church's spiritual vitality and relevance.

External Conflicts:

The Ethiopian Orthodox Church has also faced numerous external conflicts throughout its history. In the medieval period, the church had to contend with the expansion of Islam, which posed a threat to its dominance in the region. The Ethiopian-Adal War in the 16th century was a major conflict between Christian Ethiopia and the Muslim Adal Sultanate, resulting in significant loss of life and destruction. However, Ethiopia's victory in this war, attributed in part to divine intervention, solidified the Church's position and strengthened its bond with the Ethiopian people.

In the modern era, the Church faced the challenge of European colonialism, which sought to impose Western values and religious practices on Ethiopia. The Italian occupation in the 20th century was a particularly dark period, as the Church was persecuted and its leaders were martyred. However, the Church's resilience and its role in rallying the resistance movement ultimately contributed to Ethiopia's liberation.

Resolutions and Reconciliation:

The Ethiopian Orthodox Tewahedo Church has a long tradition of resolving conflicts through dialogue, compromise, and reconciliation. Internal disputes have often been resolved through Church councils and synods, where theological differences were debated and resolutions were reached. The Church's emphasis on forgiveness, reconciliation, and communal harmony has also played a crucial role in healing divisions and restoring unity.

In the face of external threats, the Church has often rallied the Ethiopian people, inspiring them to resist aggression and defend their faith and freedom. The Church's leaders have also played a crucial role in mediating conflicts and promoting peace, both within Ethiopia and in the wider region.

The Church's ability to resolve conflicts and promote reconciliation is rooted in its deep understanding of the human condition and its commitment to the Gospel's message of love, forgiveness, and peace. This commitment has enabled the Church to overcome numerous challenges throughout its history, emerging stronger and more united.

Lessons Learned:

The Ethiopian Orthodox Tewahedo Church's history of conflicts and resolutions offers valuable lessons for the present and the future. It highlights the importance of dialogue, compromise, and reconciliation in addressing differences and resolving disputes. It also underscores the Church's crucial role in promoting peace, justice, and unity in a world often marred by conflict and division.

As the Church continues to navigate the complexities of the modern world, it can draw upon its rich history of conflict resolution to address new challenges and build bridges of understanding with other faiths and communities. By embracing its tradition of dialogue and reconciliation, the Church can continue to be a beacon of hope and a force for positive change in Ethiopia and beyond.

Modern Era Changes

20th- and 21st-century developments:

The dawn of the 20th century ushered in an era of unprecedented change and upheaval for the Ethiopian Orthodox Tewahedo Church. The winds of modernization, political transformation, and global events swept through the ancient land, challenging the Church's traditions, structures, and relationship with the state. Yet, amidst these trials, the Church demonstrated remarkable resilience, adapting to the changing times while preserving its spiritual essence and cultural heritage.

The early 20th century saw Ethiopia grappling with the pressures of modernization and the encroachment of European colonialism. Emperor Haile Selassie, a devout Orthodox Christian, sought to modernize the nation while maintaining the Church's central role in society. He initiated reforms aimed at improving education, healthcare, and social services, often in collaboration with the Church. However, the Italian occupation of Ethiopia in 1935 disrupted these efforts and plunged the nation into a period of turmoil.

During the Italian occupation, the Ethiopian Orthodox Church faced persecution and suppression. Many churches and monasteries were destroyed or damaged, and religious leaders were imprisoned or exiled. Yet, the Church remained a symbol of national resistance, with its leaders inspiring the faithful to fight for their freedom and cultural identity. The Church's resilience during this dark period further solidified its bond with the Ethiopian people.

The post-war era saw the restoration of Ethiopian independence and the return of Emperor Haile Selassie. The Church, though weakened by the occupation, embarked on a process of rebuilding and renewal. It expanded its educational and social service programs, reaching out to communities across the country. The Church also played a crucial role in the nation's political and social development, advocating for peace, justice, and national unity.

The 1974 Ethiopian Revolution, which overthrew the monarchy and established a Marxist-Leninist regime, brought new challenges for the Church. The new government nationalized Church lands and properties, restricted its activities, and sought to limit its influence. However, the Church remained a spiritual and cultural force, providing solace and guidance to the people during a time of political turmoil and social upheaval.

The fall of the Derg regime in 1991 marked a turning point for the Ethiopian Orthodox Church. The Church regained its autonomy and embarked on a process of revitalization. It rebuilt its institutions, expanded its educational and social programs, and re-established its role as a leading voice in Ethiopian society. The Church also embraced new technologies, using radio, television, and the internet to reach wider audiences and spread its message.

The 21st century has seen the Ethiopian Orthodox Church continue to adapt and evolve. It has faced new challenges, such as the rise of Pentecostalism and other evangelical movements, as well as the ongoing struggle to address poverty, inequality, and social injustice. However, the Church has also embraced new opportunities, such as the growing Ethiopian diaspora, which has established vibrant Orthodox communities around the world.

The Church has also played a crucial role in promoting peace and reconciliation in Ethiopia, particularly in the aftermath of the recent conflict in the Tigray region. Its leaders have called for dialogue, forgiveness, and unity, reminding the nation of its shared spiritual heritage and the importance of peaceful coexistence.

In recent years, the Ethiopian Orthodox Tewahedo Church has witnessed a resurgence of interest in its ancient traditions and practices. Young people, in particular, are rediscovering the richness of their spiritual heritage, drawn to the Church's emphasis on community, spirituality, and social justice. This renewed interest offers hope for the Church's continued vitality and relevance in the 21st century.

The Ethiopian Orthodox Tewahedo Church's journey through the 20th and 21st centuries is a testament to its resilience, adaptability, and enduring appeal. It has faced numerous challenges, from political upheavals to social transformations, but it has emerged from each trial with renewed strength and a deeper commitment to its faith and its people. As Ethiopia continues to evolve, the Church remains a steadfast presence, a source of spiritual guidance, cultural preservation, and social progress.

Key reforms and modern challenges

The Ethiopian Orthodox Tewahedo Church, an ancient institution steeped in tradition, has not remained stagnant in the face of modernity. The 20th and 21st centuries have ushered in an era of significant reforms and adaptations as the Church grapples with the complexities of a rapidly changing world. These reforms, while aimed at preserving the Church's spiritual essence, have also sparked debates and presented new challenges.

Key Reforms:

1. **Educational Reforms:** Recognizing the importance of education in the modern era, the Church has made significant strides in expanding its educational institutions and programs. The establishment of the Theological College of the Holy Trinity in 1961 marked a major milestone, providing formal theological education to clergy and laity. The Church has also established numerous schools and colleges across the country, offering both religious and secular education to thousands of students.

2. **Social Service Initiatives:** The Church has expanded its social service initiatives, reaching out to communities in need through healthcare, poverty alleviation, and humanitarian aid programs. It has established hospitals, clinics, orphanages, and shelters for the homeless, providing essential services to the most vulnerable members of society. These initiatives not only reflect the Church's commitment to social justice but also strengthen its bond with the Ethiopian people.

3. **Embracing Technology:** In an effort to reach wider audiences and adapt to the digital age, the Church has embraced technology. It has utilized radio, television, and the internet to broadcast sermons, religious teachings, and cultural programs. The Church has also established a strong online presence through websites and social media platforms, engaging with younger generations and fostering a sense of community among the diaspora.

4. **Interfaith Dialogue:** The Church has actively participated in interfaith dialogue, seeking to build bridges of understanding and cooperation with other Christian denominations and religious traditions. It has engaged in theological discussions, joint projects, and peace initiatives, contributing to a more harmonious and inclusive religious landscape in Ethiopia.

5. **Women's Empowerment:** The Church has taken steps to empower women within its ranks, recognizing their valuable contributions to the spiritual and social life of the community. While challenges remain, there has been a growing recognition of the need for greater gender equality within the Church, and efforts are underway to promote women's leadership and participation in decision-making processes.

Modern Challenges:

1. **Secularism and Modernization:** The rise of secularism and the influence of Western values have posed challenges to the Church's traditional authority and practices. The younger generation, exposed to diverse ideas and lifestyles, may question or challenge some of the Church's teachings and practices. The Church must find ways to remain relevant and engaging to young people while preserving its core values and traditions.

2. **Internal Divisions:** The Church has faced internal divisions and theological debates, particularly regarding the interpretation of scripture and the role of tradition. These divisions, while not new, have been exacerbated by the pressures of modernization and the influence of external ideas. The Church must find ways to

address these divisions through dialogue, reconciliation, and a renewed commitment to unity.

3. **Political Interference:** The Church's relationship with the state has been complex and at times fraught with tension. While the Church has regained its autonomy in recent years, there have been instances of political interference in its affairs. The Church must navigate this delicate relationship, maintaining its independence while also engaging with the state on issues of mutual concern.

4. **Financial Sustainability:** The Church relies heavily on donations and contributions from its members to fund its various programs and initiatives. However, economic challenges and the growing needs of the community have put a strain on the Church's financial resources. The Church must find innovative ways to ensure its financial sustainability while continuing to serve the needs of its followers.

5. **The Diaspora Challenge:** The growing Ethiopian diaspora presents both opportunities and challenges for the Church. While diaspora communities have helped to spread the Ethiopian Orthodox faith and culture around the world, they also face issues of assimilation, generational differences, and maintaining their connection to the mother Church. The Church must find ways

to support and engage with the diaspora while also addressing their unique needs and concerns.

The Ethiopian Orthodox Tewahedo Church stands at a crossroads, navigating the complexities of the modern world while striving to preserve its ancient traditions. The reforms and adaptations it has undertaken in recent decades are a testament to its resilience and its commitment to remaining relevant in a changing world. However, the challenges it faces are significant, and its future will depend on its ability to address these challenges with wisdom, compassion, and a renewed commitment to its spiritual mission.

Archaeological Discoveries

Archaeological discoveries have been instrumental in illuminating the rich and complex history of the Ethiopian Orthodox Tewahedo Church. These tangible remnants of the past, unearthed from the depths of time, offer invaluable insights into the Church's evolution, its interactions with other cultures, and its enduring impact on Ethiopian society.

1. **Aksumite Stelae and Inscriptions:** The ancient city of Aksum, once the heart of a powerful empire, has yielded a treasure trove of archaeological finds that shed light on the early days of Christianity in Ethiopia. The towering

stelae, some reaching over 100 feet in height, are not only architectural marvels but also bear inscriptions that provide valuable clues about the Aksumite kings' conversion to Christianity and their patronage of the Church. These inscriptions, written in Ge'ez, the ancient Ethiopian language, offer glimpses into the religious beliefs, practices, and social structures of the time.

2. **Ancient Churches and Monasteries:** The ruins of ancient churches and monasteries scattered across Ethiopia provide tangible evidence of the Church's early expansion and its architectural ingenuity. These structures, often built with locally sourced materials and adorned with intricate carvings and murals, reflect the Church's deep integration into the cultural and artistic landscape of the region. The discovery of ancient manuscripts, icons, and liturgical objects within these ruins has further enriched our understanding of the Church's early history and its spiritual practices.

3. **The Ark of the Covenant:** One of the most intriguing archaeological quests related to the Ethiopian Orthodox Church is the search for the Ark of the Covenant. According to Ethiopian tradition, the Ark, a sacred chest believed to contain the Ten Commandments, was brought to Ethiopia by Menelik I, the son of King Solomon and the Queen of Sheba. While its existence

remains shrouded in mystery, the belief in its presence in Ethiopia has fueled numerous archaeological expeditions and continues to captivate the imagination of believers and scholars alike.

4. **The Gunda Gunde Monastery Complex:** The Gunda Gunde Monastery complex, located in the Tigray region of Ethiopia, is a remarkable archaeological site that offers insights into the daily lives and spiritual practices of Ethiopian monks. The complex, which dates back to the 16th century, includes numerous buildings, churches, and underground tunnels. The discovery of well-preserved manuscripts, religious artifacts, and skeletal remains has shed light on the monastery's history, its role in preserving knowledge, and the challenges it faced during times of conflict and upheaval.

5. **The Yeha Temple:** The Yeha Temple, located in northern Ethiopia, is one of the oldest standing structures in the country. Believed to have been built in the 8th century BC, the temple predates the arrival of Christianity in Ethiopia. However, its architectural style and religious symbolism have influenced the design of later Ethiopian Orthodox churches. The temple's preservation offers a glimpse into the pre-Christian religious practices of the region and their potential influence on the development of Ethiopian Christianity.

Impact on Understanding the Church's History:

These archaeological discoveries have significantly enriched our understanding of the Ethiopian Orthodox Tewahedo Church's history. They have provided tangible evidence of the Church's early establishment, its evolution over time, and its interactions with other cultures. The inscriptions on Aksumite stelae, for example, have confirmed the Aksumite kings' conversion to Christianity and their patronage of the Church. The ruins of ancient churches and monasteries have revealed the Church's architectural ingenuity and its role in preserving knowledge and cultural heritage.

Archaeological finds have also shed light on the Church's theological development, its liturgical practices, and its relationship with the state and society. The discovery of ancient manuscripts and religious artifacts has provided valuable insights into the Church's doctrinal beliefs, its rituals and ceremonies, and its social and political influence.

Furthermore, archaeological discoveries have helped to illuminate the lives of ordinary believers, revealing their daily practices, their struggles, and their aspirations. The skeletal remains found in the Gunda Gunde Monastery complex, for example, offer a poignant reminder of the sacrifices made by monks in their pursuit of spiritual enlightenment.

In conclusion, archaeological discoveries have played a crucial role in unveiling the rich tapestry of the Ethiopian Orthodox Tewahedo Church's history. They have provided tangible evidence of the Church's enduring legacy, its deep roots in Ethiopian society, and its contributions to the nation's spiritual, cultural, and intellectual development. As archaeologists continue to explore Ethiopia's rich historical landscape, we can expect further discoveries that will shed new light on this ancient and vibrant faith.

The echoes of these pivotal moments resonate through the centuries, shaping the Ethiopian Orthodox Tewahedo Church into the vibrant and resilient institution it is today. From the early days of Aksum to the challenges and triumphs of the modern era, the Church has consistently demonstrated its ability to adapt, evolve, and maintain its central role in Ethiopian society.

As we move forward, we will delve deeper into the heart of Ethiopian Orthodoxy, exploring the intricate tapestry of its doctrines and beliefs. We will uncover the theological foundations that underpin its unique identity, its distinct interpretations of scripture, and its profound impact on the spiritual lives of millions. Prepare to be immersed in a world of ancient wisdom, profound mysteries, and unwavering faith.

In the next chapter, we will embark on a journey into the spiritual heart of Ethiopian Orthodoxy, where we will uncover the core doctrines that have shaped its identity and guided the faith of millions for centuries. From the profound mystery of the Holy Trinity to the unique interpretation of Christ's nature, we will explore the theological foundations that distinguish Ethiopian Orthodoxy and illuminate its place in the broader Christian tradition.

Chapter 3

Doctrines and Beliefs

At the heart of Ethiopian Orthodox Tewahedo theology lies the fundamental doctrine of the Holy Trinity, a cornerstone of Christian faith shared across denominations. Yet, as with many aspects of this ancient tradition, the Ethiopian Orthodox Church embraces the Trinity with a unique perspective, weaving together biblical teachings, patristic interpretations, and indigenous cultural nuances.

The Ethiopian Orthodox Church firmly upholds the belief in one God existing in three co-equal and co-eternal persons: Father, Son, and Holy Spirit. This triune nature of God is not seen as a division but rather a harmonious unity, a divine dance of love and communion. The Father is the source of all being, the Son is the incarnate Word of God, and the Holy Spirit is the life-giving breath that animates creation and dwells within the hearts of believers.

This Trinitarian understanding is deeply rooted in the Scriptures, particularly the New Testament, where Jesus speaks of the Father and the Holy Spirit as distinct persons yet united in purpose and essence. The Ethiopian Orthodox Church, however, goes beyond a mere recitation of biblical verses, delving into the rich theological tradition of the early Church Fathers, who grappled with the mystery of the Trinity and sought to articulate its profound implications for Christian faith and life.

One of the distinctive features of Ethiopian Orthodox Trinitarian theology is its emphasis on the unity of the Godhead. While acknowledging the distinct roles and attributes of each person of the Trinity, the Church emphasizes their inseparable unity and their shared divine essence. This emphasis on unity is reflected in the Church's liturgical language, Ge'ez, which often uses the term "Egzi-abher" (Lord) to refer to God as a unified entity, encompassing all three persons of the Trinity.

The Ethiopian Orthodox Church also places a strong emphasis on the role of the Holy Spirit in the life of the Church and the individual believer. The Holy Spirit is seen as the source of spiritual renewal, enlightenment, and sanctification. It is through the Holy Spirit that believers are united with Christ and empowered to live a life of faith and obedience. The Church's liturgical practices, such as the Divine Liturgy and the sacraments, are seen as channels of divine grace, through which the Holy Spirit works to transform and sanctify the faithful.

The Ethiopian Orthodox understanding of the Trinity is not merely an intellectual exercise but a lived reality that permeates every aspect of the Church's life and worship. It is reflected in the Church's art, music, and architecture, which often depict the Trinity as a harmonious unity of three persons. It is also evident in the Church's social teachings, which emphasize the importance of community, compassion, and love for one's neighbor, reflecting the Trinitarian model of divine love and communion.

The Ethiopian Orthodox Church's Trinitarian theology is a rich and nuanced tapestry, woven together from biblical teachings, patristic interpretations, and indigenous cultural insights. It is a theology that is both deeply rooted in tradition and yet open to new interpretations and understandings. As we delve deeper into the Church's doctrines and beliefs, we will see how this Trinitarian foundation underpins its unique identity and shapes its spiritual practices.

Christology and the concept of Miaphysitism

Central to the Ethiopian Orthodox Tewahedo Church's theological tapestry is its Christology, the understanding of the nature and person of Jesus Christ. The Church adheres to a doctrine known as Miaphysitism, a term derived from the Greek words "mia" (one) and "physis" (nature). This doctrine, while shared with other Oriental Orthodox churches, holds a unique significance within Ethiopian

Orthodoxy, shaping its liturgical practices, theological discourse, and spiritual identity.

Miaphysitism, in essence, asserts the unity of Christ's divine and human natures. It posits that Jesus Christ is both fully God and fully human, not two separate entities but one indivisible person. This understanding stands in contrast to the Chalcedonian definition of Christ, which emphasizes the distinction between Christ's two natures.

The Ethiopian Orthodox Church's embrace of Miaphysitism is deeply rooted in its theological tradition, drawing upon the teachings of early Church Fathers such as St. Cyril of Alexandria. These theologians emphasized the unity of Christ's person, arguing that His divinity and humanity were inseparable and perfectly united in one hypostasis, or individual existence.

This understanding of Christ's nature has profound implications for Ethiopian Orthodox theology and spirituality. It emphasizes the Incarnation, the belief that God became flesh in the person of Jesus Christ, as a central tenet of faith. It also highlights the importance of Christ's humanity, emphasizing his suffering, death, and resurrection as the means of salvation for all humankind.

The concept of Miaphysitism is not merely an abstract theological concept but a lived reality for Ethiopian Orthodox Christians. It is reflected in their liturgical practices, which emphasize the unity of Christ's divine and human natures. For example, the Divine Liturgy, the central act of worship in the Ethiopian Orthodox Church, includes prayers and hymns that extol Christ's dual nature and His role as the mediator between God and humanity.

The Church's art and iconography also reflect its Miaphysite Christology. Icons of Christ often depict him with both divine and human attributes, emphasizing the unity of his person. The use of colors, symbols, and gestures in these icons conveys the theological depth and spiritual significance of Miaphysitism.

The Ethiopian Orthodox Church's adherence to Miaphysitism has not been without controversy. It has led to theological debates and disagreements with other Christian denominations, particularly those that adhere to the Chalcedonian definition of Christ. However, the Church has remained steadfast in its Miaphysite beliefs, viewing them as essential to its identity and spiritual heritage.

In recent years, there have been efforts towards dialogue and reconciliation between the Ethiopian Orthodox Church and other Christian denominations. These dialogues, while acknowledging theological differences, have also highlighted areas of common ground and shared values. The Ethiopian Orthodox Church's participation in the ecumenical movement is a testament to its willingness to engage with other Christian traditions and to seek unity in diversity.

The concept of Miaphysitism, as embraced by the Ethiopian Orthodox Tewahedo Church, is a rich and complex theological doctrine with profound implications for the Church's faith, practice, and identity. It is a doctrine that has been shaped by centuries of theological reflection, liturgical practice, and cultural adaptation. As we continue our exploration of Ethiopian Orthodoxy, we will see how this Miaphysite understanding of Christ permeates every aspect of the Church's life and worship, shaping its unique spiritual path and its enduring legacy.

Core Doctrines

The Nature of Christ:

The EOTC teaches that Jesus Christ has one unified nature that is both fully divine and fully human. This miaphysite belief sets it apart from the Chalcedonian definition of Christ as having two natures, divine and human, in one person.

Holy Trinity

The Church professes belief in the Holy Trinity: one God in three persons—Father, Son, and Holy Spirit. This is a foundational Christian doctrine, shared across all major Christian traditions.

Role of Mary and other unique beliefs

The Ethiopian Orthodox Tewahedo Church holds a distinctive veneration for Mary, the mother of Jesus, that sets it apart from other Christian traditions. This veneration, deeply rooted in theological understanding and cultural practices, is a testament to the Church's unique perspective on the role of Mary in salvation history.

Mary, the Mother of God (Theotokos): The Ethiopian Orthodox Church unequivocally affirms Mary's title as "Theotokos," the God-bearer. This title, while accepted by many Christian denominations, holds a special significance in Ethiopian Orthodoxy. It emphasizes Mary's unique role in the Incarnation, the belief that God became flesh in the person of Jesus Christ. Mary is not merely seen as the mother of Jesus's human nature but as the mother of God incarnate. This understanding is reflected in the Church's liturgical language, art, and iconography, where Mary is often depicted as a queenly figure, adorned with regal attire and surrounded by angels.

The Ark of the New Covenant: The Ethiopian Orthodox Church also venerates Mary as the "Ark of the New Covenant." This title draws a parallel between Mary and the Ark of the Covenant, the sacred chest that housed the Ten Commandments in the Old Testament. Just as the Ark contained the Word of God in the form of the tablets, Mary carried the Word of God in her womb in the form of Jesus Christ. This analogy underscores Mary's central role in salvation history and her unique relationship with the divine.

The Intercession of Saints and Angels: In addition to its veneration of Mary, the Ethiopian Orthodox Church also holds a strong belief in the intercession of saints and angels. Saints, who are believed to have lived exemplary lives of faith and devotion, are seen as intercessors between God and humanity. They are invoked in prayers, their icons are venerated, and their feast days are celebrated with great fervor. Angels, as messengers of God, are also believed to play a crucial role in the spiritual life of believers, offering guidance, protection, and intercession.

Unique Feast Days and Traditions: The Ethiopian Orthodox Church has several unique feast days and traditions dedicated to Mary and the saints. One such feast is the "Feast of the Assumption of Mary," which celebrates Mary's bodily ascension into heaven. Another unique tradition is the use of "tabots," replicas of the Ark of the Covenant, in every Ethiopian Orthodox church. These tabots are considered sacred and are central to the Church's liturgical practices.

The Role of Tradition and Scripture: The Ethiopian Orthodox Church's unique theological perspectives are deeply rooted in both scripture and tradition. The Church's interpretation of scripture is guided by the teachings of the early Church Fathers, who provided a rich theological framework for understanding the mysteries of faith.

The Church also places a strong emphasis on oral tradition, which has been passed down through generations and is considered an integral part of its spiritual heritage.

The Ethiopian Orthodox Tewahedo Church's unique theological perspectives, including its veneration of Mary, the intercession of saints and angels, and its distinctive feast days and traditions, offer a glimpse into the rich tapestry of this ancient faith. These beliefs and practices, while sometimes differing from other Christian traditions, are deeply meaningful to Ethiopian Orthodox Christians and reflect their unique understanding of the divine, their relationship with the spiritual realm, and their path to salvation.

Sacraments and Mysteries

The Ethiopian Orthodox Tewahedo Church, like other apostolic churches, recognizes seven key sacraments, also known as mysteries, as central to the spiritual life of its followers. These sacraments are not mere rituals but channels of divine grace, through which believers encounter the living Christ and participate in the life of the Church.

1. **Baptism:** Baptism is the first and foundational sacrament, marking the entry into the Christian community. It is believed to cleanse the soul from original sin and initiate the believer into a new life in Christ. The act of immersion in water

symbolizes the washing away of sin and the rebirth into a new spiritual identity.

2. **Confirmation (Chrismation):** Immediately following baptism, the sacrament of Chrismation is administered. This involves the anointing of the believer with holy oil, symbolizing the sealing of the Holy Spirit upon them. Chrismation is believed to strengthen the newly baptized and empower them for a life of faith and service. It is seen as a confirmation of the baptismal grace and a deepening of the believer's relationship with the Holy Spirit.

3. **Holy Eucharist (Qurban):** The Eucharist, also known as Holy Communion, is the central act of worship in the Ethiopian Orthodox Church. It is a reenactment of the Last Supper, where bread and wine are consecrated and become the body and blood of Christ. Partaking in the Eucharist is seen as a means of spiritual nourishment and union with Christ. The Ethiopian Orthodox Church uses leavened bread and wine made from grapes for the Eucharist, following ancient traditions. This sacrament is considered the most sacred and essential for spiritual growth and communion with God.

4. **Confession:** Confession is a sacrament of repentance and forgiveness. Believers confess their sins to a priest, who offers absolution and spiritual guidance. Confession is seen as a means of

spiritual healing and reconciliation with God and the community. It is a way for believers to acknowledge their shortcomings, seek forgiveness, and receive spiritual counsel for a renewed life in Christ.

5. **Matrimony:** Marriage is a sacred union between a man and a woman, blessed by the Church and seen as a reflection of Christ's love for his Church. The Ethiopian Orthodox Church emphasizes the importance of marriage as a lifelong commitment and a source of mutual support and spiritual growth. It is a sacrament that signifies the joining of two individuals into one flesh, blessed by God for the purpose of procreation and mutual support in faith.

6. **Holy Orders:** Holy Orders is the sacrament through which men are ordained as deacons, priests, and bishops. These ordained ministers are entrusted with the responsibility of leading the Church, administering the sacraments, and teaching the faith. The Ethiopian Orthodox Church has a hierarchical structure, with the Patriarch as the head of the Church and bishops overseeing dioceses. This sacrament is seen as a divine calling and a lifelong commitment to serve God and the Church.

7. **Unction of the Sick:** Unction of the Sick, also known as the Anointing of the Sick, is a sacrament of healing and comfort for those who

are ill or suffering. It involves the anointing of the sick with holy oil, accompanied by prayers for their physical and spiritual well-being. This sacrament is seen as a means of divine grace and a source of strength and comfort in times of illness and suffering. It is a reminder of God's love and care for the sick and a source of hope for healing and restoration.

These seven sacraments, deeply rooted in the Ethiopian Orthodox tradition, are not merely rituals but encounters with the divine. They mark significant moments in the lives of believers, offering them spiritual nourishment, healing, and guidance. Through these sacraments, the Ethiopian Orthodox Tewahedo Church continues to nurture the faith of its followers, guiding them on their spiritual journey and strengthening their bond with God and the community.

Sacred Scriptures

Overview of the Ethiopian Orthodox Bible.

The Ethiopian Orthodox Bible, a treasure trove of spiritual wisdom and historical narratives, stands as a testament to the Church's rich and diverse heritage. It is not merely a collection of texts but a living testament to the faith and traditions of the Ethiopian people, a sacred repository of their spiritual identity and cultural memory.

The Ethiopian Orthodox Bible, also known as the Ethiopian Orthodox Canon, is a unique and expansive collection of sacred texts that differs in several ways from the canons of other Christian traditions. It encompasses a wider range of books than the standard Western Bible, including several apocryphal and deuterocanonical texts that are not found in other Christian canons. This broader canon reflects the Ethiopian Orthodox Church's deep respect for ancient traditions and its openness to diverse sources of spiritual wisdom.

The core of the Ethiopian Orthodox Bible consists of the Old and New Testaments, which are shared with other Christian traditions. However, the Ethiopian version of these texts often includes additional books and chapters not found in other Bibles. For example, the Ethiopian Old Testament includes the Book of Enoch, the Book of Jubilees, and the Book of Ezra Sutuel, which offer unique insights into Ethiopian religious beliefs and practices.

The New Testament in the Ethiopian Orthodox Bible also includes some unique features. It contains a book called the "Sinodos," which is a collection of canons and decrees from early Church councils. It also includes the "Qalementos," a collection of writings attributed to Clement of Rome, an early Church Father. These additional texts provide valuable insights into the early development of Christianity and the Ethiopian Orthodox Church's unique theological perspectives.

The Ethiopian Orthodox Bible is not merely a collection of texts but a living tradition that is deeply embedded in the Church's liturgy, rituals, and daily life. The readings from the Bible are an integral part of every church service, and the faithful are encouraged to study and meditate on the scriptures. The Church also has a rich tradition of biblical interpretation, with commentaries and homilies that offer insights into the deeper meanings of the texts.

The language of the Ethiopian Orthodox Bible is Ge'ez, an ancient Semitic language that is no longer spoken in everyday life but remains the liturgical language of the Church. The use of Ge'ez in the Bible and liturgy adds to the sacredness and mystique of the texts, connecting the faithful to their ancient roots and spiritual heritage.

The Ethiopian Orthodox Bible is not only a source of spiritual guidance but also a cultural treasure. Its rich language, poetic imagery, and historical narratives have inspired generations of Ethiopian artists, writers, and musicians. The Bible's stories and characters have become deeply ingrained in the cultural consciousness of the Ethiopian people, shaping their values, beliefs, and worldview.

The Ethiopian Orthodox Bible is a testament to the Church's rich and diverse heritage, its openness to different sources of spiritual wisdom, and its deep connection to Ethiopian culture and identity. It is a sacred text that continues to inspire and guide the faithful, offering them a glimpse into the divine mysteries and a path towards spiritual enlightenment.

Importance of the Ge'ez language.

Ge'ez, an ancient Semitic language no longer spoken in everyday life, holds a sacred and revered place in the heart of the Ethiopian Orthodox Tewahedo Church. Its importance transcends the merely linguistic, as it is intertwined with the spiritual, cultural, and historical identity of both the Church and the Ethiopian nation.

Often referred to as the "language of angels" by the faithful, Ge'ez is the language of the Church's liturgy, prayer, and scripture. Its melodious sounds resonate in the ancient chants and hymns that have been passed down through generations, connecting believers to their ancestral roots and rich spiritual heritage. The use of Ge'ez in the liturgy not only adds an aura of sacredness and mystery to religious services but also serves as a powerful reminder of the continuity and timelessness of the Ethiopian Orthodox faith.

Beyond its liturgical use, Ge'ez is also the language of ancient Ethiopian manuscripts, containing a wealth of theological, historical, and cultural knowledge. These manuscripts, written on parchment and beautifully illuminated, are national treasures that preserve Ethiopia's collective memory and bear witness to the Church's rich intellectual and spiritual tradition. The study and translation of these Ge'ez texts have been fundamental in understanding the history, doctrines, and practices of the Ethiopian Orthodox Church throughout the centuries.

Ge'ez has also played a crucial role in preserving Ethiopian cultural identity. Although no longer spoken in daily life, its influence endures in the vocabulary, grammar, and syntax of Amharic, the official language of Ethiopia. Ge'ez is also a source of inspiration for Ethiopian literature, poetry, and music, enriching these forms of artistic expression with its beauty and depth.

In essence, Ge'ez is much more than a language for the Ethiopian Orthodox Tewahedo Church; it is a sacred link to the past, a vehicle for spiritual expression, and a symbol of Ethiopian cultural identity. Its preservation and study are essential for understanding the rich heritage of the Church and its profound impact on the life of the nation.

This deep connection to language and history sets the stage for our exploration of the Ethiopian Orthodox Bible, a collection of sacred texts unique to this ancient tradition. In the next section, we will delve into the specific books that comprise this canon, exploring their significance and how they contribute to the rich tapestry of Ethiopian Orthodox theology and spirituality.

Role of the Holy Spirit

Understanding the Holy Spirit in doctrine.

In the Ethiopian Orthodox Tewahedo Church, the Holy Spirit, the third person of the Holy Trinity, is not merely an abstract concept but a dynamic and active force that permeates every aspect of creation and the spiritual life of believers. The Church's understanding of the Holy Spirit is deeply rooted in scripture, tradition, and liturgical practice, shaping its theological discourse, spiritual experiences, and communal identity.

The Ethiopian Orthodox Church affirms the Holy Spirit's divinity and co-equality with the Father and the Son. It recognizes the Holy Spirit as the life-giving breath of God, the source of inspiration, wisdom, and sanctification. The Holy Spirit is believed to have been present and active throughout salvation history, from the creation of the world to the establishment of the Church.

One of the distinctive features of Ethiopian Orthodox pneumatology (the study of the Holy Spirit) is its emphasis on the Holy Spirit's role in the Incarnation. The Church teaches that the Holy Spirit was instrumental in the conception and birth of Jesus Christ, overshadowing the Virgin Mary and bringing about the miraculous union of divine and human natures in Christ. This understanding of the Holy Spirit's role in the Incarnation is reflected in the Church's liturgical language, art, and iconography, where the Holy Spirit is often depicted as a dove descending upon Mary.

The Ethiopian Orthodox Church also emphasizes the Holy Spirit's ongoing presence and activity in the life of the Church and the individual believer. The Holy Spirit is seen as the source of spiritual renewal, enlightenment, and sanctification. It is through the Holy Spirit that believers are united with Christ and empowered to live a life of faith and obedience. The Church's liturgical practices, such as the Divine Liturgy and the sacraments, are seen as channels of divine grace, through which the Holy Spirit works to transform and sanctify the faithful.

The Ethiopian Orthodox understanding of the Holy Spirit is not merely an intellectual exercise but a lived reality that permeates every aspect of the Church's life and worship. It is reflected in the Church's emphasis on communal prayer, fasting, and almsgiving, which are seen as ways of opening oneself to the Holy Spirit's guidance and grace. It is also evident in the Church's rich musical tradition, where hymns and chants are believed to be inspired by the Holy Spirit and to serve as a means of spiritual communion with the divine.

The Ethiopian Orthodox Church's pneumatology is a rich and nuanced tapestry, woven together from biblical teachings, patristic interpretations, and indigenous cultural insights. It is a theology that is both deeply rooted in tradition and yet open to new interpretations and understandings. As we continue our exploration of the Church's doctrines and beliefs, we will see how this understanding of the Holy Spirit underpins its unique identity and shapes its spiritual practices.

Practical implications for worship

The Ethiopian Orthodox Tewahedo Church's profound reverence for the Holy Spirit permeates every aspect of its worship, infusing its rituals, prayers, and hymns with a sense of divine presence and spiritual vitality. This reverence is not merely theoretical but finds practical expression in various ways, shaping the Church's liturgical practices and the spiritual experiences of its followers.

1. **Invocation and Epiclesis:** The Holy Spirit is invoked at the beginning of every liturgical service, inviting the divine presence to descend upon the congregation and sanctify their worship. The epiclesis, a prayer invoking the Holy Spirit to transform the bread and wine into the body and blood of Christ during the Eucharist, is a central moment in the Divine Liturgy, highlighting the Holy Spirit's role in the sacramental life of the Church.

2. **Chants and Hymns:** The Church's rich musical tradition, with its mesmerizing chants and hymns, is seen as a manifestation of the Holy Spirit's inspiration. The rhythmic patterns, melodic contours, and poetic lyrics of these compositions are believed to uplift the soul, create a sense of

spiritual ecstasy, and facilitate communion with the divine.

3. **Use of Incense:** The burning of incense during liturgical services is not merely a sensory experience but a symbolic representation of the Holy Spirit's presence. The fragrant smoke rising towards heaven is seen as a symbol of prayers ascending to God, carried by the Holy Spirit.

4. **Spiritual Gifts:** The Ethiopian Orthodox Church recognizes the diverse gifts of the Holy Spirit, such as prophecy, healing, and speaking in tongues. These gifts are believed to be bestowed upon believers for the edification of the Church and the service of others. The Church encourages its members to seek these gifts through prayer, fasting, and spiritual discipline.

5. **Personal Piety:** The Holy Spirit is not only present in communal worship but also in the individual lives of believers. The Church encourages its members to cultivate a personal relationship with the Holy Spirit through prayer, meditation, and the study of scripture. This personal piety is seen as essential for spiritual growth and transformation.

6. **Community Life:** The Holy Spirit is also seen as the bond that unites the community of believers. The Church emphasizes the importance of communal worship, fellowship, and service, as expressions of the Holy Spirit's

work in the world. The spirit of unity and mutual support within the Ethiopian Orthodox community is a testament to the Holy Spirit's unifying power.

The Ethiopian Orthodox Tewahedo Church's understanding of the Holy Spirit is not confined to theological discourse but finds practical expression in its worship, spirituality, and communal life. The Holy Spirit is not merely an abstract concept but a living presence that guides, inspires, and empowers the faithful. By embracing the Holy Spirit's gifts and seeking its guidance, the Ethiopian Orthodox community continues to thrive as a vibrant and dynamic spiritual tradition.

Comparative Theology

- Differences from other Christian denominations.
- Historical and theological disputes.

The Ethiopian Orthodox Tewahedo Church, while sharing the fundamental tenets of Christianity with other denominations, possesses a distinct theological identity that sets it apart. These differences, often rooted in historical and cultural contexts, have led to theological disputes and dialogues that have shaped the Church's relationship with the broader Christian world.

Miaphysitism vs. Dyophysitism:

One of the most significant theological distinctions lies in the Church's adherence to Miaphysitism, a Christological doctrine that emphasizes the unified nature of Christ's divinity and humanity. This stands in contrast to the Dyophysite Christology embraced by many Western churches, which emphasizes the distinction between Christ's two natures. This doctrinal difference has been a source of contention throughout history, leading to the separation of Oriental Orthodox churches, including the Ethiopian Orthodox Church, from the Eastern Orthodox and Catholic churches in the 5th century.

Council of Chalcedon (451 AD):

The Council of Chalcedon, a pivotal event in Christian history, sought to resolve the Christological debates of the time. However, its definition of Christ as having two distinct natures in one person was not accepted by the Ethiopian Orthodox Church and other Oriental Orthodox churches. This disagreement led to a schism that has persisted for centuries, although recent ecumenical dialogues have sought to bridge the theological divide and promote understanding between different Christian traditions.

Unique Biblical Canon:

The Ethiopian Orthodox Bible, with its broader canon that includes books not found in other Christian Bibles, such as the Book of Enoch and the Book of Jubilees, is another distinctive feature. These additional texts, considered apocryphal by other denominations, offer unique insights into Ethiopian religious beliefs and practices. They reflect the Church's openness to diverse sources of spiritual wisdom and its deep respect for ancient traditions.

Liturgical and Ritual Practices:

The Ethiopian Orthodox Church's liturgical and ritual practices also set it apart. Its unique liturgical calendar, ancient Ge'ez language, distinctive chants and hymns, and elaborate use of incense create a sensory-rich worship experience that is deeply rooted in tradition. The Church's emphasis on fasting, pilgrimage, and veneration of saints and angels further distinguishes its spiritual practices.

Monastic Tradition:

The Ethiopian Orthodox Church's monastic tradition, with its emphasis on asceticism, communal living, and spiritual discipline, is another distinctive feature. Monasteries have played a crucial role in preserving the Church's teachings, traditions, and cultural heritage. They have also served as centers of learning, spiritual guidance, and social service, contributing to the Church's enduring influence in Ethiopian society.

Historical and Theological Disputes:

Throughout history, the Ethiopian Orthodox Church has engaged in theological disputes and dialogues with other Christian denominations. These interactions, while sometimes marked by disagreement and tension, have also fostered mutual understanding and respect. The Church's participation in the ecumenical movement in the 20th century marked a significant step towards greater cooperation and dialogue with other Christian traditions.

Contemporary Challenges and Opportunities:

In the modern era, the Ethiopian Orthodox Church faces the challenge of maintaining its unique identity and traditions while engaging with the broader Christian world. The rise of Pentecostalism and other evangelical movements, with their emphasis on personal salvation and emotional expression, has posed a challenge to the Church's traditional authority and practices. However, the Church has also found opportunities for dialogue and collaboration with these movements, recognizing the importance of diversity and inclusivity within the Christian faith.

The Ethiopian Orthodox Tewahedo Church's unique theological perspectives and historical experiences have shaped its distinct identity and its relationship with other Christian denominations. While differences remain, there is a growing recognition of the importance of dialogue, understanding, and cooperation in promoting Christian unity and addressing common challenges. The Church's willingness to engage with other traditions, while remaining true to its own unique heritage, is a testament to its resilience, adaptability, and commitment to the Gospel's message of love, peace, and reconciliation.

Influence on Culture and Society

Integration of doctrines into daily life.

The doctrines and beliefs of the Ethiopian Orthodox Tewahedo Church are not confined to the hallowed halls of churches and monasteries; they permeate the daily lives of its followers, shaping their worldview, values, and social interactions. This integration of faith into the quotidian is a testament to the Church's profound influence on Ethiopian culture and society.

Rhythms of Life: The Church's liturgical calendar, with its numerous feasts and fasts, sets the rhythm of life for many Ethiopians. Fasting, a central practice in Ethiopian Orthodoxy, is observed not only during major religious periods like Lent but also on specific days of the week. These fasting periods, which often involve abstaining from meat and dairy products, are not merely dietary restrictions but spiritual disciplines aimed at purifying the body and soul. They are a tangible expression of the Church's teachings on self-discipline, humility, and devotion.

Social Customs and Etiquette: The Church's teachings on respect for elders, hospitality, and communal harmony have shaped Ethiopian social customs and etiquette. The traditional coffee ceremony, a ritual deeply rooted in Ethiopian culture, is often infused with religious symbolism and blessings. The sharing of meals, the exchange of greetings, and the respect shown to religious leaders are all manifestations of the Church's influence on social interactions.

Art and Symbolism: The Church's doctrines and beliefs are also reflected in the art and symbolism that permeates Ethiopian culture. The intricate crosses, often worn as jewelry or displayed in homes, are not merely decorative items but symbols of faith and protection. The vibrant murals and icons that adorn churches and monasteries depict biblical stories and saints, serving as visual reminders of the Church's teachings and inspiring devotion among the faithful.

Language and Literature: The Ge'ez language, the liturgical language of the Church, has had a profound impact on Ethiopian language and literature. Many Amharic words and phrases have their roots in Ge'ez, and the Church's rich literary tradition, including hymns, prayers, and theological treatises, has shaped Ethiopian literary expression. The Ge'ez script, with its elegant characters and rich symbolism, is also used in secular contexts, further highlighting the Church's influence on Ethiopian culture.

Values and Worldview: The Church's teachings on the sanctity of life, the importance of family, and the interconnectedness of all creation have shaped the Ethiopian worldview. The Church's emphasis on compassion, forgiveness, and reconciliation has fostered a culture of tolerance and respect for diversity. The Church's teachings on social justice and the responsibility of the wealthy to care for the poor have also influenced social and economic policies in Ethiopia.

Challenges and Adaptations: The integration of the Church's doctrines into daily life is not without its challenges. In a rapidly modernizing world, some traditional practices and beliefs may be questioned or challenged. The Church must find ways to remain relevant and engaging to younger generations while preserving its core values and traditions. This requires a delicate balance between upholding ancient teachings and adapting to the changing needs and aspirations of the faithful.

The Ethiopian Orthodox Tewahedo Church's ability to integrate its doctrines into the daily lives of its followers is a testament to its enduring relevance and its deep roots in Ethiopian society. The Church's teachings, rituals, and traditions continue to shape the way Ethiopians live, work, and interact with one another. As Ethiopia continues to evolve, the Church's role in shaping the nation's cultural and social landscape remains as vital as ever.

Societal impact of theological beliefs

The Ethiopian Orthodox Tewahedo Church's theological beliefs have profoundly shaped Ethiopian society, leaving an enduring mark on its values, social structures, and cultural expressions. These beliefs, deeply ingrained in the hearts and minds of the faithful, have served as a moral compass, guiding individual behavior and shaping communal norms.

One of the most significant societal impacts of the Church's theology is its emphasis on communal values and social cohesion. This concept which emphasizes the importance of communal living, mutual support, and shared responsibility, is deeply rooted in Ethiopian Orthodox teachings. This emphasis on community has fostered a strong sense of social solidarity, where individuals are encouraged to care for one another, share resources, and work together for the common good.

The Church's teachings on social justice and equality have also had a profound impact on Ethiopian society. The concept of "mehaber," which emphasizes the inherent dignity and worth of every human being, regardless of social status or background, is a cornerstone of Ethiopian Orthodox social ethics. This belief in equality has inspired movements for social reform and has challenged discriminatory practices throughout history.

The Church's emphasis on forgiveness, reconciliation, and peaceful conflict resolution has also contributed to a culture of tolerance and respect for diversity in Ethiopia. This form of reconciliation and forgiveness is deeply ingrained in Ethiopian culture and is often facilitated by religious leaders. This emphasis on forgiveness and reconciliation has helped to heal wounds of conflict and promote social harmony.

The Church's teachings on the sanctity of life and the importance of family have also shaped Ethiopian social norms and values. The Church strongly opposes abortion and euthanasia, upholding the sanctity of life from conception to natural death. It also emphasizes the importance of marriage and family as the foundation of society, promoting traditional gender roles and family values.

The Church's influence on education and literacy has also had a significant societal impact. For centuries, the Church was the primary provider of education in Ethiopia, establishing schools and monasteries that served as centers of learning. The Church's emphasis on literacy and education has contributed to a high literacy rate in Ethiopia, even in rural areas.

However, the Church's theological beliefs have also been a source of contention and debate. Its conservative stance on social issues, such as gender roles and sexuality, has been challenged by some who advocate for more progressive interpretations of scripture and tradition. The Church's hierarchical structure and its relationship with the state have also been subjects of debate, with some calling for greater democratization and accountability.

Despite these challenges, the Ethiopian Orthodox Tewahedo Church remains a powerful force in Ethiopian society. Its theological beliefs continue to shape the nation's values, social structures, and cultural expressions. As Ethiopia continues to evolve and modernize, the Church will undoubtedly play a crucial role in shaping the nation's future, navigating the complexities of a changing world while remaining true to its ancient faith and traditions.

In this chapter, we have embarked on a theological exploration of the Ethiopian Orthodox Tewahedo Church, delving into its core doctrines and beliefs. We have traced the contours of its Trinitarian theology, its unique Christology rooted in Miaphysitism, and its profound understanding of the Holy Spirit. We have also examined the distinctive theological perspectives that set it apart from other Christian traditions, such as the doctrine of Sost Lidet and its veneration of Mary.

As we have seen, the Church's theology is not merely an abstract system of beliefs but a living reality that permeates every aspect of its life and worship. It shapes the way Ethiopians understand the divine, their relationship with God, and their place in the world. It also informs their ethical values, social norms, and cultural practices.

But theology is not the only pillar of the Ethiopian Orthodox Tewahedo Church. Its rich liturgical tradition, with its ancient rituals, vibrant ceremonies, and deep spiritual symbolism, is equally essential to understanding its essence. In the next chapter, we will step into the sacred space of Ethiopian Orthodox worship, where we will witness the beauty and mystery of the Divine Liturgy, the rhythm of the liturgical calendar, and the profound significance of sacraments. We will explore the role of music, art, and architecture in creating an atmosphere of reverence and devotion, and we will discover how the Church's liturgical practices reflect its unique theological perspectives and its deep connection to Ethiopian culture and history.

Prepare to be immersed in a sensory-rich experience, where the sights, sounds, and smells of worship transport you to a world of ancient traditions, vibrant spirituality, and profound devotion. Join us as we unlock the mysteries of Ethiopian Orthodox liturgy and worship, and discover the transformative power of sacred rituals in the lives of believers.

Chapter 4

Liturgy and Worship

The Divine Liturgy of Saint Basil

The Divine Liturgy of Saint Basil, a cornerstone of Ethiopian Orthodox worship, is a sacred symphony of rituals, prayers, and hymns that transports the faithful into the heart of divine mystery. This ancient liturgy, attributed to Saint Basil the Great, a 4th-century theologian and bishop, is a profound expression of the Church's faith, a transformative encounter with the divine, and a communal celebration of spiritual unity.

Structure:

The Divine Liturgy of Saint Basil follows a carefully choreographed structure, divided into distinct sections, each with its own symbolic meaning and spiritual significance. The liturgy begins with the Prothesis, the preparation of the bread and wine, symbolizing Christ's sacrifice. This is followed by the Liturgy of the Catechumens, which includes readings from the Old and New Testaments, hymns, and prayers. This section is open to all, including those who have not yet been baptized.

The Liturgy of the Faithful, the central part of the service, is reserved for baptized members of the Church. It begins with the Kiss of Peace, a gesture of reconciliation and unity. This is followed by the Anaphora, the Eucharistic prayer, during which the bread and wine are consecrated and become the body and blood of Christ. The faithful then partake in Holy Communion, receiving the consecrated elements as a sign of their union with Christ and with one another.

The liturgy concludes with prayers of thanksgiving, blessings, and the dismissal. The entire service is accompanied by the mesmerizing chants and hymns of the Ethiopian Orthodox tradition, creating an atmosphere of reverence, awe, and spiritual ecstasy.

Significance:

The Divine Liturgy of Saint Basil is not merely a religious ritual but a transformative experience that engages the senses, nourishes the soul, and unites the community of believers. It is a reenactment of Christ's sacrifice, a foretaste of the heavenly banquet, and a communion with the saints and angels.

The liturgy's structure, with its carefully orchestrated movements, gestures, and prayers, is designed to lead the faithful on a spiritual journey, from repentance and confession to thanksgiving and praise. The use of incense, candles, and liturgical vestments creates a sensory-rich environment that enhances the spiritual experience.

The liturgy's emphasis on communal participation fosters a sense of unity and belonging among the faithful. The congregation actively participates in the service through responses, chants, and prostrations, creating a vibrant and dynamic atmosphere of worship.

The Divine Liturgy of Saint Basil is also a treasure trove of theological and spiritual insights. Its prayers and hymns express the Church's core doctrines, such as the Trinity, the Incarnation, and the role of the Holy Spirit. The liturgy's symbolism, drawn from biblical narratives and patristic interpretations, offers a deeper understanding of the mysteries of faith.

The Divine Liturgy of Saint Basil is not merely a relic of the past but a living tradition that continues to nourish the spiritual lives of millions of Ethiopian Orthodox Christians. Its enduring appeal lies in its ability to connect the faithful to their rich spiritual heritage, to offer them a transformative encounter with the divine, and to foster a sense of community and belonging. As the Ethiopian Orthodox Church continues to evolve and adapt to the challenges of the modern world, the Divine Liturgy of

Saint Basil remains a cornerstone of its faith, a timeless expression of its spiritual identity, and a source of inspiration and renewal for generations to come.

Historical origins and evolution

The Divine Liturgy of Saint Basil, a cornerstone of Ethiopian Orthodox worship, traces its origins to the 4th century, attributed to Saint Basil the Great, a prominent theologian and bishop in Caesarea. This liturgy, celebrated in Ge'ez, the liturgical language of the Church, is a testament to the enduring power of tradition and the Church's connection to early Christianity.

Over the centuries, the Divine Liturgy of Saint Basil has evolved and adapted to the unique cultural and spiritual context of Ethiopia. While the core structure and theological essence of the liturgy have remained consistent, certain elements have been incorporated to reflect the Church's distinct identity. These include the use of traditional Ethiopian musical instruments, such as the sistrum and the kebero, the incorporation of local saints and martyrs into the liturgical calendar, and the adaptation of certain rituals to align with Ethiopian customs and practices.

The liturgy's evolution is also evident in the variations that exist between different regions and monastic traditions within Ethiopia. While the overall structure remains consistent, there are subtle differences in the chants, hymns, and rituals performed in different parts of the country. These variations reflect the rich diversity of Ethiopian culture and the Church's ability to adapt to local contexts while maintaining its core liturgical identity.

The Divine Liturgy of Saint Basil, in its Ethiopian Orthodox form, is not merely a relic of the past but a living tradition that continues to evolve and resonate with the faithful. Its ability to adapt and incorporate new elements while preserving its ancient roots is a testament to the Church's resilience and its commitment to maintaining its spiritual and cultural heritage. As the Ethiopian Orthodox Tewahedo Church continues to navigate the complexities of the modern world, the Divine Liturgy of Saint Basil remains a cornerstone of its faith, a timeless expression of its spiritual identity, and a source of inspiration and renewal for generations to come.

Liturgical Calendar and Festivals

Overview of major festivals:

The Ethiopian Orthodox Tewahedo Church's liturgical calendar is a vibrant tapestry of feasts and fasts, each marking a significant event in the life of Christ, the Virgin Mary, or the saints. These festivals, celebrated with great fervor and devotion, are not merely religious observances but also cultural celebrations that bring communities together and reinforce the Church's teachings.

1. Timkat (Epiphany): Timkat, celebrated on January 19th, commemorates the baptism of Jesus Christ in the Jordan River. It is one of the most important and colorful festivals in the Ethiopian Orthodox calendar. The celebration involves processions, chanting, and the symbolic re-enactment of baptism. The faithful gather at rivers and lakes, where priests bless the water and sprinkle it on the congregation. Timkat is a time of spiritual renewal and purification, as believers reaffirm their faith and commitment to Christ.

2. Meskel (Feast of the Finding of the True Cross): Meskel, celebrated on September 27th, commemorates the discovery of the True Cross by Empress Helena, the mother of Emperor Constantine. The festival involves the burning of a large bonfire, symbolizing the finding of the cross. The faithful gather around the bonfire, singing hymns and offering prayers. Meskel is a time of reflection on the significance of the cross in Christian faith and a celebration of the triumph of good over evil.

3. Genna (Christmas): Genna, celebrated on January 7th, marks the birth of Jesus Christ. It is a time of joy and celebration, with families gathering for feasts and exchanging gifts. The celebration includes special church services, processions, and the singing of Christmas hymns. Genna is a time for reflection on the Incarnation, the belief that

God became flesh in the person of Jesus Christ, and its significance for human salvation.

4. Fasika (Easter): Fasika, the most important festival in the Ethiopian Orthodox calendar, celebrates the resurrection of Jesus Christ. It is preceded by a 55-day Lenten fast, a period of introspection and spiritual preparation. The celebration of Fasika includes special church services, the breaking of the fast with festive meals, and the exchange of greetings and gifts. Fasika is a time of great joy and hope, as believers celebrate the triumph of life over death and the promise of eternal salvation.

5. Kulubi Gabriel (Feast of Saint Gabriel): This festival, celebrated on December 28th, honors Saint Gabriel, the archangel who is believed to have appeared to the Virgin Mary to announce the birth of Jesus. The celebration includes special church services, processions, and the veneration of icons depicting Saint Gabriel. Kulubi Gabriel is a time for reflection on the role of angels in God's plan of salvation and their intercession on behalf of believers.

6. Hidar Tsion (Feast of Our Lady Mary of Zion): This festival, celebrated on November 21st, honors Mary, the mother of Jesus, and her association with the ancient city of Aksum, believed to be the resting place of the Ark of the Covenant. The celebration includes special church

services, processions, and the veneration of icons depicting Mary. Hidar Tsion is a time for reflection on Mary's role in salvation history and her intercession on behalf of believers.

These are just a few of the major festivals celebrated by the Ethiopian Orthodox Tewahedo Church. Each festival, with its unique rituals, traditions, and spiritual significance, offers a glimpse into the rich tapestry of Ethiopian Orthodox faith and culture. They are not merely religious observances but communal celebrations that bring people together, strengthen their faith, and reinforce their cultural identity.

Liturgical year structure

The Ethiopian Orthodox Tewahedo Church follows a unique liturgical calendar that guides the rhythm of its spiritual life throughout the year. This calendar, a harmonious blend of solar and lunar cycles, is a testament to the Church's rich heritage and its deep connection to the natural world.

1. **Major Feasts of the Lord**
   A. **Feasts of the Incarnation (Birth)**
      - *Annunciation* – Megabit 29 (March 25)
      - *Nativity of Christ* (ገና) – Tahisas 29 (January 7)

- *Epiphany (Timket)* (ጥምቀት) – Tir 11 (January 19)
- *Presentation of Christ in the Temple* – Yekatit 23 (March 2)

B. **Feasts of the Passion (Death and Resurrection)**
- *Palm Sunday* (ሆሣዕና) – One week before Easter
- *Good Friday* (ስቅለት) – Two days before Easter
- *Resurrection (Easter)* (ፋሲካ) – Date varies annually (between late March and late April)

C. **Feasts of the Second Coming**
- *Feast of the Ascension* – 40 days after Easter
- *Pentecost* – 50 days after Easter

2. **Feasts of the Virgin Mary:**

A. The Church honors the Virgin Mary through numerous feasts, including:
- *Kidane Mehret* – Yekatit 16 (February 23)
- *Her Nativity* – Nehasé 1 (August 15)
- *Her Presentation in the Temple*– Yekatit 3 (February 10)
- *Her Dormition (Filseta)* – Nehasé 16 (August 22)

3. **Fasting Periods**

A. Fasting is a central part of the Ethiopian Orthodox calendar, including:
- *Great Lent (Abiy Tsom)* – 55 days before Easter

- *Fast of the Apostles (Sene Tsom)* – After Pentecost, length varies
- *Fast of the Assumption (Filseta Tsom)* – 16 days in August
- *Fast of Nineveh (Ba'ale Wold)* – 3 days before the Great Lent
- *Advent Fast (Tsome Gena)* – 40 days before Christmas
- *Wednesdays and Fridays* – Weekly fasts except during feasting seasons.

4. **Feasts of Saints**

   A. The EOTC calendar commemorates saints daily, with major celebrations including:
      - *St. George (Giorgis)* – Miazia 23 (April 28)
      - *St. Michael* – Monthly, especially Hedar 12 (November 21) and Sene 12 (June 19)
      - *St. Tekle Haymanot* – Nehasé 24 (August 30)

5. **Liturgical Year (Zemene Mahlet)**

   A. The liturgical year begins in Meskerem (September), aligning with the Ethiopian New Year. It is divided into:
      - *Seasons of Nativity (Qidasew Beal)* – Focus on Christ's birth and manifestation.
      - *Season of Passion (Himamat)* – Focus on the suffering, death, and resurrection of Christ.
      - *Season of Pentecost (Paraklitos)* – Focus on the descent of the Holy Spirit and the life of the Church.

6. **Special Celebrations**
   A. They include:
      - *Meskel (Finding of the True Cross)* –
        Meskerem 17 (September 27 or 28 during
        leap years).
      - *Enkutatash (New Year)* – Meskerem 1
        (September 11 or 12 during leap years).
      - *Hosanna (Palm Sunday)* – Celebrated one
        week before Easter.

The liturgical calendar is further divided into weeks, each dedicated to a specific theme or saint. Sundays are particularly important, as they commemorate the resurrection of Christ and are marked by special church services and communal gatherings.

The Ethiopian Orthodox liturgical year is a cyclical journey, a continuous rhythm of feasts and fasts that guide the faithful through the seasons of their spiritual lives. It is a time for celebration, reflection, repentance, and renewal, a constant reminder of God's presence and the promise of salvation.

Role of Icons and Religious Art

Importance of religious imagery:

In the Ethiopian Orthodox Tewahedo Church, icons and religious art are not mere decorations; they are windows into the divine, visual manifestations of spiritual truths, and conduits of grace. The reverence for religious imagery is deeply ingrained in the Church's tradition, stemming from a theological understanding that transcends the material and embraces the spiritual significance of artistic expression.

Icons, in particular, hold a place of profound veneration in Ethiopian Orthodoxy. These sacred images, often depicting Christ, the Virgin Mary, or the saints, are not seen as mere representations but as living presences of the divine. They are believed to be imbued with spiritual power, capable of mediating between the earthly and the heavenly realms. The faithful venerate icons by bowing before them, kissing them, and lighting candles in front of them. This act of veneration is not worship of the image itself but an expression of devotion to the person or event depicted in the icon.

The importance of religious imagery in the Ethiopian Orthodox Church can be understood through several key aspects:

1. Theological Significance: Icons are seen as visual expressions of theological truths. They depict biblical narratives, the lives of saints, and the mysteries of faith in a way that is accessible and meaningful to believers. The colors, symbols, and gestures used in icons are not arbitrary but carry deep theological significance. For example, the use of gold backgrounds in icons symbolizes the

divine light, while the halos around the heads of saints represent their holiness and closeness to God.

2. Spiritual Function: Icons are not merely decorative but serve a spiritual function in the life of the Church. They are believed to be channels of divine grace, through which believers can connect with the spiritual realm. The act of venerating an icon is seen as a way of participating in the divine life and receiving blessings from God. Icons are also used in liturgical processions and ceremonies, adding to the solemnity and spiritual significance of these events.

3. Educational Role: Icons serve as visual aids for religious instruction, particularly for those who are illiterate or have limited access to written texts. The stories and teachings depicted in icons are easily understood and remembered, making them an effective tool for transmitting the faith to future generations. Icons also serve as a visual catechism, teaching believers about the lives of saints, the events of salvation history, and the mysteries of faith.

4. Cultural Expression: Religious art, including icons, murals, and illuminated manuscripts, is a vibrant expression of Ethiopian culture and identity. The unique artistic style of Ethiopian icons, with its elongated figures, expressive eyes,

and vibrant colors, reflects the Church's rich cultural heritage and its adaptation to local artistic traditions. The use of indigenous materials, such as wood, paint, and parchment, further reinforces the connection between faith and culture.

5. Aesthetic Beauty: Beyond their theological and spiritual significance, icons and religious art are also valued for their aesthetic beauty. The intricate details, vibrant colors, and symbolic representations found in Ethiopian religious art are a testament to the skill and creativity of the artists who created them. These works of art not only inspire devotion but also enrich the cultural landscape of Ethiopia.

The Ethiopian Orthodox Tewahedo Church's reverence for religious imagery is a testament to its deep understanding of the power of art to communicate spiritual truths, inspire devotion, and foster a sense of community. Icons and religious art are not merely objects of veneration but living expressions of faith, connecting the faithful to the divine and enriching their spiritual lives.

Art forms and their meanings

The Ethiopian Orthodox Tewahedo Church's artistic expressions are not merely decorative; they are visual narratives that convey theological depth, spiritual significance, and cultural identity. Each art form, meticulously crafted and imbued with symbolism, serves as a window into the Church's rich heritage and its enduring faith.

1. **Icons:** Icons, often painted on wood panels or parchment, are revered as sacred images that depict Christ, the Virgin Mary, saints, and angels. They are not meant to be realistic portrayals but rather stylized representations that convey spiritual truths. The elongated figures, almond-shaped eyes, and vibrant colors of Ethiopian icons are distinctive features that reflect the Church's unique artistic tradition. Icons are not merely objects of veneration but are believed to be conduits of divine grace, mediating between the earthly and the heavenly realms.

2. **Murals and Frescoes:** The walls of Ethiopian Orthodox churches and monasteries are adorned with vibrant murals and frescoes that depict biblical scenes, the lives of saints, and theological teachings. These murals, often painted in a naive style with bold colors and expressive figures, serve as visual aids for religious instruction and inspire devotion among the faithful. They are a testament to the Church's rich artistic heritage and its commitment to preserving its traditions through visual storytelling.

3. **Illuminated Manuscripts:** Ethiopian illuminated manuscripts, with their intricate calligraphy, vibrant colors, and elaborate

illustrations, are among the most exquisite examples of religious art. These manuscripts, often containing biblical texts, liturgical books, or hagiographies (lives of saints), were meticulously crafted by skilled scribes and artists. They are not only valuable historical documents but also works of art that reflect the Church's deep reverence for the written word and its commitment to preserving its spiritual heritage.

4. **Crosses:** The cross, a central symbol of Christianity, holds a special significance in Ethiopian Orthodoxy. Ethiopian crosses are renowned for their intricate designs, often incorporating geometric patterns, floral motifs, and symbolic representations. They are not merely decorative objects but are believed to possess protective powers and are worn as jewelry or displayed in homes and churches. The cross is a constant reminder of Christ's sacrifice and the central message of salvation in the Ethiopian Orthodox faith.

5. **Church Architecture:** Ethiopian church architecture is a unique blend of indigenous and foreign influences. The traditional round churches, with their conical thatched roofs and intricate wooden carvings, are a testament to the Church's adaptation to the local environment and its cultural heritage. The rock-hewn churches of Lalibela, carved out of solid rock, are a marvel of

engineering and a testament to the Church's spiritual ambition and artistic vision. These architectural wonders not only serve as places of worship but also as cultural landmarks that attract pilgrims and tourists from around the world.

The Ethiopian Orthodox Tewahedo Church's artistic expressions are a testament to its rich spiritual heritage, its deep connection to Ethiopian culture, and its enduring faith. These art forms, imbued with symbolism and meaning, continue to inspire and uplift the faithful, serving as visual reminders of the Church's teachings and its central role in Ethiopian society.

Sacraments in Worship

Detailed exploration of liturgical practices:

The sacraments, or mysteries, are not merely symbolic rituals in the Ethiopian Orthodox Tewahedo Church; they are profound encounters with the divine, conduits of grace, and transformative experiences that shape the spiritual lives of believers. These sacred rites, deeply rooted in tradition and imbued with spiritual significance, are woven into the fabric of the Church's liturgical practices, enriching its worship and fostering a sense of communion with God.

Baptism: The journey of faith begins with baptism, a sacrament that signifies spiritual rebirth and cleansing from sin. The Ethiopian Orthodox Church practices baptism by immersion, typically in a pool or natural body of water. The priest, adorned in liturgical vestments, immerses the candidate three times while invoking the Holy Trinity. This act of immersion symbolizes the washing away of sin and the emergence of a new creation in Christ. The newly baptized is then anointed with holy oil, signifying the sealing of the Holy Spirit.

Chrismation: Immediately following baptism, the sacrament of Chrismation is administered. The priest anoints the forehead, eyes, ears, nose, mouth, hands, and feet of the newly baptized with holy oil, invoking the Holy Spirit to strengthen and guide them in their spiritual journey. This anointing is seen as a confirmation of the baptismal grace and a deepening of the believer's relationship with the Holy Spirit.

Eucharist (Qurban): The Eucharist, the central act of worship in the Ethiopian Orthodox Church, is a profound mystery that unites the faithful with Christ and with one another. The liturgy of the Eucharist, known as the Divine Liturgy of Saint Basil, is a rich tapestry of prayers, chants, and rituals that culminate in the consecration of bread and wine into the body and blood of Christ. The faithful partake in Holy Communion, receiving the consecrated elements as a sign of their participation in the divine life and their communion with the Church.

Confession: Confession, a sacrament of repentance and forgiveness, is an integral part of Ethiopian Orthodox spiritual practice. Believers confess their sins to a priest, who offers absolution and spiritual guidance. This act of confession is seen as a means of spiritual healing and reconciliation with God and the community. The priest, acting as a mediator between the penitent and God, offers words of comfort, encouragement, and absolution, restoring the believer to a state of grace.

Matrimony: Marriage, a sacred union between a man and a woman, is celebrated with great joy and solemnity in the Ethiopian Orthodox Church. The wedding ceremony, rich in symbolism and tradition, includes the exchange of rings, the crowning of the couple, and the sharing of bread and wine. The Church views marriage as a lifelong commitment, a reflection of Christ's love for his Church, and a source of mutual support and spiritual growth for the couple.

Holy Orders: The sacrament of Holy Orders is a sacred rite through which men are ordained as deacons, priests, and bishops. The ordination ceremony involves the laying on of hands, the anointing with holy oil, and the bestowal of liturgical vestments. The ordained clergy are entrusted with the responsibility of leading the Church, administering the sacraments, and teaching the faith. They are seen as shepherds of the flock, guiding the faithful on their spiritual journey and serving as intermediaries between God and humanity.

Unction of the Sick (Qandil): The Unction of the Sick, a sacrament of healing and comfort, is administered to those who are ill or suffering. The priest anoints the sick with holy oil, accompanied by prayers for their physical and spiritual well-being. This sacrament is seen as a means of divine grace, offering comfort, strength, and the hope of healing. It is a reminder of God's love and care for the sick and a source of solace in times of suffering.

Role of sacraments in daily worship

While the Divine Liturgy, with the Eucharist at its heart, is the central act of worship in the Ethiopian Orthodox Tewahedo Church, the sacraments are not confined to this singular event. They permeate the daily spiritual life of the faithful, serving as constant reminders of God's grace, the community's interconnectedness, and the ongoing journey of faith.

Baptism and Chrismation, while often associated with infancy or conversion, are not isolated events but the beginning of a lifelong spiritual journey. The blessings and prayers associated with these sacraments are echoed in daily devotions, reminding believers of their commitment to Christ and their membership in the Church.

Confession, while not a daily practice for most, is encouraged as a regular means of spiritual cleansing and renewal. The act of confessing one's sins and receiving absolution is seen as a way to maintain a healthy relationship with God and the community.

Marriage, though a one-time sacrament, is a constant source of spiritual strength and support for couples. The Church's teachings on the sanctity of marriage and the importance of mutual love and respect guide couples in their daily lives, fostering a sense of unity and purpose.

Holy Orders, while specific to ordained clergy, impacts the daily worship of all believers. The priests and deacons who have received this sacrament lead the community in prayer, administer the sacraments, and offer spiritual guidance, enriching the daily spiritual lives of the faithful.

The Unction of the Sick, though administered in times of illness or suffering, is a reminder of God's constant presence and care. The prayers and anointing offered during this sacrament bring comfort and hope to the sick, reminding them of the Church's support and the promise of healing.

In essence, the sacraments are not isolated events but threads that weave together the daily spiritual life of Ethiopian Orthodox Christians. They are constant reminders of God's grace, the community's interconnectedness, and the ongoing journey of faith. Through these sacraments, the Church nurtures the spiritual growth of its followers, guiding them on their path towards salvation and union with God.

Prayer and Chanting

Traditional prayers and chants:

In the Ethiopian Orthodox Tewahedo Church, prayer and chanting are not merely acts of devotion; they are the lifeblood of spiritual expression, the rhythmic pulse that connects the earthly with the divine. Rooted in ancient traditions and imbued with profound symbolism, these vocal offerings create an atmosphere of reverence, awe, and spiritual ecstasy, transporting the faithful into the heart of divine mystery.

Traditional Prayers:

Ethiopian Orthodox prayers are a tapestry of biblical verses, patristic teachings, and poetic expressions of faith. They are often recited in Ge'ez, the liturgical language of the Church, adding a layer of sacredness and mystery to their recitation. These prayers encompass a wide range of themes, from praise and thanksgiving to supplication and intercession. They are offered for personal needs, communal well-being, and the salvation of the world.

The Lord's Prayer, a cornerstone of Christian prayer, holds a special place in Ethiopian Orthodox worship. It is recited in Ge'ez, its ancient words echoing through the centuries, connecting the faithful to the earliest days of Christianity. Other common prayers include the Hail Mary, the Nicene Creed, and various prayers to saints and angels.

Chants and Hymns:

Chants and hymns, known as "zema" in Ge'ez, are an integral part of Ethiopian Orthodox worship. These melodic compositions, often accompanied by traditional instruments like the sistrum and the kebero, create a mesmerizing soundscape that uplifts the soul and fosters a sense of spiritual communion. The zema, with their intricate melodies and poetic lyrics, express the Church's theological teachings, recount biblical stories, and celebrate the lives of saints.

The most renowned composer of Ethiopian Orthodox chants is Saint Yared, a 6th-century saint and scholar who is revered as the father of Ethiopian church music. His compositions, known for their complexity, beauty, and spiritual depth, continue to be sung in churches and monasteries throughout Ethiopia.

The Power of Vocal Expression:

In the Ethiopian Orthodox tradition, prayer and chanting are not merely individual acts of devotion but communal expressions of faith. The congregation actively participates in the liturgy, responding to the priest's prayers, joining in the chants, and prostrating themselves in reverence. This communal participation creates a vibrant and dynamic atmosphere of worship, where the voices of the faithful blend together in a harmonious chorus of praise and supplication.

The power of vocal expression in Ethiopian Orthodox worship is not limited to its aesthetic appeal. It is believed that the act of praying and chanting has a transformative effect on the soul, purifying it from sin, opening it to divine grace, and drawing it closer to God. The rhythmic patterns, melodic contours, and repetitive nature of the chants are believed to induce a state of spiritual ecstasy, allowing the faithful to transcend the mundane and experience a glimpse of the divine.

Role of music in worship

In the Ethiopian Orthodox Tewahedo Church, music is not merely an accompaniment to worship; it is an integral part of the spiritual experience, a vehicle for divine communication, and a powerful expression of faith. The Church's musical tradition, deeply rooted in ancient melodies and rhythms, creates an atmosphere of reverence, awe, and spiritual ecstasy, transporting the faithful into the heart of divine mystery.

The role of music in Ethiopian Orthodox worship is multifaceted:

1. **Enhancing Prayer and Devotion:** The rhythmic patterns, melodic contours, and repetitive nature of Ethiopian Orthodox chants and hymns are believed to have a meditative effect, calming the mind, opening the heart, and

fostering a deeper connection with the divine. The music serves as a vehicle for prayer, allowing the faithful to express their devotion, supplication, and gratitude through song.

2. **Transmitting Theological Teachings:** The lyrics of the chants and hymns are often rich in theological content, conveying the Church's teachings on the Trinity, the Incarnation, the life of Christ, and the lives of saints. The music thus serves as a form of oral tradition, transmitting the faith from one generation to the next.

3. **Creating a Sense of Community:** Communal singing is a hallmark of Ethiopian Orthodox worship. The congregation actively participates in the liturgy, joining their voices in a harmonious chorus of praise and supplication. This shared musical experience fosters a sense of unity and belonging, strengthening the bonds between the faithful and creating a vibrant atmosphere of worship.

4. **Evoking Spiritual Ecstasy:** The hypnotic rhythms and soaring melodies of Ethiopian Orthodox music are believed to induce a state of spiritual ecstasy, allowing the faithful to transcend the mundane and experience a glimpse of the divine. This ecstatic experience is often accompanied by spontaneous bodily movements, such as swaying, clapping, and dancing, further enhancing the sense of spiritual fervor.

5. **Preserving Cultural Heritage:** The Church's musical tradition is a treasure trove of Ethiopian cultural heritage. The use of traditional instruments, such as the sistrum and the kebero, the preservation of ancient melodies, and the transmission of musical knowledge through oral tradition all contribute to the richness and diversity of Ethiopian musical expression.

The Ethiopian Orthodox Tewahedo Church's musical tradition is a testament to the power of music to uplift the soul, inspire devotion, and foster a sense of community. It is a living tradition that continues to evolve and adapt, while remaining deeply rooted in the Church's ancient heritage. As the Church navigates the challenges of the modern world, its musical tradition remains a source of strength, identity, and spiritual renewal.

Community Participation

Involvement of the laity:

In the Ethiopian Orthodox Tewahedo Church, the laity's active participation is not merely encouraged; it is woven into the very fabric of worship, creating a vibrant and dynamic communal experience. The liturgy is not a spectator sport but a participatory symphony, where the voices of the faithful blend with the melodies of the deacons and priests, creating a harmonious chorus of praise and supplication.

The involvement of the laity is evident in various aspects of the Divine Liturgy:

1. **Responses and Antiphons:** Throughout the liturgy, the congregation actively responds to the prayers and chants of the clergy, creating a call-and-response pattern that engages the entire community. These responses, often short phrases or verses from scripture, are not mere repetitions but affirmations of faith and expressions of devotion.

2. **Chanting and Singing:** The laity joins the deacons and priests in singing the hymns and chants that are an integral part of the liturgy. The rich musical tradition of the Ethiopian Orthodox Church, with its unique scales, rhythms, and melodies, is not confined to the clergy but is shared by the entire congregation. This communal singing creates a powerful sense of unity and spiritual upliftment.

3. **Prostrations and Gestures:** The physical act of worship is also emphasized in the Ethiopian Orthodox tradition. The faithful engage in prostrations, bowing, and making the sign of the cross at various points during the liturgy. These gestures are not merely outward expressions but are believed to have a spiritual significance,

humbling the body and focusing the mind on the divine.

4. **Reading of Scripture:** Laypeople are often invited to participate in the reading of scripture during the liturgy. This practice not only emphasizes the importance of the Bible in the life of the Church but also empowers the laity to engage with the sacred texts and share their insights with the community.

5. **Offering of Incense:** The offering of incense, a symbolic act of prayer and devotion, is not limited to the clergy. Laypeople are also invited to participate in this ritual, offering incense as a sign of their personal prayers and intentions.

6. **Participation in Processions:** During major festivals and celebrations, the laity actively participates in processions, carrying icons, banners, and crosses. These processions, often accompanied by music and chanting, are a vibrant expression of communal faith and a public witness to the Church's teachings.

The active involvement of the laity in Ethiopian Orthodox worship is not merely a matter of tradition but a theological imperative. The Church views the liturgy as a communal act, where the entire community participates in the offering of praise, thanksgiving, and supplication to God. This participatory approach fosters a sense of belonging, strengthens the bonds between the faithful, and creates a vibrant and dynamic spiritual community.

Importance of communal worship

The communal aspect of worship in the Ethiopian Orthodox Tewahedo Church is not merely a matter of tradition; it is a theological imperative that reflects the Church's understanding of the interconnectedness of all believers. The act of gathering together for prayer, chanting, and the sharing of the Eucharist is seen as a microcosm of the heavenly kingdom, where all are united in Christ.

Communal worship fosters a sense of belonging and shared identity among the faithful. It strengthens the bonds of community, providing a space for mutual support, encouragement, and spiritual growth. The shared experience of worship, with its rhythmic chants, fragrant incense, and vibrant rituals, creates a sense of awe and reverence, drawing the participants closer to God and to one another.

The Ethiopian Orthodox Church views the liturgy as a collective offering of praise, thanksgiving, and supplication to God. The active participation of the laity, through responses, chants, prostrations, and other gestures, is seen as essential to the efficacy of the liturgy. It is through this communal participation that the Church becomes a living body, a vibrant expression of the Holy Spirit's unifying power.

The importance of communal worship is also reflected in the Church's emphasis on hospitality and fellowship. After the Divine Liturgy, it is customary for the congregation to gather for a shared meal, known as "agape." This communal meal, often held in the church courtyard or a nearby home, is a time for socializing, sharing stories, and strengthening the bonds of community. It is a tangible expression of the Church's belief in the importance of fellowship and mutual support.

In the Ethiopian Orthodox Tewahedo Church, communal worship is not merely a religious obligation but a joyful celebration of faith, a source of spiritual nourishment, and a means of strengthening the bonds of community. It is a testament to the Church's deep understanding of the interconnectedness of all believers and its commitment to fostering a vibrant and inclusive spiritual community.

As we conclude this chapter on liturgy and worship, we have witnessed the rich tapestry of rituals, prayers, and artistic expressions that define the Ethiopian Orthodox Tewahedo Church's spiritual life. We have explored the profound significance of the Divine Liturgy, the vibrant celebrations of the liturgical calendar, and the role of icons, music, and communal participation in creating a transformative worship experience.

In the next chapter, we will delve into the sacred scriptures that form the foundation of Ethiopian Orthodox faith and practice. We will explore the unique features of the

Ethiopian Orthodox Bible, the importance of the Ge'ez language, and the Church's rich tradition of biblical interpretation. Join us as we uncover the treasures of the written word and their enduring impact on the spiritual life of the Ethiopian Orthodox community.

Chapter 5

Scriptural Canon

Overview of the Ethiopian Orthodox Bible

The Ethiopian Orthodox Tewahedo Church reveres a unique and expansive scriptural canon, a testament to its ancient heritage and distinct theological perspective. This sacred collection, known as the Ethiopian Orthodox Bible, is a treasure trove of spiritual wisdom, historical narratives, and prophetic visions that have nourished the faith of millions for centuries.

Structure:

The Ethiopian Orthodox Bible is not a single book but a compilation of 81 books, divided into two main sections: the Old Testament and the New Testament. However, its structure and contents differ significantly from the canons of other Christian traditions, reflecting the Church's unique historical and theological development.

The Old Testament in the Ethiopian Orthodox Bible includes all the books found in the Protestant Old Testament, as well as additional books and chapters that are considered apocryphal or deuterocanonical by other denominations. These additional texts, such as the Book of Enoch, the Book of Jubilees, and the Book of Ezra Sutuel, offer unique insights into Ethiopian religious beliefs and practices, providing a broader and more diverse perspective on the Old Testament narrative.

The New Testament in the Ethiopian Orthodox Bible also includes all the books found in the Protestant New Testament, but with some variations in arrangement and content. For example, the Ethiopian New Testament includes a book called the "Sinodos," a collection of canons and decrees from early Church councils, and the "Qalementos," a collection of writings attributed to Clement of Rome, an early Church Father. These additional texts provide valuable insights into the early development of Christianity and the Ethiopian Orthodox Church's unique theological perspectives.

Contents:

The Ethiopian Orthodox Bible is a rich tapestry of diverse literary genres, including historical narratives, legal codes, prophetic writings, wisdom literature, psalms, gospels, epistles, and apocalyptic visions. Each book within the canon offers a unique perspective on the divine, the human condition, and the relationship between God and humanity.

The Old Testament books, such as Genesis, Exodus, and Leviticus, recount the creation of the world, the history of the Israelites, and the laws and covenants that governed their relationship with God. The prophetic books, such as Isaiah, Jeremiah, and Ezekiel, contain warnings, exhortations, and promises of salvation. The wisdom literature, such as Proverbs, Ecclesiastes, and the Song of Songs, offers insights into the nature of wisdom, the meaning of life, and the complexities of human relationships.

The New Testament books, including the four Gospels, the Acts of the Apostles, and the Epistles, tell the story of Jesus Christ's life, ministry, death, and resurrection. They also provide guidance and instruction for the early Christian communities, addressing issues of faith, morality, and social responsibility. The Book of Revelation, with its apocalyptic visions, offers a glimpse into the end times and the ultimate triumph of good over evil.

The Ethiopian Orthodox Bible, with its unique structure and diverse contents, is a testament to the Church's rich heritage and its openness to different sources of spiritual wisdom. It is a sacred text that has nourished the faith of millions for centuries, providing guidance, inspiration, and a sense of connection to the divine. As we delve deeper into the specific books of the Ethiopian Orthodox canon, we will uncover the treasures of wisdom, history, and prophecy that have shaped the Church's identity and continue to inspire its followers today.

Unique books in the canon

The Ethiopian Orthodox Tewahedo Church's scriptural canon, a testament to its ancient heritage and unique theological perspective, includes several books not found in other Christian Bibles. These unique texts, often referred to as "deutero-canonical" or "extra-canonical," offer valuable insights into Ethiopian religious beliefs, practices, and historical narratives.

1. **The Book of Enoch:** This ancient Jewish apocalyptic text, attributed to Enoch, the great-grandfather of Noah, is considered canonical by the Ethiopian Orthodox Church. It contains vivid descriptions of the heavenly realms, the fallen angels, and the final judgment. The Book of Enoch's inclusion in the Ethiopian canon reflects the Church's openness to apocalyptic literature and its belief in the ongoing struggle between good and evil.

2. **The Book of Jubilees:** Also known as "Little Genesis," this book provides an alternative account of the events described in the biblical book of Genesis. It offers a more detailed chronology of events, expands on certain narratives, and provides additional insights into

Jewish laws and customs. The Book of Jubilees is valued for its historical and theological perspectives, shedding light on the development of Jewish and Christian traditions.

3. **The Book of Ezra Sutuel:** This book, unique to the Ethiopian Orthodox canon, contains a collection of prayers, hymns, and liturgical texts. It is believed to have been written by Ezra the Scribe, a key figure in Jewish history who is credited with restoring the Torah after the Babylonian exile. The Book of Ezra Sutuel is valued for its liturgical and devotional content, providing a glimpse into the spiritual practices of the early Ethiopian Church.

4. **The Book of Joseph ben Gurion:** This historical narrative recounts the exploits of the Jewish general Joseph ben Gurion during the Roman occupation of Judea. It is a tale of heroism, resistance, and martyrdom, offering a unique perspective on Jewish history and the struggle for freedom. The book's inclusion in the Ethiopian canon reflects the Church's respect for Jewish traditions and its recognition of the shared heritage of Judaism and Christianity.

5. **The Book of Meqabyan:** This book, also known as the Ethiopian Maccabees, tells the story of the Maccabean Revolt, a Jewish uprising against the Seleucid Empire in the 2nd century BC. It is a tale of courage, faith, and the struggle

for religious freedom. The Book of Meqabyan is valued for its historical and inspirational content, highlighting the importance of resisting oppression and defending one's faith.

These unique books, while not universally accepted by all Christian denominations, hold a special place in the Ethiopian Orthodox tradition. They offer valuable insights into the Church's theological perspectives, its historical development, and its relationship with other religious traditions. They also provide a glimpse into the rich literary and cultural heritage of Ethiopia, reflecting the diversity and depth of its spiritual traditions.

Ge'ez Language Importance

Historical and religious significance:

The Ge'ez language, with its elegant script and rich vocabulary, is far more than a relic of the past; it is a living testament to Ethiopia's ancient heritage and the bedrock upon which the Ethiopian Orthodox Tewahedo Church's unique identity is built. Its historical and religious significance is so profound that it has been dubbed the "language of angels" by the faithful, a testament to its perceived divine origins and its role as a conduit for spiritual expression.

Historically, Ge'ez served as the official language of the Aksumite Empire, a powerful kingdom that flourished in northern Ethiopia from the 1st to the 8th centuries AD. It was the language of royal inscriptions, legal documents, and historical chronicles, documenting the empire's achievements and cultural legacy. The adoption of Christianity in the 4th century further elevated Ge'ez's status, as it became the language of the Bible, liturgical texts, and theological treatises.

The Church's decision to adopt Ge'ez as its liturgical language was a pivotal moment in its history. It not only ensured the preservation of ancient Christian texts but also fostered a sense of continuity and connection to the early Church. The use of Ge'ez in worship created a sacred linguistic space, setting the Church apart from the surrounding cultures and reinforcing its unique identity.

The religious significance of Ge'ez extends beyond its liturgical use. It is believed to be the language spoken by God and the angels, a divine language that carries a special spiritual potency. The faithful believe that prayers and hymns recited in Ge'ez are more effective in reaching God and invoking his blessings. The language's rich vocabulary and poetic expressions are seen as a means of expressing the ineffable mysteries of faith and connecting with the divine.

The Ge'ez script, with its unique characters and intricate calligraphy, is also revered as a sacred art form. The scribes who meticulously copied and illuminated manuscripts in Ge'ez were not merely artisans but spiritual practitioners, their work imbued with religious devotion and artistic skill. These manuscripts, often adorned with vibrant colors and intricate designs, are not only repositories of knowledge but also works of art that reflect the Church's rich cultural heritage.

The importance of Ge'ez in Ethiopian Orthodox tradition is not confined to the past. It continues to be the language of the Church's liturgy, prayer, and theological discourse. The study of Ge'ez is an essential part of theological education, and its preservation is seen as a sacred duty. The Church's commitment to maintaining the Ge'ez language ensures that its ancient traditions and spiritual heritage are passed on to future generations.

Role in liturgy and scripture

Ge'ez serves as the foundation upon which the Ethiopian Orthodox Tewahedo Church's liturgical and scriptural traditions are built. Its significance is not merely linguistic but deeply spiritual and cultural, shaping the way the faithful engage with the divine and understand their place in the world.

In the liturgy, Ge'ez is the language of prayer, hymns, and chants. Its ancient words, imbued with centuries of devotion, create an atmosphere of reverence and spiritual connection. The rhythmic cadence and melodic flow of Ge'ez enhance the liturgical experience, transporting the faithful to a realm where the earthly and the divine intertwine. The use of Ge'ez in the liturgy not only preserves the Church's ancient heritage but also fosters a sense of continuity and timelessness, connecting present-day worshippers with the traditions of their ancestors.

In the realm of scripture, Ge'ez is the language of the Ethiopian Orthodox Bible, a unique and expansive canon that includes texts not found in other Christian traditions. The Ge'ez Bible, with its rich vocabulary and poetic expressions, is considered a sacred treasure, a repository of divine wisdom and spiritual guidance. The act of reading and studying the scriptures in Ge'ez is not merely an intellectual exercise but a spiritual practice, a way of encountering the divine word and deepening one's faith.

The use of Ge'ez in both liturgy and scripture creates a sacred linguistic space that sets the Ethiopian Orthodox Tewahedo Church apart from other Christian traditions. It is a language that embodies the Church's unique identity, its rich history, and its deep connection to Ethiopian culture. The preservation and study of Ge'ez are not merely academic pursuits but acts of spiritual devotion, ensuring that the Church's ancient traditions and teachings continue to inspire and guide the faithful for generations to come.

Canonical Books

Key texts and their themes:

The Ethiopian Orthodox Tewahedo Church's scriptural canon, a testament to its ancient heritage and unique theological perspective, encompasses a rich tapestry of texts that have nourished the faith of millions for centuries. These canonical books, both shared with other Christian traditions and unique to Ethiopian Orthodoxy, offer profound insights into the Church's spiritual worldview, ethical teachings, and historical narratives.

Old Testament:

The Ethiopian Orthodox Old Testament, while sharing many books with other Christian traditions, also includes several unique texts that hold special significance for the Church.

- **The Book of Enoch:** This apocalyptic text, attributed to Enoch, the great-grandfather of Noah, offers a glimpse into the heavenly realms, the angelic hierarchy, and the final judgment. It emphasizes the importance of righteousness, warns against the dangers of sin, and offers hope for the ultimate triumph of good over evil.
- **The Book of Jubilees:** This text, also known as "Little Genesis," provides an alternative account of the events described in the biblical book of Genesis. It offers a more detailed chronology of events, expands on certain narratives, and provides additional insights into Jewish laws and customs. The Book of Jubilees is valued for its historical and theological perspectives, shedding

light on the development of Jewish and Christian traditions.

- **The Book of Ezra Sutuel:** This unique book, found only in the Ethiopian Orthodox canon, contains a collection of prayers, hymns, and liturgical texts attributed to Ezra the Scribe. It is a valuable resource for understanding the early liturgical practices and spiritual traditions of the Ethiopian Church.

New Testament:

The Ethiopian Orthodox New Testament, while largely consistent with other Christian canons, also includes some unique features and additional texts.

- **The Four Gospels:** The Gospels of Matthew, Mark, Luke, and John, which recount the life, teachings, death, and resurrection of Jesus Christ, are central to Ethiopian Orthodox faith and worship. They are read and studied extensively, providing the foundation for the Church's theological understanding and spiritual practices.
- **The Acts of the Apostles:** This book narrates the early history of the Christian Church, focusing on the missionary journeys of the apostles and the spread of the Gospel throughout the Roman Empire. It serves as a model for evangelism and

church growth, inspiring the Ethiopian Orthodox Church's own missionary endeavors.

- **The Epistles:** The letters of Paul, Peter, James, John, and other apostles offer guidance and instruction to the early Christian communities, addressing issues of faith, morality, and social responsibility. These epistles are valued for their theological insights, ethical teachings, and practical advice for Christian living.

- **The Book of Revelation:** This apocalyptic text, with its vivid imagery and symbolic language, offers a glimpse into the end times and the ultimate triumph of good over evil. It is a source of hope and encouragement for believers, reminding them of God's ultimate victory over sin and death.

Other Canonical Texts:

In addition to the Old and New Testaments, the Ethiopian Orthodox canon includes several other books, such as the Didascalia Apostolorum (Teachings of the Apostles), the Shepherd of Hermas, and the Book of Clement. These texts, while not considered canonical by all Christian traditions, are valued for their historical and theological insights, providing a broader perspective on the development of early Christianity.

The Ethiopian Orthodox Tewahedo Church's scriptural canon, with its unique books and diverse contents, is a testament to the Church's rich heritage and its openness to different sources of spiritual wisdom. It is a sacred treasure that has nourished the faith of millions for centuries, providing guidance, inspiration, and a sense of connection to the divine.

Differences from other Christian Bibles

The Ethiopian Orthodox Bible, a testament to the Church's ancient heritage and unique theological perspective, distinguishes itself from other Christian Bibles in several key aspects:

1. **Expanded Canon:** The Ethiopian Orthodox Bible boasts a broader canon than most other Christian traditions, encompassing 81 books compared to the 66 books found in Protestant Bibles and the 73 books in Catholic Bibles. This expanded canon includes several books not found in other Bibles, such as the Book of Enoch, the Book of Jubilees, and the Book of Ezra Sutuel. These additional texts, often referred to as "deutero-canonical" or "extra-canonical," offer unique insights into Ethiopian religious beliefs, practices, and historical narratives.

2. **Order and Arrangement:** The order and arrangement of books within the Ethiopian Orthodox Bible also differ from other Christian Bibles. For instance, the Book of Job is placed

after the Psalms, and the books of Ezra and Nehemiah are combined into a single book. These variations reflect the Church's distinct liturgical traditions and its understanding of the biblical narrative.

3. **Additional Chapters and Verses:** Some books in the Ethiopian Orthodox Bible contain additional chapters and verses not found in other versions. For example, the Book of Esther includes six additional chapters that provide further details about the story of Esther and Mordecai. These additions offer a broader perspective on the biblical narrative and enrich the Church's understanding of these texts.

4. **Unique Interpretations:** The Ethiopian Orthodox Church has its own interpretive traditions and theological perspectives that shape its understanding of the Bible. These interpretations, often rooted in the teachings of the early Church Fathers and the Church's unique historical and cultural context, may differ from the interpretations of other Christian denominations. For example, the Church's understanding of the Book of Revelation, with its emphasis on the role of Ethiopia in salvation history, is distinct from other interpretations.

5. **Liturgical Use:** The Ethiopian Orthodox Bible is not merely a text for private study but is deeply integrated into the Church's liturgical life. The

readings from the Bible are an integral part of every church service, and the faithful are encouraged to memorize and recite passages from scripture. The Church's unique chants and hymns, often based on biblical texts, further reinforce the Bible's central role in Ethiopian Orthodox worship.

These differences, while significant, do not diminish the Ethiopian Orthodox Bible's spiritual value or its contribution to the broader Christian tradition. Rather, they highlight the diversity and richness of Christian faith and practice, demonstrating how different communities have interpreted and applied the scriptures in their unique cultural and historical contexts. The Ethiopian Orthodox Bible, with its expanded canon, unique interpretations, and deep integration into liturgical life, stands as a testament to the Church's rich heritage and its enduring commitment to the Word of God.

Translation and Interpretation

History of Bible translations:

The history of Bible translations in the Ethiopian Orthodox Tewahedo Church is a testament to the Church's dedication to preserving and disseminating the sacred scriptures in a language accessible to its followers. This journey of translation, spanning centuries, reflects the

Church's commitment to both linguistic accuracy and cultural relevance.

The earliest translations of the Bible into Ge'ez, the liturgical language of the Church, are shrouded in some mystery. Tradition holds that the first translations were made as early as the 4th century AD, attributed to figures like St. Frumentius, the "Apostle of Ethiopia." However, the earliest surviving manuscripts date back to the 6th and 7th centuries, suggesting a long and continuous tradition of biblical translation and transmission.

These early translations were primarily based on Greek versions of the Bible, reflecting the Church's close ties to the Coptic Orthodox Church of Alexandria. However, they also incorporated elements of Hebrew and Syriac traditions, demonstrating the Church's openness to diverse sources of biblical scholarship.

Over the centuries, the Ge'ez Bible underwent revisions and refinements, as scholars and scribes sought to ensure its accuracy and clarity. The 14th century saw a significant effort to standardize the biblical text, resulting in the production of several authoritative manuscripts that served as the basis for subsequent translations.

The advent of printing in the 19th century revolutionized the dissemination of the Bible in Ethiopia. The first printed edition of the Ge'ez Bible was published in 1840, making the scriptures more accessible to the wider population. This was followed by translations into Amharic, the vernacular language of Ethiopia, in the late 19th and early 20th centuries.

The translation of the Bible into Amharic was a landmark event in the Church's history. It made the scriptures accessible to a wider audience, including those who did not understand Ge'ez. This led to a greater understanding and appreciation of the Bible among the laity, fostering a deeper engagement with the faith.

In recent decades, the Ethiopian Orthodox Tewahedo Church has continued its efforts to translate and disseminate the Bible in various languages spoken in Ethiopia. This includes translations into Oromo, Tigrinya, Somali, and other regional languages. These translations not only make the scriptures accessible to diverse communities but also contribute to the preservation and promotion of Ethiopia's rich linguistic diversity.

The history of Bible translations in the Ethiopian Orthodox Tewahedo Church is a testament to the Church's unwavering commitment to the Word of God and its dedication to making the scriptures accessible to all its followers. It is a story of linguistic preservation, cultural adaptation, and spiritual renewal, reflecting the Church's enduring vitality and its central role in Ethiopian society.

Interpretive traditions:

The Ethiopian Orthodox Tewahedo Church boasts a rich and nuanced tradition of biblical interpretation, shaped by centuries of theological reflection, monastic scholarship, and cultural adaptation. This interpretive tradition, while rooted in the teachings of the early Church Fathers, also incorporates unique Ethiopian perspectives and insights, resulting in a vibrant and dynamic approach to understanding the Scriptures.

Theological Foundations:

The Ethiopian Orthodox Church's interpretive tradition is grounded in the principles of patristic exegesis, drawing upon the writings and commentaries of early Church Fathers such as St. Athanasius, St. Cyril of Alexandria, and St. John Chrysostom. These theologians, revered for their wisdom and spiritual insight, provided a framework for understanding the Bible's deeper meanings and its relevance to Christian life.

The Church also places a strong emphasis on the authority of tradition, recognizing the accumulated wisdom of generations of believers and scholars. This respect for tradition ensures continuity and consistency in biblical interpretation while also allowing for flexibility and adaptation to new contexts and challenges.

Unique Ethiopian Perspectives:

While drawing upon the broader Christian tradition, the Ethiopian Orthodox Church also brings its unique perspectives and insights to biblical interpretation. These perspectives are shaped by the Church's historical experiences, cultural context, and theological understanding.

One distinctive feature of Ethiopian biblical interpretation is its emphasis on typology, a method of interpreting the Old Testament as a prefiguration of the New Testament. Ethiopian scholars and theologians often see events, characters, and symbols in the Old Testament as foreshadowing the life, ministry, and teachings of Jesus Christ. This typological approach enriches the Church's understanding of the Bible and its relevance to the Christian life.

Another unique aspect of Ethiopian biblical interpretation is its openness to mystical and allegorical interpretations. The Church recognizes that the Bible contains deeper meanings that are not always immediately apparent. It encourages believers to seek these hidden truths through prayer, meditation, and spiritual discernment. This mystical approach to interpretation allows for a deeper engagement with the scriptures and a more profound understanding of their spiritual significance.

Oral Tradition and Commentary:

In addition to written commentaries, the Ethiopian Orthodox Church also has a rich tradition of oral interpretation. Sermons, homilies, and teachings by religious leaders play a crucial role in transmitting the Church's understanding of the Bible to the faithful. These oral interpretations often incorporate local stories, proverbs, and cultural references, making the scriptures more accessible and relevant to the Ethiopian context.

Modern Developments:

In recent decades, the Ethiopian Orthodox Tewahedo Church has witnessed a renewed interest in biblical studies and interpretation. The establishment of theological colleges and seminaries has provided a platform for scholarly research and the training of clergy in modern exegetical methods. This has led to a deeper engagement with the scriptures and a more nuanced understanding of their historical and cultural contexts.

The Ethiopian Orthodox Church's interpretive tradition is a dynamic and evolving process, shaped by centuries of theological reflection, cultural adaptation, and spiritual insight. It is a tradition that values both the authority of scripture and the wisdom of tradition, while also remaining open to new interpretations and understandings. This approach ensures that the Bible remains a living and relevant source of spiritual guidance for the Ethiopian Orthodox community, enriching their faith and shaping their lives.

Apocryphal Texts

- Overview of accepted apocryphal books.
- Their role and significance.

While not considered canonical by all Christian traditions, these apocryphal texts hold a special place within the Ethiopian Orthodox Tewahedo Church, enriching its theological tapestry and providing unique insights into its spiritual worldview. Their role and significance can be understood through several key aspects:

1. **Historical and Cultural Context:** These texts offer valuable insights into the historical and cultural context in which Ethiopian Christianity developed. They reflect the Church's engagement with Jewish and early Christian traditions, as well as its openness to diverse sources of spiritual wisdom. The Book of Enoch, for example, provides a glimpse into the apocalyptic worldview that was prevalent in the ancient world, while the Book of Jubilees offers a unique perspective on Jewish history and law.

2. **Theological and Spiritual Significance:** These texts often contain theological concepts and spiritual teachings that are not found in the canonical books of the Bible. For example, the Book of Enoch elaborates on the nature of angels and demons, the afterlife, and the final judgment. The Book of Jubilees provides a detailed calendar of religious festivals and observances, offering insights into the early development of Jewish and Christian liturgical practices. These texts, while not considered

authoritative in the same way as the canonical scriptures, nonetheless enrich the Church's theological understanding and spiritual practices.

3. **Liturgical and Devotional Use:** Some of these apocryphal texts are incorporated into the Church's liturgical readings and prayers, particularly during specific feasts and fasts. For example, the Book of Enoch is often read during the Lenten season, while the Book of Jubilees is read during the Feast of the Cross. This liturgical use of apocryphal texts highlights their importance in the spiritual life of the Ethiopian Orthodox community.

4. **Artistic and Literary Inspiration:** The vivid imagery, symbolic language, and dramatic narratives found in these texts have inspired generations of Ethiopian artists, writers, and musicians. The Book of Enoch, with its descriptions of heavenly journeys and angelic encounters, has been a particularly rich source of artistic inspiration. The influence of these texts can be seen in the Church's iconography, illuminated manuscripts, and liturgical music.

5. **Identity and Heritage:** The inclusion of these unique texts in the Ethiopian Orthodox canon is a testament to the Church's distinct identity and its rich cultural heritage. These texts, often rooted in Ethiopian traditions and historical narratives, reinforce the Church's connection to its ancient

past and its unique place in the Christian world. They also serve as a source of pride and cultural identity for Ethiopian Orthodox Christians, distinguishing them from other Christian communities.

The Ethiopian Orthodox Tewahedo Church's embrace of apocryphal texts is a testament to its openness to diverse sources of spiritual wisdom and its willingness to engage with different religious traditions. While these texts may not hold the same canonical status as the Old and New Testaments, they nonetheless play a significant role in the Church's liturgical life, theological understanding, and cultural identity. They offer a unique window into the rich and complex world of Ethiopian Orthodoxy, revealing its deep roots, its spiritual depth, and its enduring appeal.

Scriptural Study and Education

- Methods of teaching scripture.
- Role in religious education.

In the Ethiopian Orthodox Tewahedo Church, the study and teaching of scripture are not merely academic pursuits but deeply spiritual practices, aimed at nurturing faith, deepening understanding, and fostering a lifelong commitment to the Word of God. The Church employs a variety of methods to transmit the sacred texts to its followers, ensuring that the scriptures remain a living and relevant source of guidance and inspiration.

Methods of Teaching Scripture:

1. **Oral Tradition:** The Ethiopian Orthodox Church has a rich tradition of oral transmission of scripture, where biblical stories, teachings, and interpretations are passed down through generations by word of mouth. This oral tradition, often accompanied by music, poetry, and storytelling, makes the scriptures accessible to all, regardless of literacy levels. It also fosters a sense of community and shared heritage, as the faithful gather to listen to the sacred texts and engage in discussions about their meaning and relevance.

2. **Liturgical Readings:** The Divine Liturgy, the central act of worship in the Ethiopian Orthodox Church, includes extensive readings from the Old and New Testaments. These readings, often chanted in Ge'ez, the liturgical language, are not merely recitations but opportunities for spiritual reflection and contemplation. The clergy often provide commentary and interpretations, helping the congregation to understand the deeper meanings of the texts and their relevance to their lives.

3. **Church Schools and Seminaries:** The Church operates a network of church schools and seminaries that provide formal religious education to children, youth, and adults. These institutions offer courses on biblical studies, theology, church history, and liturgical practices. They also train clergy and lay leaders, equipping them with the knowledge and skills to teach and interpret the scriptures.

4. **Home-Based Study:** The Ethiopian Orthodox Church encourages families to study the Bible together at home. This practice, often involving the reading of scripture passages, discussions, and prayers, fosters a deeper understanding of the faith and strengthens family bonds. It also instills in children a love for the scriptures and a lifelong commitment to their study.

5. **Commentaries and Homilies:** The Church has a rich tradition of biblical commentaries and homilies, written by scholars and theologians throughout its history. These commentaries provide in-depth interpretations of the scriptures, drawing upon patristic teachings, historical context, and spiritual insights. They are valuable resources for both clergy and laity, offering guidance and inspiration for understanding the Bible's deeper meanings.

6. **Use of Technology:** In recent years, the Church has embraced technology as a tool for scriptural

study and education. Websites, social media platforms, and mobile applications offer access to biblical texts, commentaries, and educational resources. Online forums and discussion groups provide opportunities for virtual learning and engagement with the scriptures.

Role in Religious Education:

The study and teaching of scripture play a central role in religious education within the Ethiopian Orthodox Tewahedo Church. The Church views the Bible as the inspired Word of God, a source of divine revelation and spiritual guidance. It emphasizes the importance of understanding the scriptures in their historical and cultural context, as well as their relevance to contemporary life.

Religious education in the Ethiopian Orthodox Church begins at a young age, with children attending church schools and participating in Sunday school programs. These programs introduce children to the basic stories and teachings of the Bible, using age-appropriate methods and materials. As children grow older, they are encouraged to deepen their understanding of the scriptures through more advanced study and participation in liturgical life.

The Church also offers religious education programs for adults, including Bible study groups, seminars, and workshops. These programs provide opportunities for adults to deepen their knowledge of the scriptures, explore theological concepts, and engage in discussions about the relevance of the Bible to their lives.

The Ethiopian Orthodox Tewahedo Church's commitment to scriptural study and education is a testament to its belief in the transformative power of the Word of God. By providing its followers with the tools and resources to engage with the scriptures, the Church empowers them to deepen their faith, strengthen their spiritual lives, and live out the teachings of Christ in their daily lives.

Comparison with Other Traditions

- Comparative analysis with other Christian canons.
- Historical reasons for differences.

The Ethiopian Orthodox Tewahedo Church's scriptural canon, a testament to its ancient heritage and unique theological perspective, stands as a fascinating point of comparison with other Christian canons. These differences, while sometimes a source of theological debate, offer valuable insights into the diverse ways in which Christianity has been interpreted and practiced throughout history.

Canonization Process and Historical Context:

One of the primary reasons for the differences between the Ethiopian Orthodox canon and other Christian canons lies in the historical context of their formation. The Ethiopian Orthodox Church, due to its geographical isolation and unique historical trajectory, developed its canon independently of the Western and Eastern churches. This isolation allowed for the inclusion of texts that were not universally accepted by other Christian communities, such as the Book of Enoch and the Book of Jubilees. These texts, while considered apocryphal by some, hold deep spiritual and historical significance for Ethiopian Orthodox Christians.

The process of canonization itself also played a role in the differences between canons. The Ethiopian Orthodox Church, like other Eastern churches, did not have a single, definitive council that established a fixed canon. Instead, the canon evolved over time, with certain books gaining acceptance through liturgical use, theological consensus, and the influence of monastic communities. This organic process of canonization allowed for greater flexibility and diversity in the selection of texts.

Theological and Cultural Influences:

Theological and cultural influences also contributed to the differences between canons. The Ethiopian Orthodox Church's unique theological perspective, rooted in Miaphysite Christology and its emphasis on the Old Testament, led to the inclusion of texts that resonated with its doctrinal understanding. For example, the Book of Enoch, with its emphasis on angels and demons, aligns with the Church's belief in the spiritual realm and the ongoing struggle between good and evil.

Cultural factors also played a role. The Ethiopian Orthodox Church has a deep respect for tradition and a strong sense of cultural identity. This led to the inclusion of texts that were considered part of the Ethiopian literary and historical heritage, even if they were not universally accepted by other Christian communities. The Kebra Nagast, for example, a 14th-century epic that narrates the story of the Queen of Sheba and King Solomon, is considered a national treasure and a source of spiritual inspiration for many Ethiopians.

Impact on Biblical Interpretation:

The differences in canons have also led to variations in biblical interpretation. The Ethiopian Orthodox Church's broader canon provides a wider range of texts for theological reflection and spiritual guidance. The inclusion of apocryphal texts, such as the Book of Enoch and the Book of Jubilees, has enriched the Church's understanding of the biblical narrative and its theological implications.

The Church's unique interpretive traditions, shaped by its historical and cultural context, also contribute to its distinct understanding of the Bible. The emphasis on typology, allegory, and mystical interpretation allows for a deeper engagement with the scriptures and a more nuanced understanding of their spiritual significance.

Ecumenical Dialogue and Reconciliation:

The differences between the Ethiopian Orthodox canon and other Christian canons have been a source of theological debate and occasional tension throughout history. However, in recent decades, there has been a growing movement towards ecumenical dialogue and reconciliation between different Christian traditions. The Ethiopian Orthodox Church has actively participated in these dialogues, seeking to build bridges of understanding and cooperation with other churches.

While theological differences remain, there is a growing recognition of the importance of respecting diverse interpretations and appreciating the richness of the Christian tradition in its various expressions. The Ethiopian Orthodox Church's unique canon, with its broader range of texts and distinctive interpretive traditions, offers a valuable contribution to the ongoing dialogue about the meaning and relevance of the Bible in the modern world.

Conclusion

In this chapter, we have embarked on a journey through the sacred scriptures of the Ethiopian Orthodox Tewahedo Church, a journey that has taken us from the ancient language of Ge'ez to the unique books and interpretive traditions that distinguish this faith. We have explored the Church's expansive canon, delving into the Old and New Testaments, as well as the apocryphal texts that hold a special place in Ethiopian Orthodoxy. We have witnessed the importance of Ge'ez, not only as a liturgical language but also as a vessel for preserving the Church's rich theological and cultural heritage.

As we move forward, we will leave the realm of the written word and enter the vibrant world of Ethiopian Orthodox worship. We will witness the liturgy come alive, a symphony of rituals, prayers, and hymns that transport the faithful into the heart of divine mystery. We will explore the liturgical calendar, a rhythmic cycle of feasts and fasts that mark the seasons of the Church's spiritual life. We will also delve into the role of icons, religious art, and music in creating an atmosphere of reverence, awe, and spiritual ecstasy.

Prepare to be immersed in a sensory-rich experience, where the sights, sounds, and smells of worship transport you to a world of ancient traditions, vibrant spirituality, and profound devotion. Join us as we unlock the mysteries of Ethiopian Orthodox liturgy and worship, and discover the transformative power of sacred rituals in the lives of believers.

Chapter 6

Church and State

Historical Relationship

The relationship between the Ethiopian Orthodox Tewahedo Church and the Ethiopian state has been a complex and dynamic interplay of cooperation, tension, and mutual influence spanning centuries of shared history. This intricate dance between the spiritual and temporal authorities has shaped the nation's political landscape, cultural identity, and social fabric.

In the early days of the Aksumite Empire, the Church and state were closely intertwined, forming a symbiotic relationship that benefited both institutions. The Aksumite kings, recognizing the unifying power of Christianity, embraced the faith and became patrons of the Church, providing it with resources, protection, and political support. In return, the Church legitimized the monarchs' rule, offering spiritual guidance and moral authority. This close alliance between the Church and state fostered a sense of national unity and identity, with Christianity becoming deeply ingrained in the cultural and social fabric of the empire.

The rise of the Solomonic dynasty in the 13th century further solidified the Church's position as a pillar of the state. The Solomonic kings, claiming descent from the biblical King Solomon and the Queen of Sheba, embraced the Church as a source of legitimacy and a symbol of their divine right to rule. The Church, in turn, supported the monarchy, providing spiritual guidance and moral authority. This close relationship between the Church and state continued for centuries, with the Church playing a crucial role in shaping the nation's laws, customs, and social values.

However, the relationship between the Church and state was not always harmonious. During the Zemene Mesafint, a period of political fragmentation and regional rivalries in the 18th and 19th centuries, the Church's influence became more decentralized. Regional lords and princes exerted greater control over ecclesiastical affairs, leading to a decline in the Church's central authority. This period of political instability and competition for power often put the Church in a precarious position, as it had to navigate complex alliances and rivalries while maintaining its spiritual independence.

The modern era brought new challenges and opportunities for the Church-state relationship. The rise of European colonialism and the subsequent Italian occupation of Ethiopia in the 20th century tested the Church's resilience and its relationship with the state. During the occupation, the Church became a symbol of national resistance, with its leaders inspiring the faithful to fight for their freedom and cultural identity. However, the post-war era saw a shift in the Church-state dynamics, with the rise of secular nationalism and the emergence of new political ideologies.

The Ethiopian Revolution of 1974, which overthrew Emperor Haile Selassie and established a Marxist-Leninist regime, marked a turning point in the Church-state relationship. The new government nationalized Church lands and properties, restricted its activities, and sought to limit its influence. The Church, however, remained a resilient force, adapting to the changing political landscape and continuing to provide spiritual guidance and support to the Ethiopian people.

The fall of the Derg regime in 1991 and the establishment of a new government ushered in a new era for the church-state relationship. The Church regained its autonomy and embarked on a process of renewal and reform. The new constitution guaranteed freedom of religion, allowing the Church to operate independently of the state. However, the relationship between the Church and state remains complex, with ongoing debates about the role of religion in public life and the extent of the Church's influence on political and social issues.

Key historical events shaping this relationship

The intricate dance between the Ethiopian Orthodox Tewahedo Church and the Ethiopian state has been punctuated by key historical events that have shaped their relationship, leaving an enduring mark on the nation's political and spiritual landscape. These events, spanning centuries, reveal a dynamic interplay of cooperation, tension, and mutual influence.

1. **Conversion of King Ezana (4th Century):** The baptism of King Ezana of Aksum by St. Frumentius marked a turning point in Ethiopian history. This event not only established Christianity as the state religion but also forged a close alliance between the Church and the monarchy, setting the stage for centuries of intertwined destinies.

2. **Establishment of the Solomonic Dynasty (13th Century):** The rise of the Solomonic dynasty, claiming descent from King Solomon and the Queen of Sheba, further solidified the Church's position. The Solomonic kings, viewing themselves as divinely ordained rulers, sought the Church's blessing and support, while the Church, in turn, gained royal patronage and protection.

3. **Gondar Period and Royal Patronage (17th Century):** The establishment of Gondar as the imperial capital in the 17th century ushered in an era of heightened royal patronage for the Church. Emperors like Fasilides and Iyasu the Great built magnificent churches and monasteries, solidifying Gondar as a center of religious learning and authority.

4. **Zemene Mesafint (Era of the Princes) (18th-19th Centuries):** This era of political fragmentation and regional rivalries led to a decentralization of power, impacting the Church-state relationship. Regional lords and princes exerted greater control over ecclesiastical affairs, challenging the Church's central authority and leading to a period of relative autonomy for regional churches.

5. **Emperor Tewodros II and Centralization Efforts (19th Century):** Emperor Tewodros II, a reformer who sought to modernize and centralize Ethiopia, attempted to curtail the Church's power and wealth. His efforts, however, were met with resistance from the clergy, highlighting the ongoing tension between the spiritual and temporal authorities.

6. **Italian Occupation and the Church's Resistance (1935-1941):** The Italian occupation of Ethiopia was a dark chapter in the nation's history, but it also witnessed the Church's

unwavering resilience and its role in rallying the people against foreign aggression. The Church's leaders, including Abune Petros, who was martyred by the Italians, became symbols of national resistance and spiritual strength.

7. **The Ethiopian Revolution and Nationalization of Church Lands (1974):** The 1974 revolution, which overthrew Emperor Haile Selassie and established a Marxist-Leninist regime, led to the nationalization of Church lands and properties. This marked a significant shift in the church-state relationship, as the Church lost much of its economic power and political influence.

8. **Post-1991 Era and Restoration of Church Autonomy:** The fall of the Derg regime in 1991 and the adoption of a new constitution ushered in a new era for the Church. The constitution guaranteed freedom of religion and restored the Church's autonomy, allowing it to operate independently of the state. However, the relationship between the Church and state remains complex, with ongoing negotiations and discussions about their respective roles and responsibilities.

These key historical events, while not exhaustive, provide a glimpse into the intricate dance between the Ethiopian Orthodox Tewahedo Church and the Ethiopian state.

They reveal a relationship that has been shaped by both cooperation and conflict, mutual influence and periods of tension. As we delve deeper into this relationship, we will uncover the nuances and complexities that have defined this unique partnership throughout history.

Influence on Politics

The role of the church in political decisions:

The Ethiopian Orthodox Tewahedo Church, with its deep-rooted history and spiritual authority, has consistently held a significant role in shaping Ethiopia's political landscape. This influence, while fluctuating throughout the ages, has been a constant thread woven into the fabric of the nation's governance and decision-making processes.

In the early days of the Aksumite Empire, the Church and state were closely intertwined, with monarchs often seeking the Church's blessing and counsel on matters of governance. The Church's spiritual authority legitimized the rule of kings and emperors, and its teachings on justice, morality, and social responsibility provided a framework for ethical leadership. The Church's influence was not merely advisory; it actively participated in shaping laws and policies, particularly those concerning marriage, family, and social welfare.

During the medieval period, the Church's influence on politics continued, with emperors often consulting with religious leaders on matters of war and peace, diplomacy, and internal affairs. The Church's monasteries and schools served as centers of learning, producing scholars and advisors who played key roles in the royal court. The Church's vast landholdings and economic resources also gave it considerable leverage in political matters.

The Zemene Mesafint, a period of political fragmentation and regional rivalries, saw a shift in the Church's political role. With the weakening of central authority, regional lords and princes sought to control ecclesiastical affairs, leading to a decentralization of the Church's power. However, the Church continued to exert influence through its spiritual authority and its role as a mediator in conflicts.

In the modern era, the Church's political influence has been more nuanced. During the Italian occupation, the Church played a crucial role in mobilizing resistance and preserving national unity. Its leaders, such as Abune Petros, became symbols of defiance and spiritual strength, inspiring the Ethiopian people to fight for their freedom.

The Ethiopian Orthodox Tewahedo Church's role in political decisions is a complex and evolving one. It is shaped by historical traditions, theological principles, and the changing socio-political landscape of Ethiopia. While the Church maintains its independence from the state, it recognizes its responsibility to speak out on issues of justice, morality, and the well-being of the Ethiopian people. Its voice, rooted in centuries of spiritual authority and cultural influence, continues to resonate in the halls of power, shaping the nation's political discourse and decision-making processes.

Examples of significant political interventions

Throughout Ethiopia's history, the Ethiopian Orthodox Tewahedo Church has not shied away from engaging in the political arena when the well-being of its people or the preservation of its traditions were at stake. These interventions, often driven by a deep sense of moral responsibility and a commitment to justice, have left a lasting impact on the nation's political landscape.

1. **Resistance to the Gragn Mohammed Invasion (16th Century):** When the Muslim armies of Gragn Mohammed threatened Ethiopia's sovereignty and Christian heritage, the Church rallied the faithful to resist the invasion. Emperor Lebna Dengel, with the Church's blessing and support, led the Ethiopian forces in a protracted war that ultimately resulted in the defeat of Gragn Mohammed and the preservation of Ethiopia's independence.

2. **Mediation in Political Conflicts:** During the Zemene Mesafint, a period of political fragmentation and regional rivalries, the Church often played the role of mediator, seeking to resolve conflicts and prevent bloodshed. Religious

leaders, respected for their wisdom and impartiality, facilitated negotiations between warring factions, helping to maintain a semblance of order and stability in a turbulent era.

3. **Opposition to Italian Occupation:** The Italian occupation of Ethiopia in the 20th century was met with fierce resistance from the Church. Religious leaders, such as Abune Petros, openly condemned the occupation and inspired the faithful to fight for their freedom. Abune Petros's martyrdom at the hands of the Italians further galvanized the resistance movement and solidified the Church's role as a symbol of national unity and defiance.

4. **Advocacy for Human Rights and Social Justice:** In the post-war era, the Church emerged as a vocal advocate for human rights and social justice. It spoke out against the Derg regime's oppressive policies, calling for an end to violence and political repression. The Church also played a crucial role in providing humanitarian aid and support to those affected by the regime's atrocities.

5. **Promotion of Peace and Reconciliation:** In recent years, the Church has been actively involved in promoting peace and reconciliation in Ethiopia, particularly in the aftermath of the conflict in the Tigray region. Its leaders have called for dialogue, forgiveness, and unity, emphasizing the importance of healing the

wounds of war and building a more inclusive and harmonious society.

These examples illustrate the Ethiopian Orthodox Tewahedo Church's significant political interventions throughout history. The Church's unwavering commitment to justice, peace, and the well-being of the Ethiopian people has made it a powerful force for good in the nation's political landscape. Its voice, rooted in spiritual authority and moral conviction, continues to resonate in the halls of power, shaping the nation's political discourse and decision-making processes.

Cultural Influence

Impact on Ethiopian cultural policies:

The Ethiopian Orthodox Tewahedo Church's influence extends beyond the spiritual and political realms, deeply permeating the cultural policies that have shaped the nation's identity and heritage. This influence is a testament to the Church's enduring role as a custodian of tradition, a moral compass, and a source of cultural inspiration.

1. **Preservation of Cultural Heritage:** The Church has been instrumental in preserving Ethiopia's rich cultural heritage, advocating for the protection of historical sites, artifacts, and traditions. Its monasteries and churches, often

repositories of ancient manuscripts, icons, and religious art, have been recognized as UNESCO World Heritage sites, ensuring their preservation for future generations. The Church's advocacy for the preservation of Ge'ez, the ancient liturgical language, has also been crucial in maintaining Ethiopia's linguistic and literary heritage.

2. **Promotion of Traditional Arts and Crafts:** The Church has actively promoted traditional Ethiopian arts and crafts, recognizing their intrinsic value and their role in expressing the nation's cultural identity. The intricate designs of Ethiopian crosses, the vibrant murals adorning churches, and the exquisite craftsmanship of religious artifacts are all testaments to the Church's patronage of the arts. The Church's support for traditional music, dance, and storytelling has also been instrumental in preserving these art forms and ensuring their transmission to future generations.

3. **Influence on Education Policy:** The Church has historically played a significant role in education, establishing schools and monasteries that served as centers of learning for centuries. While the state now plays a more prominent role in education, the Church continues to influence education policy by advocating for the inclusion of religious instruction in schools and promoting the teaching of Ge'ez and Ethiopian history. The

Church also operates its own schools and colleges, providing both religious and secular education to thousands of students.

4. **Social Welfare and Development:** The Church's teachings on social justice, compassion, and the importance of community have influenced Ethiopia's social welfare and development policies. The Church has been a vocal advocate for the poor, the marginalized, and the vulnerable, calling for policies that address poverty, inequality, and social injustice. Its extensive network of social service institutions, including hospitals, clinics, orphanages, and shelters for the homeless, provides essential services to communities across the country.

5. **Promotion of National Unity and Identity:** The Church has played a crucial role in promoting national unity and identity, particularly in times of political turmoil and ethnic conflict. Its leaders have consistently called for peace, reconciliation, and dialogue, emphasizing the importance of shared values and common heritage. The Church's emphasis on Ethiopian traditions, language, and history has also fostered a sense of national pride and belonging among Ethiopians of diverse backgrounds.

The Ethiopian Orthodox Tewahedo Church's influence on Ethiopian cultural policies is a testament to its enduring role as a custodian of tradition, a moral compass, and a source of cultural inspiration. Its advocacy for the preservation of cultural heritage, promotion of traditional arts and crafts, influence on education policy, commitment to social welfare, and promotion of national unity have all contributed to shaping Ethiopia's cultural landscape. As Ethiopia continues to evolve and face new challenges, the Church's cultural influence remains a vital force in preserving the nation's identity and ensuring its continued vibrancy and relevance in the modern world.

Integration of religious practices into cultural norms

The Ethiopian Orthodox Tewahedo Church's influence on cultural norms is so profound that it's difficult to discern where faith ends and tradition begins. The Church's teachings, rituals, and values have become so deeply ingrained in Ethiopian society that they are often indistinguishable from cultural practices. This seamless integration is a testament to the Church's enduring power and its ability to shape the very fabric of Ethiopian life.

1. **Daily Rhythms:** The Church's liturgical calendar, with its numerous feasts and fasts, dictates the rhythm of daily life for many Ethiopians. Fasting, a central tenet of Orthodox practice, is not merely a religious obligation but a cultural norm observed by believers and non-

believers alike. The aroma of incense wafting from homes during prayer times, the rhythmic sounds of prayer bells echoing through villages, and the communal gatherings for feasts and holidays are all manifestations of the Church's influence on the daily rhythms of Ethiopian life.

2. **Social Values and Etiquette:** The Church's teachings on respect for elders, hospitality, and communal harmony have shaped Ethiopian social values and etiquette. The act of bowing to elders, kissing their hands, and seeking their blessings is a deeply ingrained cultural practice rooted in the Church's emphasis on honoring one's elders. The Ethiopian coffee ceremony, a cherished tradition that involves the roasting, grinding, and brewing of coffee, is often accompanied by prayers and blessings, highlighting the Church's influence on social rituals.

3. **Family and Community:** The Church's emphasis on the importance of family and community has shaped Ethiopian social structures and relationships. The extended family unit, with its emphasis on mutual support and shared responsibility, is a cornerstone of Ethiopian society. The Church's teachings on marriage, procreation, and the raising of children have also influenced family dynamics and gender roles. The Church's role in mediating conflicts and promoting reconciliation has further strengthened

communal bonds and fostered a sense of social cohesion.

4. **Art and Symbolism:** The Church's rich artistic tradition, with its intricate crosses, vibrant murals, and illuminated manuscripts, has permeated Ethiopian culture. The cross, a symbol of faith and protection, is ubiquitous in Ethiopian homes, businesses, and public spaces. The vibrant colors and symbolic motifs found in Ethiopian art often reflect biblical stories and the lives of saints, serving as visual reminders of the Church's teachings and inspiring devotion among the faithful.

5. **Language and Literature:** The Ge'ez language, the liturgical language of the Church, has had a profound impact on Ethiopian language and literature. Many Amharic words and phrases have their roots in Ge'ez, and the Church's vast literary corpus, including hymns, prayers, and theological treatises, has shaped Ethiopian literary expression. The Ge'ez script, with its elegant characters and rich symbolism, is also used in secular contexts, further highlighting the Church's influence on Ethiopian culture.

The Ethiopian Orthodox Tewahedo Church's integration into cultural norms is a testament to its enduring power and its ability to adapt and evolve while remaining true to its core values. It is a living tradition that continues to shape the lives of millions, providing spiritual guidance, cultural identity, and a sense of community. As Ethiopia navigates the complexities of the modern world, the Church's influence on cultural norms remains a vital force in preserving the nation's heritage and shaping its future.

Church Leadership and State

Interaction between church leaders and state officials:

The interplay between church leaders and state officials in Ethiopia has been a dynamic and often complex dance throughout the nation's history. This intricate relationship, shaped by both cooperation and tension, has played a crucial role in shaping the country's political and spiritual landscape.

In the early days of the Aksumite Empire, the lines between church and state were often blurred. Monarchs, recognizing the spiritual authority and influence of the church, sought the blessings and counsel of religious leaders on matters of governance. In turn, church leaders often served as advisors to the throne, offering wisdom and guidance on matters of law, ethics, and social policy. This symbiotic relationship fostered a sense of mutual respect and cooperation, with both institutions working together to maintain social order and promote the welfare of the people.

During the medieval period, this close relationship continued, with emperors often consulting with the Abuna, the head of the Ethiopian Orthodox Tewahedo Church, on matters of war and peace, diplomacy, and internal affairs. The Church's monasteries and schools produced scholars and advisors who played key roles in the royal court, further solidifying the Church's influence in the political sphere.

However, the Zemene Mesafint, a period of political fragmentation and regional rivalries, saw a shift in this dynamic. As central authority weakened, regional lords and princes sought to exert greater control over ecclesiastical affairs, leading to a more decentralized and at times contentious relationship between church and state. Church leaders often had to navigate complex political alliances and rivalries, balancing their spiritual authority with the demands of secular rulers.

In the modern era, the interaction between church leaders and state officials has continued to evolve. During the Italian occupation, the Church emerged as a symbol of national resistance, with its leaders openly defying the occupying forces and inspiring the faithful to fight for their freedom. This period saw a resurgence of the Church's moral authority and its role as a unifying force in the face of external aggression.

Following the restoration of independence, the Church continued to play a significant role in political discourse, advocating for social justice, human rights, and national unity. Church leaders often served as mediators in conflicts, offering counsel and guidance to both government officials and opposition groups. However, the rise of secularism and the establishment of a socialist government in 1974 led to a period of tension between the Church and state, with the government seeking to limit the Church's influence in political affairs.

The fall of the Derg regime in 1991 and the adoption of a new constitution ushered in a new era for the Church-state relationship. The constitution guaranteed freedom of religion, allowing the Church to operate independently of the state. However, the Church continues to engage with the government on issues of mutual concern, such as education, healthcare, and social welfare. Church leaders often meet with government officials to discuss these issues and offer their perspectives and recommendations.

In recent years, the Church has become more vocal on political matters, speaking out against corruption, injustice, and human rights abuses. Its leaders have called for greater accountability and transparency in government and have advocated for policies that promote social welfare and economic development. The Church's influence is also evident in the growing number of religious leaders who have entered politics, bringing their moral and ethical perspectives to the political arena.

Historical figures who influenced both realms

Throughout Ethiopian history, certain figures have emerged who, through their piety, wisdom, and leadership, have wielded influence in both the ecclesiastical and political spheres. These individuals, often revered as saints or national heroes, have left an enduring legacy on the Church-state relationship and the nation's trajectory.

1. **Abba Selama (St. Frumentius):** As the "Apostle of Ethiopia," Abba Selama's influence transcended the religious sphere. His close relationship with King Ezana of Aksum led to the adoption of Christianity as the state religion, establishing a precedent for the Church's involvement in political affairs. His wisdom and counsel were sought by rulers, and his teachings on justice and morality shaped the ethical framework of the Aksumite Empire.

2. **Emperor Gebre Meskel Lalibela (12th Century):** Renowned for his architectural vision and spiritual devotion, Lalibela's construction of the rock-hewn churches was not merely a religious endeavor but also a political statement. The churches, designed to replicate the holy city of Jerusalem, symbolized Ethiopia's spiritual independence and its unique place in the Christian world. Lalibela's reign marked a period of close cooperation between the Church and

state, with the emperor actively supporting the Church's growth and development.

3. **Emperor Zara Yaqob (15th Century):** A devout and scholarly king, Zara Yaqob's reign was marked by a deep engagement with theological matters and a strong emphasis on the Church's role in society. He convened the Council of Debre Mitmaq, which addressed theological disputes and reaffirmed the Church's adherence to Miaphysite Christology. His writings and teachings on faith, morality, and governance further solidified the Church's influence on political and social life.

4. **Emperor Tewodros II (19th Century):** A reformer who sought to modernize and centralize Ethiopia, Tewodros II had a complex relationship with the Church. While he recognized the Church's importance, he also sought to curtail its power and wealth. His efforts to reform the Church and limit its landholdings led to tensions and conflicts, highlighting the delicate balance between the spiritual and temporal authorities.

5. **Emperor Haile Selassie (20th Century):** Haile Selassie, a devout Orthodox Christian, sought to maintain the Church's central role in society while also modernizing the nation. He initiated reforms in education, healthcare, and social services, often in collaboration with the Church. However, his reign also saw periods of tension between the Church and state, particularly

regarding issues of land ownership and political influence.

These historical figures, each in their own way, have shaped the complex and dynamic relationship between the Ethiopian Orthodox Tewahedo Church and the Ethiopian state. Their actions and decisions have left a lasting legacy on the nation's political and spiritual landscape, demonstrating the intricate interplay between faith and power, tradition and progress.

Separation and Integration

Periods of separation and integration:

The intricate dance between the Ethiopian Orthodox Tewahedo Church and the Ethiopian state has not always been harmonious. There have been periods of both separation and integration, each leaving a distinct mark on the Church's autonomy, influence, and relationship with the ruling powers.

Periods of Separation:

- **Zemene Mesafint (Era of the Princes):** This era, marked by political fragmentation and regional rivalries, led to a significant degree of separation between the Church and the weakened central authority. Regional lords and princes exerted greater control over ecclesiastical affairs, appointing bishops and abbots, and influencing Church policies. This decentralization of power allowed for greater regional autonomy within the Church but also weakened its overall influence on national politics.

- **The Derg Regime (1974-1991):** The Marxist-Leninist Derg regime, which overthrew Emperor Haile Selassie in 1974, sought to curtail the Church's power and influence. The regime nationalized Church lands and properties, restricted its activities, and attempted to suppress its voice in political matters. This period of forced separation was a challenging time for the Church, as it struggled to maintain its autonomy and spiritual integrity under a hostile government.

Periods of Integration:

- **Aksumite and Solomonic Eras:** During the Aksumite and Solomonic eras, the Church and state enjoyed a close and symbiotic relationship. Monarchs often acted as patrons and protectors of the Church, providing it with resources and political support. In return, the Church legitimized the monarchs' rule, offering spiritual guidance and moral authority. This integration fostered a sense of national unity and identity, with Christianity becoming deeply ingrained in the cultural and social fabric of the empire.

- **Post-1991 Era:** The fall of the Derg regime in 1991 and the adoption of a new constitution ushered in a new era of religious freedom and autonomy for the Church. While the Church and state are now officially separated, their relationship remains intertwined. The Church continues to play a significant role in social and political discourse, advocating for peace, justice, and human rights. The government, in turn, recognizes the Church's important role in society and often seeks its cooperation on various issues.

The ebb and flow between separation and integration have shaped the Church's role in Ethiopian society. Periods of separation have often led to greater internal autonomy and diversity within the Church, while periods of integration have allowed the Church to exert greater influence on national policies and social values. This dynamic interplay between the spiritual and temporal authorities continues to shape the Ethiopian Orthodox Tewahedo Church's identity and its relationship with the Ethiopian state.

Effects on both the Church and the state

The ebb and flow between separation and integration have profoundly shaped both the Ethiopian Orthodox Tewahedo Church and the Ethiopian state, leaving lasting imprints on their identities, functions, and interactions.

Effects on the Church:

- **Autonomy and Identity:** Periods of separation, such as the Zemene Mesafint and the Derg regime, fostered a sense of autonomy within the Church. This allowed for the development of diverse theological interpretations, liturgical practices, and monastic traditions, enriching the Church's spiritual and cultural landscape. However, it also led to internal divisions and a weakening of central authority.
- **Resilience and Adaptation:** The Church's ability to navigate periods of separation and persecution, such as during the Italian occupation and the Derg regime, demonstrates its resilience and adaptability. The Church emerged from these challenges with a renewed sense of purpose and a deeper connection to the Ethiopian people.
- **Social Engagement:** Periods of integration, particularly in the post-1991 era, have allowed the Church to expand its social engagement and influence. The Church has been able to establish schools, hospitals, and other social service institutions, reaching out to communities across the country and addressing critical needs.
- **Political Advocacy:** The Church's engagement with the state has also allowed it to advocate for social justice, human rights, and the well-being of the Ethiopian people. Church leaders have

become vocal on political issues, using their moral authority to influence policy debates and promote peace and reconciliation.

Effects on the State:

- **Legitimacy and Authority:** The Church's support and blessing have historically been crucial for the legitimacy and authority of Ethiopian rulers. The Church's spiritual authority has often been invoked to justify political decisions and to garner popular support for the monarchy or government.
- **Social Stability and Cohesion:** The Church's emphasis on communal values, social harmony, and respect for authority has contributed to social stability and cohesion in Ethiopia. Its teachings on forgiveness, reconciliation, and peaceful conflict resolution have helped to mitigate social tensions and promote national unity.
- **Cultural Preservation:** The Church's role in preserving Ethiopia's cultural heritage, including its language, literature, art, and architecture, has been invaluable. The Church's institutions have served as repositories of knowledge and tradition, ensuring the continuity of Ethiopia's rich cultural legacy.
- **Challenges to Secular Authority:** At times, the Church's influence has also posed challenges

to secular authority. During periods of integration, the Church's involvement in political affairs has sometimes led to tensions and conflicts with the state. The Church's advocacy for social justice and human rights has also occasionally put it at odds with government policies.

- The complex interplay between the Ethiopian Orthodox Tewahedo Church and the Ethiopian state has shaped the nation's history, culture, and identity. This dynamic relationship, characterized by both cooperation and tension, continues to evolve, reflecting the changing political and social landscape of Ethiopia. As the nation navigates the challenges of the 21st century, the Church's role as a spiritual guide, cultural custodian, and advocate for social justice remains as vital as ever.

Modern Dynamics

Current relationship with the state:

The current relationship between the Ethiopian Orthodox Tewahedo Church and the Ethiopian state is a multifaceted one, characterized by a delicate balance of cooperation, autonomy, and occasional tension. The Church, while officially separated from the state, continues to wield significant influence in the social and political spheres, while the state recognizes the Church's important role in society and often seeks its cooperation on various issues.

The Ethiopian constitution guarantees freedom of religion, allowing the Church to operate independently and manage its own affairs. This autonomy has enabled the Church to revitalize its institutions, expand its social services, and engage in interfaith dialogue. However, the Church's relationship with the state is not without its complexities.

However, there have also been instances of tension and disagreement between the Church and state. The Church has been vocal in criticizing government policies that it deems unjust or harmful to the interests of the people. It has also raised concerns about the government's interference in religious affairs, particularly in the appointment of bishops and the management of Church properties.

Contemporary issues and challenges

In the contemporary era, the Ethiopian Orthodox Tewahedo Church faces a myriad of challenges that test its resilience, adaptability, and relevance in a rapidly changing world. These challenges, both internal and external, require the Church to navigate complex social, political, and theological landscapes while remaining true to its ancient traditions and spiritual mission.

1. **Religious Pluralism and Competition:**
   The rise of Pentecostalism and other evangelical

movements in Ethiopia has challenged the Church's traditional dominance. These movements, with their emphasis on personal salvation, emotional expression, and charismatic leadership, have attracted a growing number of followers, particularly among the youth. The Church must find ways to engage with these new religious expressions, offering a compelling alternative that resonates with the spiritual needs and aspirations of the younger generation.

2. **Secularism and Modernization:** The forces of secularism and modernization have also posed challenges to the Church's authority and influence. The increasing emphasis on individual autonomy, scientific rationalism, and material progress has led some Ethiopians to question or reject traditional religious beliefs and practices. The Church must find ways to adapt its message and ministry to the modern context, addressing the concerns and aspirations of a more secularized society.

3. **Ethnic and Political Tensions:** Ethiopia's diverse ethnic and political landscape has also presented challenges for the Church. The Church, while striving to be a unifying force, has sometimes been caught in the crossfire of ethnic conflicts and political rivalries. It must navigate these tensions carefully, promoting peace,

reconciliation, and dialogue while maintaining its spiritual independence and moral authority.

4. **Economic Challenges:** The Church, like many institutions in Ethiopia, faces economic challenges. The need to maintain its vast network of churches, monasteries, schools, and social service institutions requires significant financial resources. The Church must find sustainable ways to fund its operations and ensure its continued service to the community.

5. **The Diaspora Challenge:** The growing Ethiopian diaspora, while a source of strength and support for the Church, also presents challenges. Diaspora communities often face issues of assimilation, generational differences, and maintaining their connection to the mother Church. The Church must find ways to engage with the diaspora, providing spiritual guidance and support while also respecting their unique cultural contexts.

6. **Environmental Degradation:** The environmental crisis, with its devastating impact on Ethiopia's natural resources and livelihoods, is another challenge that the Church cannot ignore. The Church has a responsibility to raise awareness about environmental issues, advocate for sustainable practices, and mobilize its resources to protect the environment.

These contemporary issues and challenges require the Ethiopian Orthodox Tewahedo Church to adapt, innovate, and engage with the world in new ways. The Church must find a balance between preserving its ancient traditions and addressing the needs and aspirations of a rapidly changing society. By embracing dialogue, fostering unity, and promoting social justice, the Church can continue to be a beacon of hope and a source of spiritual guidance for the Ethiopian people.

Conclusion

In this chapter, we have traced the intricate relationship between the Ethiopian Orthodox Tewahedo Church and the Ethiopian state, a relationship that has been both symbiotic and fraught with tension throughout history. We have witnessed the Church's profound influence on political decisions, its role as a moral compass and advocate for social justice, and the dynamic interplay between church leaders and state officials. We have also explored the historical events that have shaped this relationship, from the early days of Aksum to the complexities of the modern era.

As we move forward, we will delve deeper into the cultural dimensions of the Ethiopian Orthodox Tewahedo Church, exploring its profound impact on Ethiopian society and its role in shaping the nation's cultural identity. We will uncover the intricate ways in which the Church's teachings, rituals, and values have permeated the daily lives of Ethiopians, influencing their social customs, artistic expressions, and even their understanding of the natural world. Join us as we embark on this cultural exploration, discovering the rich tapestry of traditions, beliefs, and practices that have made the Ethiopian Orthodox Tewahedo Church an integral part of Ethiopia's cultural landscape.

Chapter 7

Cultural Dimensions

Interweaving of Culture and Religion

In the heart of Ethiopia, where faith and tradition intertwine, the Ethiopian Orthodox Tewahedo Church has woven its vibrant threads into the very fabric of the nation's cultural tapestry. This interweaving is so profound that it is often difficult to discern where religion ends and culture begins. The Church's teachings, rituals, and values have permeated every aspect of Ethiopian life, shaping its customs, arts, social structures, and even its daily rhythms.

One of the most striking examples of this interweaving is the ubiquitous presence of the cross in Ethiopian culture. The cross, a central symbol of Christianity, is not merely a religious emblem but a cultural icon that adorns homes, businesses, and public spaces. It is worn as jewelry, etched onto everyday objects, and even incorporated into traditional hairstyles. This widespread use of the cross reflects the deep-rooted faith of the Ethiopian people and the Church's central role in their lives.

The Church's liturgical calendar, with its numerous feasts and fasts, also shapes the rhythm of daily life in Ethiopia. Fasting, a central practice in Ethiopian Orthodoxy, is observed not only during major religious periods like Lent but also on specific days of the week. These fasting periods, which often involve abstaining from meat and dairy products, are not merely dietary restrictions but spiritual disciplines aimed at purifying the body and soul. They are a tangible expression of the Church's teachings on self-discipline, humility, and devotion.

The Ethiopian coffee ceremony, a cherished tradition that involves the roasting, grinding, and brewing of coffee, is another example of the Church's influence on cultural practices. This elaborate ritual, often accompanied by prayers and blessings, is not merely a social gathering but a spiritual experience that fosters community and reinforces the Church's values of hospitality and generosity.

The Church's teachings on respect for elders, hospitality, and communal harmony have also shaped Ethiopian social customs and etiquette. The act of bowing to elders, kissing their hands, and seeking their blessings is a deeply ingrained cultural practice rooted in the Church's emphasis on honoring one's elders. The communal meals shared after church services, known as "agapes," are another example of the Church's influence on social interactions, fostering a sense of community and shared identity.

The Church's artistic tradition, with its intricate crosses, vibrant murals, and illuminated manuscripts, has also permeated Ethiopian culture. The vibrant colors and symbolic motifs found in Ethiopian art often reflect biblical stories and the lives of saints, serving as visual reminders of the Church's teachings and inspiring devotion among the faithful. The Church's patronage of traditional music, dance, and storytelling has also been instrumental in preserving these art forms and ensuring their transmission to future generations.

The Ge'ez language, the liturgical language of the Church, has had a profound impact on Ethiopian language and literature. Many Amharic words and phrases have their roots in Ge'ez, and the Church's vast literary corpus, including hymns, prayers, and theological treatises, has shaped Ethiopian literary expression. The Ge'ez script, with its elegant characters and rich symbolism, is also used in secular contexts, further highlighting the Church's influence on Ethiopian culture.

The Ethiopian Orthodox Tewahedo Church's teachings on the sanctity of life, the importance of family, and the interconnectedness of all creation have also shaped the Ethiopian worldview. The Church's emphasis on compassion, forgiveness, and reconciliation has fostered a culture of tolerance and respect for diversity. The Church's teachings on social justice and the responsibility of the wealthy to care for the poor have also influenced social and economic policies in Ethiopia.

In conclusion, the Ethiopian Orthodox Tewahedo Church's influence on Ethiopian culture is so pervasive that it is difficult to imagine one without the other. The Church's teachings, rituals, and values have become so deeply ingrained in Ethiopian society that they are often indistinguishable from cultural practices. This seamless integration is a testament to the Church's enduring power and its ability to shape the very fabric of Ethiopian life.

Integration into daily life

The Ethiopian Orthodox Tewahedo Church's embrace extends far beyond the church walls, weaving its traditions into the everyday lives of its followers. This integration is so seamless that separating the sacred from the mundane becomes a nuanced endeavor.

Rhythms of Time: The Church's liturgical calendar, a harmonious blend of solar and lunar cycles, governs the rhythm of life for many Ethiopians. Feasts and fasts punctuate the year, dictating not only spiritual observances but also social gatherings and dietary habits. The aroma of incense fills homes during designated prayer times, the rhythmic tolls of church bells mark the passage of time, and the vibrant tapestry of religious festivals paints the backdrop of daily life.

Spiritual Sustenance: The faithful carry their devotion beyond the church doors, incorporating spiritual practices into their homes and daily routines. Many Ethiopians maintain a dedicated prayer corner adorned with icons and crosses, where they offer personal devotions and seek solace in moments of reflection. The act of fasting, a cornerstone of Orthodox discipline, is not confined to religious periods but is often integrated into weekly routines, fostering a sense of spiritual discipline and self-control.

Social Fabric: The Church's teachings on community, hospitality, and respect for elders are deeply ingrained in Ethiopian social customs. The act of bowing to elders, kissing their hands as a sign of respect, and seeking their blessings are commonplace gestures that reflect the Church's emphasis on honoring one's elders. The Ethiopian coffee ceremony, a cherished tradition that transcends religious boundaries, is often infused with prayers and blessings, highlighting the Church's influence on social rituals and the importance of communal bonding.

Life Cycle Rituals: The Church's presence is felt most profoundly during significant life cycle events. From birth to death, the Church's rituals mark these milestones, offering blessings, guidance, and solace. Baptism and Chrismation welcome newborns into the faith community, while marriage ceremonies sanctify the union of couples. Funerals, conducted with solemn prayers and rituals, provide comfort and hope to the bereaved, ensuring a smooth transition for the departed soul.

Pilgrimage and Sacred Spaces

The Ethiopian landscape is dotted with sacred sites, churches, and monasteries that hold deep spiritual significance for the faithful. Pilgrimages to these holy places are not merely religious acts but cultural journeys that connect individuals to their spiritual heritage and the broader community of believers. The arduous trek to Lalibela's rock-hewn churches or the pilgrimage to the monastery of Debre Damo are transformative experiences that deepen faith and foster a sense of belonging.

In essence, the Ethiopian Orthodox Tewahedo Church is not confined to the walls of its sacred buildings; it is a living, breathing entity that permeates the daily lives of its followers. Its teachings, rituals, and values are woven into the fabric of Ethiopian society, shaping its cultural norms, social interactions, and spiritual landscape. This seamless integration of faith and life is a testament to the Church's enduring power and its ability to adapt and remain relevant in a constantly evolving world.

Ethiopian Church Calendar and Festivals

Description of major festivals:

The Ethiopian Orthodox Tewahedo Church's calendar is a vibrant tapestry woven with numerous feasts and fasts, each holding deep spiritual significance and cultural relevance. These celebrations punctuate the rhythm of life for the faithful, offering moments of communal joy, spiritual reflection, and renewed devotion.

1. **Timkat (Epiphany):** Celebrated on January 19th, Timkat commemorates the baptism of Jesus Christ in the Jordan River. This grand festival is a time of spiritual renewal and purification, marked by vibrant processions, the chanting of ancient hymns, and the symbolic re-enactment of baptism. The faithful gather at rivers and lakes, where priests bless the water and sprinkle it on the congregation, signifying the washing away of sins and the rebirth into a new life in Christ.

2. **Meskel (Feast of the Finding of the True Cross):** Meskel, celebrated on September 27th, commemorates the discovery of the True Cross by Empress Helena, the mother of Emperor Constantine. This joyous festival is marked by the burning of a large bonfire, symbolizing the finding of the cross and the triumph of good over evil. The faithful gather around the bonfire, singing hymns and offering prayers, their faces illuminated by the flickering flames.

3. **Genna (Christmas):** Celebrated on January 7th, Genna marks the birth of Jesus Christ. It is a time of family gatherings, festive meals, and the exchange of gifts. Special church services, adorned with colorful decorations and filled with the sounds of traditional music, celebrate the

Incarnation, the miraculous union of divine and human natures in the person of Christ.

4. **Fasika (Easter):** The most important festival in the Ethiopian Orthodox calendar, Fasika celebrates the resurrection of Jesus Christ. It is preceded by a 55-day Lenten fast, a period of introspection, prayer, and spiritual preparation. The culmination of this fast is the joyous celebration of Easter, marked by special church services, the breaking of the fast with festive meals, and the exchange of greetings and gifts. Fasika is a time of great hope and renewal, as believers celebrate the triumph of life over death and the promise of eternal salvation.

These major festivals, along with numerous other feasts and fasts throughout the year, create a vibrant and dynamic liturgical calendar that guides the spiritual life of the Ethiopian Orthodox community. They are not merely religious observances but cultural celebrations that bring people together, strengthen their faith, and reinforce their shared identity.

Cultural significance and celebrations

The Ethiopian Orthodox Tewahedo Church's festivals are not merely religious observances; they are vibrant cultural celebrations that pulsate with the rhythm of faith, tradition, and communal joy. These festivals, deeply ingrained in the Ethiopian psyche, offer a glimpse into the rich tapestry of the nation's spiritual and cultural heritage.

Timkat (Epiphany): A jubilant celebration of Christ's baptism, Timkat is a sensory feast that unfolds across Ethiopia. Processions of priests, adorned in resplendent vestments and carrying sacred tabots (replicas of the Ark of the Covenant), wind their way through towns and villages, accompanied by the rhythmic beat of drums and the harmonious chants of the faithful. The highlight of the festival is the ritual re-enactment of Christ's baptism, where priests bless the waters and sprinkle them on the jubilant crowds, symbolizing spiritual renewal and purification.

Meskel (Feast of the Finding of the True Cross): Meskel, a festival steeped in symbolism and reverence, commemorates the discovery of the True Cross by Empress Helena. The centerpiece of the celebration is the burning of a massive bonfire, known as the "Demera," which illuminates the night sky with its radiant glow. As the flames dance and crackle, the faithful gather around, singing hymns and offering prayers, their faces aglow with the warmth of faith and tradition.

Genna (Christmas): Genna, the Ethiopian Christmas, is a time of family gatherings, festive meals, and the exchange of gifts. The celebrations begin on Christmas Eve with a midnight mass, where the faithful gather in churches illuminated by countless candles, their voices raised in joyous hymns. The next day, families feast on traditional dishes, such as "doro wat" (spicy chicken stew) and "injera" (sourdough flatbread), and exchange gifts, fostering a sense of warmth and togetherness.

Fasika (Easter): The most important festival in the Ethiopian Orthodox calendar, Fasika celebrates the resurrection of Jesus Christ. It is preceded by a 55-day Lenten fast, a period of introspection, prayer, and spiritual preparation. The culmination of this fast is the joyous celebration of Easter, marked by special church services, the breaking of the fast with festive meals, and the exchange of greetings and gifts. The air is filled with the sounds of ululation, the rhythmic clapping of hands, and the joyous cries of "Christ is risen!"

These major festivals, along with numerous other feasts and fasts throughout the year, create a vibrant tapestry of spiritual and cultural expression. They are not merely religious observances but communal celebrations that bring people together, strengthen their faith, and reinforce their shared identity. The vibrant colors, rhythmic music, and elaborate rituals of these festivals create a sensory feast that captivates the heart and soul, leaving an enduring impression on all who witness them.

Role in Shaping Cultural Practices

Influence on Ethiopian arts, music, and literature.

The Ethiopian Orthodox Tewahedo Church's influence on the arts is so profound that it has shaped not only the sacred but also the secular artistic expressions of the Ethiopian people. The Church's patronage, theological teachings, and liturgical practices have inspired generations of artists, musicians, and writers, resulting in a rich and diverse cultural heritage that continues to thrive today.

Art:

Ethiopian Orthodox art is a visual feast, a symphony of colors, symbols, and narratives that reflect the Church's deep-rooted faith and its unique cultural identity. Icons, murals, and illuminated manuscripts are not merely decorative objects but windows into the spiritual world, conveying theological truths and inspiring devotion among the faithful.

- **Icons:** Ethiopian icons, with their distinctive style characterized by elongated figures, almond-shaped eyes, and vibrant colors, are revered as sacred images that mediate between the earthly and the divine. They depict Christ, the Virgin Mary, saints, and angels, not as realistic portrayals but as stylized representations that convey spiritual truths. The use of gold leaf, intricate patterns, and symbolic gestures adds to the icons' aesthetic beauty and theological depth.
- **Murals and Frescoes:** The walls of Ethiopian Orthodox churches and monasteries are adorned

with vibrant murals and frescoes that depict biblical scenes, the lives of saints, and theological teachings. These murals, often painted in a naïve style with bold colors and expressive figures, serve as visual aids for religious instruction and inspire devotion among the faithful. They are a testament to the Church's rich artistic heritage and its commitment to preserving its traditions through visual storytelling.

- **Illuminated Manuscripts:** Ethiopian illuminated manuscripts, with their intricate calligraphy, vibrant colors, and elaborate illustrations, are among the most exquisite examples of religious art. These manuscripts, often containing biblical texts, liturgical books, or hagiographies (lives of saints), were meticulously crafted by skilled scribes and artists. They are not only valuable historical documents but also works of art that reflect the Church's deep reverence for the written word and its commitment to preserving its spiritual heritage.

Music:

The Ethiopian Orthodox Church's musical tradition is a unique and vibrant expression of faith, characterized by its distinctive scales, rhythms, and instruments. The Church's liturgical music, known as "zema," is an integral part of worship, creating an atmosphere of reverence, awe, and spiritual ecstasy.

- **Zema:** The zema, a collection of chants and hymns, are sung in Ge'ez, the liturgical language of the Church. These chants, often accompanied by traditional instruments like the sistrum and the kebero, are not merely musical performances but acts of devotion, expressing the Church's theological teachings and inspiring spiritual fervor among the faithful.
- **Qene:** Qene is a form of religious poetry that is often sung or chanted. It is characterized by its intricate rhyme schemes, metaphors, and allusions to biblical stories and theological concepts. Qene is not only a form of artistic expression but also a means of transmitting the Church's teachings and preserving its cultural heritage.

Literature:

The Ethiopian Orthodox Church has a rich literary tradition, encompassing a wide range of genres, including biblical commentaries, theological treatises, hagiographies, and historical chronicles. These texts, written primarily in Ge'ez, are not only sources of religious instruction but also valuable historical documents that shed light on the Church's development and its interaction with Ethiopian society.

The Church's literary tradition has also influenced secular literature, with many Ethiopian writers and poets drawing inspiration from biblical stories, religious themes, and the Ge'ez language. This cross-pollination between religious and secular literature has enriched Ethiopian literary expression and contributed to the nation's cultural identity.

Specific cultural practices rooted in religion

The Ethiopian Orthodox Tewahedo Church's influence extends beyond grand festivals and into the minutiae of daily life, shaping cultural practices that have been passed down through generations. These practices, often imbued with deep spiritual symbolism, are a testament to the Church's enduring impact on Ethiopian society.

1. **Fasting:** The Ethiopian Orthodox Church observes numerous fasting periods throughout the year, including Lent, Wednesdays, Fridays, and various saints' days. These fasts, which often involve abstaining from meat and dairy products, are not merely dietary restrictions but spiritual disciplines aimed at purifying the body and soul, fostering humility, and drawing closer to God. Fasting is deeply ingrained in Ethiopian culture, with many non-Orthodox Ethiopians also observing these practices, highlighting the Church's influence on societal norms.

2. **Pilgrimage:** Pilgrimages to holy sites, such as the rock-hewn churches of Lalibela or the ancient monasteries of Debre Damo and Debre Libanos, are an integral part of Ethiopian Orthodox spirituality. These journeys, often arduous and demanding, are seen as acts of devotion and a means of seeking blessings and spiritual renewal. The communal aspect of pilgrimage, with groups of pilgrims traveling together, singing hymns, and sharing stories, reinforces the Church's emphasis on community and shared faith.

3. **Veneration of Saints:** The Ethiopian Orthodox Church venerates a vast array of saints, each associated with specific miracles, virtues, or historical events. The faithful seek the intercession of these saints through prayers, offerings, and pilgrimages to their shrines. This veneration of saints is not only a religious practice but also a cultural phenomenon, with many Ethiopians bearing the names of saints and celebrating their feast days with communal gatherings and festivities.

4. **Use of Holy Water:** Holy water, blessed by priests during religious ceremonies, is considered a source of spiritual purification and protection. It is used in various rituals, such as baptism, blessing of homes, and healing ceremonies. The use of holy water is deeply ingrained in Ethiopian culture,

with many people carrying small bottles of holy water for personal blessings and protection.

5. **Traditional Medicine and Healing Practices:** The Ethiopian Orthodox Church has a long tradition of using traditional medicine and healing practices, often intertwined with religious rituals and prayers. Priests and monks, knowledgeable in herbal remedies and spiritual healing techniques, play a crucial role in providing healthcare to communities, particularly in rural areas. This integration of faith and healing reflects the Church's holistic approach to well-being, addressing both the physical and spiritual needs of its followers.

These cultural practices, deeply rooted in the teachings and traditions of the Ethiopian Orthodox Tewahedo Church, are a testament to its enduring influence on Ethiopian society. They reflect the Church's ability to integrate faith into the daily lives of its followers, shaping their values, customs, and worldview. As Ethiopia continues to evolve and modernize, these cultural practices remain a vital link to the nation's rich spiritual heritage, providing a sense of continuity, identity, and belonging.

Traditional Clothing and Symbols

Religious Significance of Traditional Attire:

In the Ethiopian Orthodox Tewahedo Church, traditional clothing transcends its utilitarian purpose, becoming a visual tapestry woven with threads of symbolism and spiritual meaning. Each element of attire, from the intricate embroidery to the vibrant colors, speaks volumes about the wearer's faith, status, and devotion.

1. **The Shamma:** The shamma, a ubiquitous garment worn by both men and women, is more than just a shawl; it is a symbol of purity, humility, and reverence. Its pristine white color signifies the wearer's spiritual cleanliness and their commitment to a life of righteousness. The shamma's draping over the shoulders and body is reminiscent of the wings of angels, signifying the wearer's aspiration to emulate their heavenly counterparts.

2. **The Qamis:** The long, flowing robe worn by priests and deacons, known as the qamis, is a symbol of their sacred office and their dedication to serving God. The white color of the qamis represents purity and holiness, while its flowing design evokes the image of a shepherd guiding his flock. The qamis is not merely a garment but a visual representation of the priest's spiritual authority and their role as a mediator between the divine and the human.

3. **The Sinete:** The belt worn by priests and deacons, known as the senete, is a symbol of their

spiritual strength and their commitment to upholding the Church's teachings. The act of tying the senete around the waist signifies the wearer's readiness to serve God and the community, girding themselves for the spiritual battles that lie ahead.

4. **The Qob:** The conical hat worn by priests and bishops, known as the qob, is a symbol of their authority and their role as leaders of the Church. The qob's elaborate embroidery and embellishments often depict crosses, biblical scenes, and other religious motifs, further emphasizing the wearer's spiritual status and their connection to the divine.

5. **Colors and Motifs:** The colors and motifs used in Ethiopian Orthodox attire are rich in symbolism. White, the predominant color, signifies purity, holiness, and divine light. Gold, often used in embroidery and embellishments, represents the glory of God and the heavenly realm. Red, sometimes used in liturgical vestments, symbolizes the blood of Christ and the sacrifice he made for humanity. The intricate patterns and geometric designs found in Ethiopian textiles often have symbolic meanings, representing spiritual concepts such as the Trinity, the Incarnation, and the interconnectedness of all creation.

The symbolic meanings embedded in Ethiopian Orthodox attire are not merely decorative but serve a deeper purpose. They are visual reminders of the Church's teachings, its rich history, and its enduring traditions. By wearing these garments, the faithful not only express their devotion to God but also connect themselves to a vibrant spiritual heritage that has been passed down through generations. The attire becomes a tangible expression of faith, a visible manifestation of the wearer's spiritual identity and their place within the community of believers.

Religious Art and Architecture: Overview of religious art forms.

The Ethiopian Orthodox Tewahedo Church stands as a custodian of a rich artistic heritage, where faith and creativity intertwine to create a visual symphony of devotion and cultural expression. Religious art forms, imbued with symbolism and spiritual significance, adorn the sacred spaces of Ethiopia, inviting the faithful into a world of divine beauty and contemplation.

1. **Icons:** Icons, often painted on wood panels or parchment, are revered as windows into the divine. These sacred images, depicting Christ, the Virgin Mary, saints, and angels, are not mere representations but living presences of the divine. The elongated figures, almond-shaped eyes, and vibrant colors of Ethiopian icons are distinctive

features that reflect the Church's unique artistic tradition.

2. **Murals and Frescoes:** The walls of Ethiopian Orthodox churches and monasteries come alive with vibrant murals and frescoes that narrate biblical stories, depict the lives of saints, and illustrate theological teachings. These paintings, often characterized by their bold colors, expressive figures, and naïve style, serve as visual aids for religious instruction and inspire devotion among the faithful.

3. **Illuminated Manuscripts:** Ethiopian illuminated manuscripts are exquisite treasures, meticulously crafted by skilled scribes and artists. These manuscripts, often containing biblical texts, liturgical books, or hagiographies (lives of saints), are adorned with intricate calligraphy, vibrant colors, and elaborate illustrations. They are not only valuable historical documents but also works of art that reflect the Church's deep reverence for the written word and its commitment to preserving its spiritual heritage.

4. **Crosses:** The cross, a central symbol of Christianity, holds a special significance in Ethiopian Orthodoxy. Ethiopian crosses are renowned for their intricate designs, often incorporating geometric patterns, floral motifs, and symbolic representations. They are not merely decorative objects but are believed to

possess protective powers and are worn as jewelry or displayed in homes and churches. The cross is a constant reminder of Christ's sacrifice and the central message of salvation in the Ethiopian Orthodox faith.

These art forms, each with its unique style and symbolism, collectively create a visual language that speaks to the heart and soul of the Ethiopian Orthodox faithful. They are not merely aesthetic expressions but conduits of grace, inviting believers into a deeper communion with the divine and enriching their spiritual lives.

Architectural styles of churches and monasteries

Ethiopian Orthodox church architecture is a testament to the faith, ingenuity, and resourcefulness of its people. It is a unique blend of indigenous styles, ancient Aksumite influences, and later adaptations inspired by Byzantine and Arab designs. This architectural diversity reflects the Church's deep-rooted connection to the land, its historical evolution, and its openness to external influences.

1. **Aksumite Style:** The earliest Ethiopian churches, dating back to the Aksumite period (4th–8th centuries), were characterized by their basilica-like design, with rectangular structures, colonnades, and elaborate decorative elements.

These churches, often built with stone and wood, featured intricate carvings, geometric patterns, and symbolic motifs that reflected the Church's theological beliefs and cultural traditions. The most iconic examples of Aksumite architecture are the towering obelisks and stelae, which served as burial markers for royalty and religious figures.

2. **Rock-Hewn Churches:** The Zagwe dynasty (12th-13th centuries) ushered in a new era of Ethiopian church architecture with the construction of the rock-hewn churches of Lalibela. These monolithic churches, carved out of solid volcanic rock, are a marvel of engineering and a testament to the Church's spiritual ambition and artistic vision. Each church has a unique design, with intricate carvings, elaborate facades, and subterranean passages. The most famous of these churches, Bete Giyorgis (Church of St. George), is shaped like a cross and is considered a masterpiece of Ethiopian architecture.

3. **Gondarine Style:** The Gondarine period (17th-18th centuries) saw the emergence of a new architectural style characterized by its use of stone, wood, and lime mortar. Gondarine churches are typically rectangular in shape, with pitched roofs, arched doorways, and windows. They often feature elaborate decorative elements, such as frescoes, murals, and intricate woodwork. The Debre Berhan Selassie Church in Gondar,

with its stunning ceiling paintings of angels, is a prime example of Gondarine architecture.

4. **Rural Churches:** In rural areas, Ethiopian Orthodox churches often follow a more traditional style, using local materials such as wood, thatch, and mud. These churches are typically circular in shape, with conical thatched roofs and simple interiors. They often feature a central pillar, symbolizing the Tree of Life, and are adorned with colorful murals depicting biblical scenes and the lives of saints.

5. **Modern Churches:** In recent decades, the Ethiopian Orthodox Church has embraced modern architectural styles, incorporating elements of concrete, steel, and glass into its church designs. These modern churches, while often larger and more elaborate than traditional structures, still retain elements of Ethiopian architectural heritage, such as the use of domes, arches, and geometric patterns.

Ethiopian Orthodox church architecture is a testament to the Church's rich history, its deep connection to the land, and its openness to diverse influences. It is a living tradition that continues to evolve, reflecting the changing needs and aspirations of the Ethiopian people. Whether ancient or modern, rural or urban, these sacred spaces serve as places of worship, community gathering, and cultural expression, embodying the enduring spirit of Ethiopian Orthodoxy.

Oral Traditions and Storytelling: Role in Preserving and Transmitting Religious Stories

In the Ethiopian Orthodox Tewahedo Church, the oral tradition is a vibrant and dynamic force, a living repository of faith, history, and cultural identity. Passed down through generations, these spoken narratives, proverbs, and teachings serve as a vital link to the past, preserving the Church's rich heritage and ensuring its continued relevance in the present.

The oral tradition plays a crucial role in preserving and transmitting religious stories, ensuring that the faith's narratives and teachings are not confined to written texts but are woven into the very fabric of daily life. Storytelling, a cherished art form in Ethiopia, is a powerful tool for transmitting religious knowledge, moral values, and cultural identity. Elders, priests, and community leaders share stories of saints, biblical figures, and historical events, captivating their audiences and imparting wisdom that transcends generations.

These oral narratives are not merely recitations of facts but living expressions of faith, imbued with emotion, symbolism, and cultural nuances. They are often accompanied by music, dance, and dramatic gestures, creating a multisensory experience that engages the listener's heart, mind, and soul. The stories are not static but evolve and adapt over time, reflecting the changing social and cultural context of the community.

The oral tradition also serves as a means of interpreting and contextualizing the written scriptures. The Ge'ez Bible, while revered as the Word of God, is not always easily accessible to the laity due to its archaic language and complex theological concepts. Oral teachings and interpretations, often delivered in Amharic or other local languages, bridge this gap, making the scriptures relevant and understandable to the wider community.

The oral tradition is not confined to formal religious settings but permeates everyday life. Proverbs, riddles, and sayings, often rooted in biblical stories and teachings, are used in daily conversations, offering guidance, wisdom, and moral instruction. These oral expressions of faith are a constant reminder of the Church's presence in the lives of its followers, shaping their worldview and guiding their actions.

In recent years, the Ethiopian Orthodox Tewahedo Church has recognized the importance of documenting and preserving its oral tradition. Efforts are underway to record and transcribe oral narratives, ensuring that this invaluable cultural heritage is not lost to time. The Church has also established cultural centers and museums that showcase its rich oral tradition, making it accessible to a wider audience.

The oral tradition of the Ethiopian Orthodox Tewahedo Church is a living testament to the power of storytelling, the importance of cultural memory, and the enduring relevance of ancient wisdom in the modern world. It is a vibrant and dynamic force that continues to shape the faith, identity, and cultural expression of the Ethiopian people.

Cultural impact of these traditions

The oral traditions and storytelling practices of the Ethiopian Orthodox Tewahedo Church have left an enduring mark on the nation's cultural landscape, shaping its artistic expressions, social values, and collective memory.

1. **Artistic Inspiration:** The rich narratives, vivid imagery, and moral lessons embedded in oral traditions have inspired generations of Ethiopian artists, writers, and musicians. The stories of saints, biblical figures, and historical events have been immortalized in paintings, sculptures, and illuminated manuscripts, enriching Ethiopia's artistic heritage. The rhythmic patterns and poetic language of oral storytelling have also influenced traditional music and dance, creating a vibrant and dynamic cultural expression that resonates with the Ethiopian spirit.

2. **Social Values and Norms:** The oral tradition serves as a repository of social values and norms, transmitting ethical teachings, moral principles, and cultural expectations from one generation to

the next. Proverbs, riddles, and sayings, often rooted in biblical stories and teachings, are used in daily conversations, offering guidance, wisdom, and moral instruction. These oral expressions of wisdom reinforce communal values, promote social cohesion, and provide a framework for ethical behavior.

3. **Historical Consciousness and Identity:** The oral tradition plays a crucial role in preserving Ethiopia's historical consciousness and cultural identity. The stories of past kings, queens, warriors, and saints are not merely tales of the past but living narratives that shape the present and inspire the future. They instill a sense of pride in Ethiopia's rich heritage, its resilience in the face of adversity, and its unique place in the world.

4. **Intergenerational Transmission of Knowledge:** The oral tradition serves as a vital link between generations, ensuring the transmission of knowledge, wisdom, and cultural values. Elders, respected as repositories of knowledge and experience, play a crucial role in passing down oral traditions to younger generations. This intergenerational transmission of knowledge fosters a sense of continuity and belonging, connecting the present with the past and ensuring the preservation of cultural heritage.

5. **Community Building and Social Cohesion:** The communal nature of storytelling, where

people gather to listen, share, and reflect on narratives, fosters a sense of community and belonging. Storytelling events, often held in churches, community centers, or under the shade of trees, provide a space for social interaction, cultural exchange, and the strengthening of communal bonds. The shared experience of listening to and participating in storytelling creates a sense of collective identity and reinforces the values that hold the community together.

The Ethiopian Orthodox Tewahedo Church's oral traditions and storytelling practices are not merely relics of the past but living expressions of faith, culture, and identity. They continue to shape the lives of millions of Ethiopians, providing spiritual guidance, moral instruction, and a sense of connection to their rich heritage. As Ethiopia navigates the complexities of the modern world, the oral tradition remains a vital force in preserving the nation's cultural identity and ensuring its continued vibrancy and relevance.

Music and Chanting

Importance of religious music:

In the Ethiopian Orthodox Tewahedo Church, music is not merely an accessory to worship; it is the lifeblood that pulses through the veins of the liturgy, carrying the prayers of the faithful to the heavens and echoing the divine back to earth. It is a sacred language that transcends words, a symphony of devotion that stirs the soul and unites the community in a shared spiritual experience.

The importance of religious music in the Ethiopian Orthodox tradition is deeply rooted in its theological understanding and cultural heritage. Music is seen as a divine gift, a means of expressing the ineffable mysteries of faith and connecting with the transcendent. The Church's rich musical tradition, with its ancient melodies, rhythmic patterns, and evocative chants, is a testament to the power of music to uplift the spirit, inspire devotion, and foster a sense of communal unity.

The significance of religious music in the Ethiopian Orthodox Tewahedo Church can be understood through several key aspects:

1. **A Channel of Divine Communication:** Music is considered a sacred language that transcends the limitations of human speech. It is believed to be a direct channel of communication with the divine, allowing the faithful to express their deepest emotions, aspirations, and longings. The rhythmic chants and soaring melodies of Ethiopian Orthodox music are seen as a way of reaching out to God, of offering praise and thanksgiving, and of seeking solace and guidance.

2. **A Vehicle for Spiritual Expression:** Music serves as a powerful vehicle for expressing the

complex emotions and spiritual experiences that words alone cannot capture. The joy of celebration, the sorrow of repentance, the awe of encountering the divine—all find their voice in the music of the Church. The rhythmic patterns and repetitive nature of the chants create a meditative atmosphere, allowing the faithful to enter a state of deep contemplation and spiritual ecstasy.

3. **A Unifying Force:** Communal singing is a hallmark of Ethiopian Orthodox worship. The congregation actively participates in the liturgy, joining their voices in a harmonious chorus of praise and supplication. This shared musical experience fosters a sense of unity and belonging, strengthening the bonds between the faithful and creating a vibrant atmosphere of worship. The music transcends individual differences, uniting people from all walks of life in a shared spiritual experience.

4. **A Preserver of Tradition:** The Church's musical tradition is a treasure trove of cultural heritage, passed down through generations of singers, musicians, and composers. The ancient melodies, rhythmic patterns, and liturgical texts have been preserved and transmitted through oral tradition, ensuring the continuity of the Church's musical legacy. This rich musical heritage is not only a source of pride for the Ethiopian people

but also a valuable contribution to the world's musical diversity.

The importance of religious music in the Ethiopian Orthodox Tewahedo Church cannot be overstated. It is an integral part of the Church's identity, a powerful expression of its faith, and a vital tool for spiritual growth and communal unity. As the Church continues to evolve and adapt to the challenges of the modern world, its musical tradition remains a steadfast anchor, connecting the faithful to their ancient roots and providing a source of inspiration and renewal for generations to come.

Notable hymns and chants in Ethiopian Orthodoxy

The Ethiopian Orthodox Tewahedo Church's musical tradition is a treasure trove of sacred melodies, each carrying the weight of centuries of devotion and spiritual expression. These hymns and chants, often sung in the ancient Ge'ez language, are not merely musical compositions but vehicles for divine communication, instruments of spiritual upliftment, and expressions of communal faith.

1. **The Deggua:** This hymn, often referred to as the "Hymn of Praise," is a cornerstone of Ethiopian Orthodox liturgy. Its verses, rich in theological depth and poetic beauty, extol the glory of God, the majesty of Christ, and the wonders of

creation. The Deggua is typically sung during the Divine Liturgy, its soaring melodies and rhythmic patterns creating an atmosphere of reverence and awe.

2. **The Mawase'et:** This collection of hymns, attributed to Saint Yared, the father of Ethiopian church music, is a masterpiece of liturgical composition. The Mawase'et, with their intricate melodies and poetic lyrics, explore various themes, including the life of Christ, the Virgin Mary, the saints, and the mysteries of faith. They are sung during specific times of the liturgical year, enriching the worship experience and deepening the faithful's understanding of the Church's teachings.

3. **The Qene:** Qene is a form of religious poetry that is often sung or chanted during church services and religious festivals. It is characterized by its intricate rhyme schemes, metaphors, and allusions to biblical stories and theological concepts. Qene is not only a form of artistic expression but also a means of transmitting the Church's teachings and preserving its cultural heritage.

4. **The Meeraf:** The Meeraf, a collection of hymns dedicated to the Virgin Mary, is a testament to the Church's deep veneration for the Mother of God. These hymns, often sung during Marian feasts and fasts, extol Mary's virtues, her role in salvation

history, and her intercession on behalf of the faithful. The Meeraf's lyrical beauty and emotional depth evoke a sense of devotion and reverence for the Virgin Mary.

5. **The Slellase:** The Slellase, a collection of hymns dedicated to the Holy Trinity, celebrates the triune nature of God and the unique role of each person of the Trinity in the divine plan of salvation. These hymns, often sung during the Divine Liturgy and other liturgical services, emphasize the unity of the Godhead and the harmonious relationship between the Father, Son, and Holy Spirit.

These are just a few examples of the many hymns and chants that enrich the Ethiopian Orthodox Tewahedo Church's musical tradition. Each composition, with its unique melody, rhythm, and lyrical content, serves as a vehicle for spiritual expression, a conduit of divine grace, and a testament to the Church's rich cultural heritage. The music of the Ethiopian Orthodox Church is not merely an accompaniment to worship but an integral part of the spiritual experience, a powerful force that unites the faithful, uplifts their souls, and draws them closer to God.

In this chapter, we have explored the multifaceted cultural dimensions of the Ethiopian Orthodox Tewahedo Church. We have witnessed the intricate interweaving of faith and culture, the Church's profound influence on Ethiopian arts, music, and literature, and its role in shaping cultural practices and social norms. We have also delved into the significance of traditional clothing and symbols, the architectural marvels of churches and monasteries, and the power of oral traditions and storytelling in preserving the Church's rich heritage.

As we move forward, we will confront the challenges and adaptations that the Ethiopian Orthodox Tewahedo Church has faced in the modern era. We will examine the impact of social, political, and technological changes on the Church's traditions and practices, and explore its responses to these challenges. Join us as we delve into the complexities of the Church's engagement with the modern world, its efforts to maintain its relevance, and its ongoing mission to serve the spiritual needs of the Ethiopian people.

Chapter 8

Challenges and Adaptations
Historical Challenges:

The Ethiopian Orthodox Tewahedo Church, a beacon of faith and resilience, has weathered numerous storms throughout its long and illustrious history. These challenges, ranging from internal theological debates to external pressures from political and religious rivals, have tested the Church's adaptability and its ability to maintain its spiritual integrity amidst adversity.

1. **Early Challenges and Heresies:** In its formative years, the Church faced challenges from various heresies and schisms that threatened to undermine its unity and doctrinal purity. One such challenge came from the followers of Mani, a 3rd-century Persian prophet who preached a dualistic doctrine that contradicted the Church's teachings on the nature of God and the world. The Church

responded by vigorously defending its orthodox beliefs, engaging in theological debates, and excommunicating those who refused to adhere to its teachings.

2. **Islamic Expansion and Isolation:** The rise of Islam in the 7th century and the subsequent expansion of Muslim empires in the region posed a significant challenge to the Ethiopian Orthodox Church. The Church found itself increasingly isolated from the broader Christian world, cut off from its traditional sources of support and theological exchange. However, this isolation also fostered a sense of resilience and self-reliance, as the Church developed its unique traditions and practices, further solidifying its identity as a distinct branch of Christianity.

3. **The Crusades and European Influence:** The Crusades, a series of religious wars fought between Christians and Muslims in the medieval period, brought the Ethiopian Orthodox Church into contact with European Christianity. While this interaction led to some cultural and intellectual exchange, it also exposed the Church to new theological ideas and practices that challenged its traditional beliefs. The Church responded by reaffirming its adherence to Miaphysite Christology and its unique liturgical traditions, while also engaging in dialogue with European Christians.

4. **The Zemene Mesafint (Era of the Princes):**
   The Zemene Mesafint, a period of political fragmentation and regional rivalries in the 18th and 19th centuries, presented a unique set of challenges for the Church. The weakening of central authority led to increased autonomy for regional churches and monasteries, which sometimes resulted in theological disputes and power struggles. However, the Church also demonstrated its adaptability during this period, as it decentralized its administration and allowed for greater regional autonomy while maintaining its core doctrines and practices.

5. **European Colonialism and Missionary Activities:** The 19th century saw the arrival of European missionaries in Ethiopia, representing various Protestant denominations. These missionaries, while providing education and healthcare, also sought to convert Ethiopians to their own brand of Christianity. This posed a challenge to the Ethiopian Orthodox Church, which had to defend its traditions and beliefs against the proselytizing efforts of foreign missionaries. The Church responded by strengthening its educational institutions, training its clergy, and engaging in theological debates with the missionaries.

6. **Italian Occupation and Persecution:** The Italian occupation of Ethiopia in the 20th century

was a dark period for the Church. The occupying forces sought to suppress the Church's influence, persecuting its leaders and attempting to replace its traditions with Roman Catholicism. However, the Church remained a symbol of national resistance, with its clergy and laity actively participating in the struggle for independence. The Church's resilience during this period of persecution further solidified its bond with the Ethiopian people.

The Ethiopian Orthodox Tewahedo Church's ability to overcome these historical challenges is a testament to its enduring strength, adaptability, and deep roots in Ethiopian society. The Church's unwavering commitment to its faith, its willingness to engage in dialogue and adapt to changing circumstances, and its resilience in the face of adversity have all contributed to its survival and continued relevance. These historical challenges have also shaped the Church's identity, making it a unique and vibrant expression of Christianity that has withstood the test of time.

Social and Political Pressures

Contemporary social and political issues:

In the contemporary era, the Ethiopian Orthodox Tewahedo Church finds itself navigating a complex landscape of social and political pressures, both within Ethiopia and in its diaspora communities. These challenges test the Church's ability to maintain its traditions, adapt to a changing world, and fulfill its spiritual mission amidst a myriad of competing forces.

1. **Ethnic and Political Tensions:** Ethiopia's diverse ethnic landscape, while a source of cultural richness, has also been a source of political and social tensions. The Church, as a national institution with followers from various ethnic groups, has sometimes been caught in the crossfire of these tensions. It has been accused by some of favoring certain ethnic groups over others, while others have criticized it for not taking a strong enough stance on political issues. The Church must navigate these tensions carefully, promoting unity and reconciliation while respecting the diversity of its members.

2. **Religious Pluralism:** The rise of Pentecostalism and other evangelical movements in Ethiopia has challenged the Church's traditional dominance. These movements, with their emphasis on personal salvation, emotional expression, and charismatic leadership, have attracted a growing number of followers, particularly among the youth. The Church must find ways to engage with these new religious expressions, offering a compelling alternative that

resonates with the spiritual needs and aspirations of the younger generation.

3. **Gender Equality and Women's Rights:** The role of women within the Church has been a subject of ongoing debate and discussion. While women play an active role in the daily life of the Church, their participation in leadership positions remains limited. The Church faces the challenge of addressing calls for greater gender equality and empowering women to take on leadership roles within the institution.

4. **The Diaspora Challenge:** The growing Ethiopian diaspora, while a source of strength and support for the Church, also presents unique challenges. Diaspora communities often face issues of assimilation, generational differences, and maintaining their connection to the mother Church. The Church must find ways to engage with the diaspora, providing spiritual guidance and support while also respecting their unique cultural contexts.

5. **Social Justice and Human Rights:** The Church has a long history of advocating for social justice and human rights. However, it faces the challenge of addressing contemporary issues such as poverty, inequality, and access to education and healthcare. The Church must continue to be a voice for the voiceless, advocating for policies and

programs that uplift the marginalized and promote the well-being of all Ethiopians.

6. **Environmental Concerns:** The environmental crisis, with its devastating impact on Ethiopia's natural resources and livelihoods, is another pressing issue that the Church must address. The Church has a responsibility to raise awareness about environmental issues, advocate for sustainable practices, and mobilize its resources to protect the environment.

These contemporary social and political issues present both challenges and opportunities for the Ethiopian Orthodox Tewahedo Church. By engaging with these issues in a thoughtful and compassionate manner, the Church can strengthen its relevance in the modern world, foster unity among its diverse members, and continue to be a beacon of hope and inspiration for the Ethiopian people.

Church's response to these pressures

The Ethiopian Orthodox Tewahedo Church, a beacon of resilience and adaptability, has not remained passive in the face of these contemporary challenges. It has responded with a multifaceted approach that seeks to preserve its traditions while engaging with the complexities of the modern world.

1. **Embracing Dialogue and Education:**
   Recognizing the importance of dialogue and
   understanding, the Church has initiated various
   interfaith initiatives, fostering conversations with
   other Christian denominations and religious
   traditions. These dialogues aim to address
   theological differences, promote mutual respect,
   and find common ground on issues of shared
   concern. The Church has also invested in
   theological education, establishing seminaries and
   colleges to train clergy and laity in modern
   exegetical methods and equip them to engage
   with contemporary theological discourse.

2. **Youth Engagement and Outreach:** To
   address the challenge of secularism and appeal to
   younger generations, the Church has launched
   youth-oriented programs and initiatives. These
   programs focus on providing spiritual guidance,
   mentorship, and opportunities for community
   engagement. The Church has also embraced
   technology, utilizing social media and online
   platforms to reach younger audiences and share
   its message in a more accessible and engaging
   way.

3. **Strengthening Diaspora Connections:**
   Recognizing the importance of the diaspora
   community, the Church has established various
   mechanisms to maintain connections and provide
   spiritual support to Ethiopians living abroad. This

includes the establishment of diaspora churches, the appointment of bishops to oversee diaspora communities, and the organization of conferences and pilgrimages that bring together Ethiopians from around the world.

4. **Advocacy and Social Action:** The Church continues to be a vocal advocate for social justice, human rights, and environmental protection. It has spoken out against injustice, corruption, and violence, calling for peaceful resolutions to conflicts and advocating for policies that promote the well-being of all Ethiopians. The Church has also launched initiatives to address poverty, inequality, and environmental degradation, working in partnership with government agencies and civil society organizations.

The Ethiopian Orthodox Tewahedo Church's response to contemporary challenges is a testament to its resilience, adaptability, and unwavering commitment to its spiritual mission. By embracing dialogue, education, and social action, the Church is striving to remain relevant and influential in a rapidly changing world. While the challenges are significant, the Church's deep roots in Ethiopian society, its spiritual authority, and its commitment to serving the needs of its people give it a unique position to address these challenges and continue to be a beacon of hope and inspiration for generations to come.

Impact of Modernization

Effects of modernization on traditional practices:

The relentless march of modernization has cast both a shadow and a light on the time-honored traditions of the Ethiopian Orthodox Tewahedo Church. As Ethiopia embraced technological advancements, urbanization, and Western influences, the Church found itself at a crossroads, grappling with the need to adapt while preserving its spiritual essence and cultural heritage.

One of the most notable effects of modernization has been the gradual erosion of some traditional practices. The allure of urban life, with its promise of economic opportunities and modern amenities, has led to a migration of young people from rural areas, where traditional practices are often more deeply rooted. This has resulted in a decline in the observance of certain customs, such as communal fasting and feasting, pilgrimage to holy sites, and participation in traditional agricultural rituals.

The influence of Western education and secular values has also challenged some traditional beliefs and practices. The younger generation, exposed to diverse ideas and lifestyles, may question or reinterpret certain aspects of the Church's teachings, leading to a re-evaluation of long-held traditions. For instance, the Church's stance on gender roles and social issues has been subject to scrutiny and debate, as more Ethiopians embrace modern notions of equality and individual autonomy.

Modernization has also impacted the Church's liturgical practices. The introduction of modern technology, such as microphones and sound systems, has altered the acoustic experience of worship in some churches. The use of printed liturgical books, while making the texts more accessible, has also led to a decline in the oral transmission of hymns and prayers.

However, modernization has not been entirely detrimental to the Church's traditions. In fact, it has also opened up new avenues for the preservation and dissemination of its heritage. The use of technology, for example, has enabled the Church to reach wider audiences through radio, television, and the internet. The establishment of theological colleges and seminaries has provided a platform for the study and preservation of ancient manuscripts and liturgical texts.

Moreover, modernization has also led to a renewed interest in traditional practices among some segments of the population. The Ethiopian diaspora, for instance, has played a crucial role in preserving and promoting Ethiopian Orthodox traditions abroad, establishing churches, cultural centers, and educational institutions that cater to the spiritual and cultural needs of Ethiopian communities.

In conclusion, the impact of modernization on the Ethiopian Orthodox Tewahedo Church's traditional practices has been a complex and multifaceted process. While some practices have declined or been modified, others have been revitalized and adapted to the modern context. The Church's ability to navigate these changes while remaining true to its core values and spiritual essence is a testament to its resilience and adaptability. As Ethiopia continues to modernize, the Church faces the ongoing challenge of balancing tradition with progress, ensuring that its rich heritage remains relevant and meaningful in the 21st century.

Adaptations to modern societal changes

The Ethiopian Orthodox Tewahedo Church, while deeply rooted in tradition, has demonstrated a remarkable capacity for adaptation in response to the sweeping societal changes of the 20th and 21st centuries. This adaptability, driven by a desire to remain relevant and accessible to its followers, is evident in various aspects of the Church's life and ministry.

1. **Liturgical Adaptations:** While the Church's liturgical traditions remain deeply rooted in ancient practices, there have been subtle adaptations to accommodate modern sensibilities. For instance, some churches have introduced the use of microphones and sound systems to enhance the audibility of chants and sermons. The translation of liturgical texts into Amharic and

other local languages has also made the liturgy more accessible to a wider audience.

2. **Embrace of Technology:** The Church has embraced technology as a tool for outreach and communication. Many churches now have websites and social media pages, where they share information about services, events, and teachings. Some clergy have even begun using social media platforms to deliver sermons and engage with the faithful online. This technological adaptation has allowed the Church to reach a wider audience, particularly among the younger generation and the diaspora community.

3. **Social Engagement:** The Church has expanded its social engagement, addressing contemporary issues such as HIV/AIDS, poverty, and gender inequality. It has established partnerships with government agencies and non-governmental organizations to provide healthcare, education, and social services to vulnerable communities. This proactive approach to social engagement has not only helped to address pressing social needs but has also enhanced the Church's relevance and credibility in the modern world.

4. **Theological Discourse:** The Church has engaged in theological discourse with other Christian denominations and religious traditions, seeking to find common ground and promote

understanding. This openness to dialogue has enriched the Church's theological understanding and fostered a spirit of ecumenism. It has also allowed the Church to address contemporary theological challenges, such as the rise of secularism and the questioning of traditional beliefs.

5. **Education and Training:** The Church has invested in the education and training of its clergy and laity, recognizing the importance of theological knowledge and pastoral skills in addressing the needs of a modern society. The establishment of theological colleges and seminaries has provided a platform for rigorous theological training, equipping clergy to engage with contemporary issues and provide effective spiritual guidance.

These adaptations, while sometimes met with resistance from traditionalists, have been essential for the Church's survival and continued relevance in a rapidly changing world. By embracing change while remaining true to its core values and teachings, the Ethiopian Orthodox Tewahedo Church has demonstrated its ability to navigate the complexities of modernity and continue to serve as a spiritual beacon for millions of Ethiopians.

Globalization

Influence of globalization on the church:

Globalization, the interconnectedness of economies, societies, and cultures across the world, has cast a wide net over the Ethiopian Orthodox Tewahedo Church, presenting a unique set of challenges and opportunities. This phenomenon, characterized by increased mobility, cultural exchange, and the spread of ideas, has profoundly impacted the Church's traditions, practices, and global reach.

Challenges:

1. **Cultural Homogenization:** The influx of Western values and secular ideologies, often propagated through media and education, has challenged the Church's traditional values and cultural norms. The younger generation, exposed to diverse lifestyles and beliefs, may question or reinterpret certain aspects of the Church's teachings, leading to a potential erosion of cultural identity and religious practices.

2. **Theological Pluralism:** Globalization has exposed the Church to a wider range of theological perspectives and interpretations, challenging its traditional understanding of scripture and doctrine. The rise of Pentecostalism and other evangelical movements, with their

emphasis on personal salvation and emotional expression, has also created a more competitive religious landscape, requiring the Church to adapt its message and ministry to remain relevant.

3. **Brain Drain and Leadership Gap:** The migration of educated Ethiopians to Western countries, often seeking better economic opportunities, has created a leadership gap within the Church. Many young, educated individuals who could potentially become future leaders of the Church are leaving Ethiopia, leaving behind a void that is difficult to fill. This brain drain poses a challenge to the Church's ability to adapt and innovate in the face of modern challenges.

4. **Economic Pressures:** Globalization has also brought economic pressures to bear on the Church. The increasing cost of maintaining churches, monasteries, and social service institutions, coupled with the economic hardships faced by many Ethiopians, has strained the Church's financial resources. The Church must find innovative ways to generate income and ensure its financial sustainability while continuing to serve the needs of its followers.

Opportunities:

1. **Expansion of the Diaspora:** The Ethiopian diaspora, scattered across the globe, has become a

significant force in the Church's global reach. Diaspora communities have established churches, cultural centers, and educational institutions, preserving Ethiopian Orthodox traditions and providing a sense of belonging for Ethiopians living abroad. This global network of believers has not only strengthened the Church's presence worldwide but has also created opportunities for cultural exchange and interfaith dialogue.

2. **Technological Advancement:** The advent of technology, particularly the internet and social media, has provided the Church with new tools for outreach and communication. The Church has embraced these tools, using them to disseminate information, connect with the diaspora, and engage with younger generations. This technological adaptation has allowed the Church to transcend geographical boundaries and reach a global audience.

3. **Interfaith Dialogue and Cooperation:** Globalization has fostered greater interaction and dialogue between different religious traditions. The Ethiopian Orthodox Church has actively participated in interfaith initiatives, seeking to build bridges of understanding and cooperation with other Christian denominations and other faiths. This engagement has not only enriched the Church's theological understanding but has also contributed to a

more peaceful and harmonious global community.

Globalization has undeniably presented the Ethiopian Orthodox Tewahedo Church with a complex set of challenges and opportunities. The Church's response to these forces will shape its future trajectory and determine its relevance in the 21st century. By embracing the positive aspects of globalization, such as technological advancements and interfaith dialogue, while remaining steadfast in its core values and traditions, the Church can navigate the complexities of the modern world and continue to be a beacon of faith, hope, and cultural identity for millions of Ethiopians.

Challenges and opportunities presented

Globalization, the interconnectedness of economies, societies, and cultures across the world, has cast a wide net over the Ethiopian Orthodox Tewahedo Church, presenting a unique set of challenges and opportunities. This phenomenon, characterized by increased mobility, cultural exchange, and the spread of ideas, has profoundly impacted the Church's traditions, practices, and global reach.

Challenges:

1. **Cultural Homogenization:** The influx of Western values and secular ideologies, often propagated through media and education, has challenged the Church's traditional values and cultural norms. The younger generation, exposed to diverse lifestyles and beliefs, may question or reinterpret certain aspects of the Church's teachings, leading to a potential erosion of cultural identity and religious practices.

2. **Theological Pluralism:** Globalization has exposed the Church to a wider range of theological perspectives and interpretations, challenging its traditional understanding of scripture and doctrine. The rise of Pentecostalism and other evangelical movements, with their emphasis on personal salvation and emotional expression, has also created a more competitive religious landscape, requiring the Church to adapt its message and ministry to remain relevant.

3. **Brain Drain and Leadership Gap:** The migration of educated Ethiopians to Western countries, often seeking better economic opportunities, has created a leadership gap within the Church. Many young, educated individuals who could potentially become future leaders of the Church are leaving Ethiopia, leaving behind a void that is difficult to fill. This brain drain poses a challenge to the Church's ability to adapt and innovate in the face of modern challenges.

4. **Economic Pressures:** Globalization has also brought economic pressures to bear on the Church. The increasing cost of maintaining churches, monasteries, and social service institutions, coupled with the economic hardships faced by many Ethiopians, has strained the Church's financial resources. The Church must find innovative ways to generate income and ensure its financial sustainability while continuing to serve the needs of its followers.

Opportunities:

1. **Expansion of the Diaspora:** The Ethiopian diaspora, scattered across the globe, has become a significant force in the Church's global reach. Diaspora communities have established churches, cultural centers, and educational institutions, preserving Ethiopian Orthodox traditions and providing a sense of belonging for Ethiopians living abroad. This global network of believers has not only strengthened the Church's presence worldwide but has also created opportunities for cultural exchange and interfaith dialogue.

2. **Technological Advancement:** The advent of technology, particularly the internet and social media, has provided the Church with new tools for outreach and communication. The Church has embraced these tools, using them to

disseminate information, connect with the diaspora, and engage with younger generations. This technological adaptation has allowed the Church to transcend geographical boundaries and reach a global audience.

3. **Interfaith Dialogue and Cooperation:** Globalization has fostered greater interaction and dialogue between different religious traditions. The Ethiopian Orthodox Church has actively participated in interfaith initiatives, seeking to build bridges of understanding and cooperation with other Christian denominations and other faiths. This engagement has not only enriched the Church's theological understanding but has also contributed to a more peaceful and harmonious global community.

Globalization has undeniably presented the Ethiopian Orthodox Tewahedo Church with a complex set of challenges and opportunities. The Church's response to these forces will shape its future trajectory and determine its relevance in the 21st century. By embracing the positive aspects of globalization, such as technological advancements and interfaith dialogue, while remaining steadfast in its core values and traditions, the Church can navigate the complexities of the modern world and continue to be a beacon of faith, hope, and cultural identity for millions of Ethiopians.

Internal Conflicts

Internal conflicts within the church:

The Ethiopian Orthodox Tewahedo Church, like any institution with a long and rich history, has experienced its share of internal conflicts. These conflicts, often arising from theological disagreements, power struggles, or differing visions for the Church's future, have tested its unity and resilience. However, they have also served as catalysts for introspection, reform, and renewal, ultimately strengthening the Church's spiritual foundation and its bond with the Ethiopian people.

One of the most significant internal conflicts in recent history revolves around the issue of autonomy and governance. Following the restoration of the Patriarchate in 1991, after a 17-year vacancy during the Derg regime, the Church has grappled with questions of leadership, authority, and the relationship between the Holy Synod and the Patriarch. These internal power struggles have sometimes led to factionalism and disagreements, but they have also prompted the Church to re-examine its governance structures and seek ways to promote greater transparency and accountability.

Theological debates have also been a source of internal conflict within the Church. While the Church adheres to a unified set of core doctrines, there have been disagreements over the interpretation of certain theological concepts and the application of traditional practices. These debates, while sometimes heated, have also fostered intellectual inquiry and theological discourse, enriching the Church's intellectual tradition and prompting a deeper engagement with its faith.

The issue of modernization and reform has also sparked internal debates within the Church. Some members advocate for embracing modern technologies and adapting certain practices to the changing times, while others emphasize the importance of preserving traditional ways. These debates reflect the tension between preserving the Church's rich heritage and ensuring its relevance in the 21st century.

The Ethiopian diaspora, while a source of strength and support for the Church, has also been a source of internal tension. Diaspora communities, often exposed to different cultural and religious influences, may hold different perspectives on theological and social issues than those in Ethiopia. This can lead to disagreements and misunderstandings, requiring the Church to find ways to bridge the gap between the diaspora and the mother church.

Despite these internal conflicts, the Ethiopian Orthodox Tewahedo Church has demonstrated a remarkable capacity for resilience and renewal. The Church's deep-rooted faith, its commitment to dialogue and reconciliation, and its strong sense of community have helped it to overcome these challenges and emerge stronger and more united. The Church's ability to navigate internal conflicts is a testament to its enduring strength and its unwavering commitment to its spiritual mission.

Resolutions and ongoing issues

The Ethiopian Orthodox Tewahedo Church has a long-standing tradition of seeking resolutions to internal conflicts through dialogue, compromise, and reconciliation. This tradition, rooted in the teachings of Christ and the wisdom of the Church Fathers, has enabled the Church to navigate through turbulent times and emerge stronger and more united.

In the face of theological disagreements, the Church has often convened councils and synods, where clergy and scholars engage in respectful debate and seek consensus on doctrinal matters. These councils, guided by the Holy Spirit and the wisdom of tradition, have played a crucial role in resolving theological disputes and maintaining the Church's doctrinal unity.

The Church has also addressed internal power struggles and governance issues through dialogue and compromise. The establishment of the Holy Synod, a council of bishops responsible for the Church's administration, has provided a platform for collective decision-making and conflict resolution. The Church's hierarchical structure, with the Patriarch as the spiritual leader, also provides a mechanism for resolving disputes and maintaining order within the Church.

However, despite these efforts, some internal conflicts remain unresolved. The issue of autonomy and governance, particularly the relationship between the Holy Synod and the Patriarch, continues to be a source of tension. The debate over modernization and reform, with its differing perspectives on the role of tradition and the need for change, also remains a challenge. The Church must continue to engage in open and honest dialogue, seeking solutions that respect both tradition and the need for adaptation in a changing world.

The Ethiopian diaspora, with its diverse perspectives and experiences, also presents a unique set of challenges for the Church. The Church must find ways to bridge the gap between the diaspora and the mother church, fostering a sense of unity and shared purpose while respecting the diversity of its members.

The Ethiopian Orthodox Tewahedo Church's ability to address these ongoing issues will be crucial for its future. By embracing dialogue, compromise, and reconciliation, the Church can continue to be a source of spiritual guidance, unity, and hope for the Ethiopian people. It can also serve as a model for other religious institutions grappling with similar challenges in a rapidly changing world.

Technological Advancements

Use of technology in religious practices:

In the face of modern advancements, the Ethiopian Orthodox Tewahedo Church has not remained a passive observer. It has cautiously embraced technology, recognizing its potential to amplify its reach, enhance its teachings, and connect with a global community of believers. This integration of technology, while mindful of preserving the sanctity of tradition, has opened new avenues for spiritual expression and engagement.

1. **Amplifying the Word:** The Church has harnessed the power of radio, television, and the internet to broadcast sermons, hymns, and teachings to a wider audience. This has allowed the faithful in remote areas and the diaspora to connect with the Church's spiritual nourishment, fostering a sense of unity and shared experience.

2. **Digital Scripture and Education:** The digital age has ushered in a new era of accessibility to sacred texts. The Ethiopian Orthodox Bible, once confined to ancient manuscripts, is now available in digital formats, allowing for easier study and dissemination. Online platforms and mobile applications offer a wealth of resources, including commentaries, translations, and educational materials, enriching

the understanding of scripture for both clergy and laity.

3. **Virtual Community and Connection:** Social media platforms have emerged as virtual gathering spaces for the Ethiopian Orthodox community. Online forums and groups facilitate discussions, share news and events, and provide a platform for spiritual exchange. This virtual connectivity has been particularly crucial for the diaspora, allowing them to maintain their connection to the mother Church and their cultural heritage.

4. **Preserving Tradition Through Technology:** The Church has also utilized technology to preserve its rich heritage. Digitization projects have ensured the preservation of ancient manuscripts, icons, and liturgical music, safeguarding them for future generations. Virtual tours of historical churches and monasteries offer a glimpse into the Church's architectural and artistic legacy, making it accessible to a global audience.

The Ethiopian Orthodox Tewahedo Church's approach to technology is characterized by a cautious embrace, balancing innovation with tradition. While recognizing the potential of technology to enhance its ministry and reach, the Church remains mindful of the need to preserve the sanctity of its rituals and the spiritual essence of its teachings. This delicate balance ensures that technology serves as a tool for spiritual growth and communal connection, rather than a replacement for traditional practices.

Benefits and Drawbacks of Technological Integration

The Ethiopian Orthodox Tewahedo Church's cautious embrace of technology has yielded both blessings and burdens, as the digital age presents a double-edged sword for this ancient faith. While technology offers unprecedented opportunities for outreach, education, and connection, it also poses challenges to the preservation of tradition and the maintenance of spiritual authenticity.

Benefits:

1. **Amplified Reach:** Technology has shattered geographical barriers, allowing the Church to reach a global audience. Sermons, hymns, and teachings can now be broadcast through radio, television, and the internet, reaching the faithful in remote corners of Ethiopia and the diaspora. This amplified reach has fostered a sense of unity and shared experience among believers, transcending physical distance.

2. **Enhanced Education:** Digital platforms have revolutionized religious education, making a wealth of resources accessible to both clergy and

laity. Online courses, webinars, and digital libraries offer opportunities for in-depth study of scripture, theology, and Church history. This democratization of knowledge empowers individuals to deepen their understanding of the faith and engage in informed discussions about its teachings.

3. **Virtual Community Building:** Social media platforms have emerged as virtual gathering spaces for the Ethiopian Orthodox community. Online forums and groups facilitate discussions, share news and events, and provide a platform for spiritual exchange. This virtual connectivity has been particularly crucial for the diaspora, allowing them to maintain their connection to the mother Church and their cultural heritage.

4. **Preservation of Heritage:** Technology has become a powerful tool for preserving the Church's rich heritage. Digitization projects have ensured the preservation of ancient manuscripts, icons, and liturgical music, safeguarding them for future generations. Virtual tours of historical churches and monasteries offer a glimpse into the Church's architectural and artistic legacy, making it accessible to a global audience.

Drawbacks:

1. **Erosion of Tradition:** The convenience and accessibility of digital media can sometimes lead to a neglect of traditional practices. The physical act of attending church services, participating in communal prayers, and engaging in face-to-face interactions may be replaced by virtual substitutes. This can erode the sense of community and the embodied experience of worship that are central to Ethiopian Orthodox spirituality.

2. **Distraction and Superficiality:** The constant bombardment of information and entertainment in the digital age can be a source of distraction, hindering deep spiritual reflection and contemplation. The Church must navigate the fine line between utilizing technology for outreach and education, and ensuring that it does not become a source of spiritual superficiality.

3. **Misinformation and Misinterpretation:** The internet, while a valuable resource, can also be a breeding ground for misinformation and misinterpretation of religious teachings. The Church must be vigilant in monitoring online content and providing accurate information to counter any distortions or misrepresentations of its doctrines and practices.

4. **Cybersecurity and Privacy Concerns:** The Church's increasing reliance on technology also raises concerns about cybersecurity and data privacy. The sensitive personal information of

members, as well as the Church's financial records and intellectual property, must be protected from cyberattacks and unauthorized access.

The Ethiopian Orthodox Tewahedo Church's engagement with technology is a journey of discernment, balancing the benefits of innovation with the preservation of tradition. It is a delicate dance between embracing the tools of the digital age and ensuring that they serve the spiritual needs of the faithful. By approaching technology with wisdom and caution, the Church can harness its power for good, amplifying its message, strengthening its community, and preserving its rich heritage for generations to come.

Future Challenges

- Predicted future challenges.
- Strategies for future resilience and adaptation.

As the Ethiopian Orthodox Tewahedo Church journeys into the uncharted waters of the future, it faces a horizon marked by both challenges and opportunities. The winds of change, propelled by globalization, technological advancements, and shifting societal values, will continue to test the Church's resilience and adaptability. However, armed with a rich spiritual heritage, a deep-rooted connection to its people, and a willingness to embrace innovation, the Church is poised to navigate these challenges and emerge stronger and more vibrant.

Predicted Future Challenges:

1. **Secularization and Shifting Values:** The rise of secularism and the increasing influence of Western values pose a significant challenge to the Church's traditional authority and teachings. The younger generation, exposed to diverse ideologies and lifestyles, may question or even reject some of the Church's long-held beliefs and practices. This could lead to a decline in church attendance, a weakening of communal bonds, and a loss of cultural identity.

2. **Religious Pluralism and Competition:** The Ethiopian religious landscape is becoming increasingly diverse, with the rise of Pentecostalism and other evangelical movements. These movements, with their emphasis on personal salvation, emotional expression, and charismatic leadership, are attracting a growing number of followers, particularly among the youth. The Church must find ways to engage with these new religious expressions, offering a compelling alternative that resonates with the spiritual needs and aspirations of the younger generation.

3. **Technological Disruption:** The rapid pace of technological advancement presents both opportunities and challenges for the Church. While technology can be harnessed for outreach, education, and communication, it can also lead to a decline in traditional practices, such as communal worship and face-to-face interactions. The Church must find a balance between embracing technology and preserving the sanctity of its rituals and the spiritual essence of its teachings.

4. **Economic and Social Disparities:** Ethiopia's economic growth, while promising, has also led to widening disparities between rich and poor. The Church, with its commitment to social justice and the well-being of all Ethiopians, must address these disparities and advocate for policies that promote equitable development and uplift the marginalized.

5. **Environmental Degradation:** The environmental crisis, with its devastating impact on Ethiopia's natural resources and livelihoods, poses a significant challenge for the Church. The Church must raise awareness about environmental issues, advocate for sustainable practices, and mobilize its resources to protect the environment. It must also integrate environmental stewardship into its theological teachings and spiritual practices.

Strategies for Future Resilience and Adaptation:

1. **Strengthening Theological Education:** The
   Church must invest in theological education,
   equipping its clergy and laity with the knowledge
   and skills to engage with contemporary
   theological discourse and address the challenges
   of a changing world. This includes promoting
   critical thinking, interfaith dialogue, and
   contextualized interpretations of scripture that
   resonate with the lived experiences of the
   faithful.

2. **Youth Engagement and Empowerment:**
   The Church must actively engage with young
   people, providing them with opportunities for
   spiritual growth, leadership development, and
   community involvement. This can be achieved
   through youth-oriented programs, mentorship
   initiatives, and the use of technology to create
   engaging and relevant content.

3. **Promoting Gender Equality:** The Church
   must continue its efforts to promote gender
   equality within its ranks, recognizing the valuable
   contributions of women and empowering them to
   take on leadership roles. This includes revisiting
   traditional interpretations of scripture and
   tradition that may perpetuate gender inequality,
   and advocating for policies that promote women's
   rights and empowerment.

4. **Embracing Technology:** The Church must continue to embrace technology as a tool for outreach, education, and communication. This includes utilizing social media platforms, developing online educational resources, and creating virtual spaces for spiritual engagement. However, the Church must also be mindful of the potential drawbacks of technology, ensuring that it does not replace or diminish the importance of traditional practices and communal worship.

5. **Social Justice and Advocacy:** The Church must continue to be a vocal advocate for social justice, human rights, and environmental protection. This includes speaking out against injustice, corruption, and violence, advocating for policies that promote equitable development, and mobilizing its resources to address poverty, inequality, and environmental degradation.

6. **Strengthening Diaspora Connections:** The Church must continue to strengthen its connections with the Ethiopian diaspora, recognizing their important role in preserving and promoting Ethiopian Orthodox traditions and values. This can be achieved through the establishment of diaspora churches, the appointment of bishops to oversee diaspora communities, and the organization of conferences and pilgrimages that bring together Ethiopians from around the world.

The Ethiopian Orthodox Tewahedo Church, with its rich history, deep-rooted traditions, and unwavering faith, is well-equipped to face the challenges of the future. By embracing change, fostering dialogue, and remaining committed to its spiritual mission, the Church can continue to be a beacon of hope, a source of spiritual guidance, and a unifying force in Ethiopian society and beyond.

In this chapter, we have explored the multifaceted challenges and adaptations that have shaped the Ethiopian Orthodox Tewahedo Church in the modern era. From historical trials such as colonialism and political upheaval to contemporary issues like secularism and globalization, the Church has consistently demonstrated resilience and adaptability. Its responses, ranging from educational reforms and technological embrace to interfaith dialogue and social advocacy, highlight its commitment to remaining relevant and influential in a rapidly changing world.

As we move forward, our journey will take us beyond the borders of Ethiopia to explore the vibrant diaspora communities that have carried the flame of Ethiopian Orthodoxy to new lands. We will delve into their history, their struggles, their triumphs, and their ongoing efforts to preserve their faith and cultural heritage in diverse global contexts. Join us as we embark on this exploration of the Ethiopian Orthodox diaspora, a testament to the Church's enduring appeal and its ability to transcend geographical boundaries.

Chapter 9

Global Diaspora

History of Diaspora Communities

The Ethiopian Orthodox Tewahedo Church, while deeply rooted in the ancient soil of Ethiopia, has blossomed into a global faith community, its branches reaching far beyond its ancestral homeland. This chapter embarks on a journey to explore the vibrant tapestry of the Ethiopian Orthodox diaspora, tracing its historical roots, its challenges and triumphs, and its enduring impact on the global religious landscape.

The formation and growth of Ethiopian diaspora communities are a testament to the resilience, adaptability, and unwavering faith of the Ethiopian people. Throughout history, Ethiopians have migrated to various parts of the world, carrying with them their rich cultural heritage and their deep-rooted Orthodox faith. These diaspora communities, scattered across continents, have not only preserved their traditions but have also enriched their host societies with their unique cultural and spiritual contributions.

The history of the Ethiopian diaspora is a story of both voluntary and involuntary migration, driven by a complex interplay of political, economic, and social factors. The earliest waves of migration can be traced back to the ancient Aksumite period, when Ethiopian traders and merchants established communities along the Red Sea and the Indian Ocean, spreading their culture and faith to distant lands.

In the medieval period, Ethiopian pilgrims journeyed to Jerusalem and other holy sites, establishing small communities in the Holy Land and Egypt. These communities, though small in number, played a crucial role in maintaining Ethiopia's connection to the broader Christian world and in fostering cultural exchange.

The 19th and 20th centuries witnessed a significant increase in Ethiopian migration, driven by political instability, economic hardship, and the search for educational and employment opportunities. The Italian occupation of Ethiopia in the 1930s and the subsequent political upheavals led to a wave of refugees seeking asylum in neighboring countries and beyond.

The post-war era saw a further expansion of the Ethiopian diaspora, as students, professionals, and skilled workers migrated to Europe, North America, and the Middle East.

The Ethiopian Revolution of 1974 and the subsequent Derg regime, marked by political repression and economic hardship, triggered another wave of migration, with many Ethiopians seeking refuge in Western countries.

In recent decades, the Ethiopian diaspora has continued to grow, fueled by ongoing political instability, economic challenges, and the desire for a better life. Today, Ethiopian diaspora communities can be found in almost every corner of the globe, from North America and Europe to Australia and Asia. These communities, while diverse in their backgrounds and experiences, share a common bond of faith, culture, and a longing for their homeland.

Key historical migrations.

The formation of the Ethiopian diaspora is a narrative woven through the annals of history, marked by key migrations that have shaped the Church's global presence. These migrations, often driven by a complex interplay of political, economic, and social factors, have led to the establishment of vibrant Ethiopian Orthodox communities across the globe.

1. **Ancient Migrations:** The earliest traces of Ethiopian migration can be found in the annals of the Aksumite Empire. As this powerful kingdom expanded its trade networks, Ethiopian merchants and traders ventured to distant lands, establishing

communities along the Red Sea and the Indian Ocean. These early migrants carried with them their Orthodox faith, planting the seeds of Ethiopian Christianity in foreign soils.

2. **Medieval Pilgrimages:** The medieval period witnessed a surge in Ethiopian pilgrimages to the Holy Land and other sacred sites. These devout travelers, seeking spiritual enlightenment and blessings, often settled in Jerusalem, Egypt, and other parts of the Middle East, forming small but vibrant communities that maintained their faith and cultural traditions.

3. **19th and 20th Century Displacements:** The 19th and 20th centuries were marked by significant political upheavals and economic hardships in Ethiopia, leading to waves of migration. The Italian occupation in the 1930s and the subsequent political instability forced many Ethiopians to seek refuge in neighboring countries and beyond. These forced migrations, while traumatic, also led to the establishment of new Ethiopian Orthodox communities in countries like Sudan, Kenya, and Israel.

4. **Post-War Migration:** The post-war era saw a new wave of Ethiopian migration, driven by the desire for education and economic opportunities. Students, professionals, and skilled workers migrated to Europe, North America, and the Middle East, seeking a better life for themselves

and their families. These migrants, often highly educated and motivated, played a crucial role in establishing and strengthening Ethiopian Orthodox communities in their adopted countries.

5. **The Derg Regime and Refugee Crisis:** The rise of the Derg regime in 1974, with its oppressive policies and violent purges, triggered a massive refugee crisis. Thousands of Ethiopians fled the country, seeking asylum in neighboring countries and Western nations. This wave of refugees, many of whom were devout Orthodox Christians, further expanded the Ethiopian diaspora and led to the establishment of new churches and communities in various parts of the world.

These key historical migrations, while diverse in their causes and destinations, share a common thread: the unwavering faith and resilience of the Ethiopian people. Despite facing adversity and displacement, Ethiopian Orthodox Christians have maintained their religious traditions, established vibrant communities, and contributed to the cultural and spiritual enrichment of their adopted lands. Their journey is a testament to the enduring power of faith and the human spirit's ability to adapt and thrive in the face of adversity.

Cultural Preservation:

- Efforts to preserve Ethiopian Orthodox traditions abroad.
- Challenges in maintaining cultural identity.

The Ethiopian Orthodox Tewahedo Church, a beacon of ancient faith and cultural heritage, has transcended geographical boundaries, establishing vibrant diaspora communities across the globe. These communities, while embracing their new homes, have also embarked on a remarkable journey of cultural preservation, striving to maintain their unique identity and pass on their rich traditions to future generations. This endeavor, however, is not without its challenges, as the diaspora navigates the complexities of assimilation, generational shifts, and the preservation of cultural authenticity in foreign lands.

Efforts to Preserve Ethiopian Orthodox Traditions Abroad:

1. **Establishment of Churches and Cultural Centers:** The establishment of Ethiopian Orthodox churches and cultural centers in various countries has been a cornerstone of cultural preservation efforts. These institutions serve as spiritual and cultural hubs, providing a space for worship, religious education, and the celebration of Ethiopian traditions. They offer a sense of belonging and community for diaspora members,

fostering a connection to their roots and providing a platform for cultural exchange.

2. **Language Schools and Cultural Programs:** Many diaspora communities have established language schools and cultural programs to teach the Ge'ez language, Ethiopian history, and traditional arts and crafts. These initiatives aim to instill a sense of cultural pride and identity in younger generations, ensuring the transmission of cultural knowledge and values.

3. **Religious Education and Youth Programs:** Sunday schools, youth groups, and religious education programs play a crucial role in passing on the faith and traditions to the next generation. These programs not only teach the doctrines and practices of the Church but also foster a sense of community and belonging among young people, helping them to connect with their Ethiopian heritage.

4. **Festivals and Celebrations:** The celebration of Ethiopian Orthodox festivals, such as Timkat, Meskel, and Genna, is a vibrant expression of cultural identity and a way of preserving traditions in the diaspora. These festivals, often held in community centers or public parks, bring together Ethiopians of all ages and backgrounds, fostering a sense of unity and shared heritage.

5. **Media and Publications:** The diaspora has also utilized media and publications to promote

Ethiopian Orthodox traditions and culture. Websites, blogs, magazines, and social media platforms provide a platform for sharing information, stories, and perspectives, connecting Ethiopians across the globe and fostering a sense of virtual community.

,

,

Challenges in Maintaining Cultural Identity:

1. **Assimilation and Acculturation:** One of the biggest challenges facing the Ethiopian Orthodox diaspora is the pressure to assimilate into the dominant culture of their adopted countries. This can lead to a loss of cultural identity, as younger generations may adopt the language, customs, and values of their host societies, sometimes at the expense of their Ethiopian heritage.

2. **Generational Differences:** Generational differences can also pose a challenge to cultural preservation. Older generations, who may have immigrated to their adopted countries, often hold onto traditional values and practices more tightly than younger generations, who may be more influenced by Western culture. This can lead to tensions and misunderstandings within families

and communities, making it difficult to pass on traditions to the next generation.

3. **Lack of Resources:** Many diaspora communities lack the resources and infrastructure needed to support cultural preservation efforts. This includes the lack of qualified teachers for language schools, the financial burden of organizing cultural events, and the difficulty of accessing traditional materials and resources.

4. **Religious Diversity:** The Ethiopian diaspora is not a monolithic entity but a diverse community with varying levels of religious commitment and practice. Some members may be more devout than others, and there may be differences in interpretation and practice of the faith. This diversity can make it challenging to maintain a unified cultural identity and preserve traditional practices.

The Ethiopian Orthodox Tewahedo Church's diaspora communities are engaged in a dynamic and ongoing process of cultural preservation. While facing numerous challenges, they have also demonstrated remarkable resilience and creativity in adapting their traditions to new contexts. By establishing churches, cultural centers, and educational programs, they are ensuring that their rich heritage is passed on to future generations. The Church's role in supporting these efforts, through the appointment of bishops, the provision of resources, and the fostering of dialogue, is crucial for the continued vitality of Ethiopian Orthodox traditions in the diaspora.

Church Establishments Abroad:

Notable Ethiopian Orthodox churches in the diaspora.

The Ethiopian Orthodox Tewahedo Church has established a notable presence in various countries, with several churches standing as pillars of faith and cultural preservation for the diaspora community. These churches not only serve as places of worship but also as community centers, fostering a sense of belonging and preserving Ethiopian traditions in foreign lands.

1. **Debre Selam Medhane Alem Ethiopian Orthodox Tewahedo Church (Washington, D.C., USA):** Located in the heart of the United States capital, this church is a vibrant hub for the Ethiopian Orthodox community. It offers regular services, religious education programs, and cultural events, catering to the spiritual and social needs of the diaspora.

2. **Medhane Alem Ethiopian Orthodox Tewahedo Cathedral (Toronto, Canada):** This majestic cathedral, with its intricate architecture and vibrant murals, is a testament to the Ethiopian Orthodox faith in Canada. It serves as a spiritual home for thousands of Ethiopians,

offering a place of worship, community gatherings, and cultural celebrations.

3. **St. Mary Ethiopian Orthodox Tewahedo Church (London, UK):** This historic church, located in the heart of London, has been a cornerstone of the Ethiopian Orthodox community in the UK for decades. It offers regular services, religious education programs, and cultural events, providing a sense of belonging and continuity for Ethiopians living in the UK.

4. **Holy Trinity Ethiopian Orthodox Tewahedo Church (Stockholm, Sweden):** This church, located in the vibrant city of Stockholm, serves as a spiritual and cultural center for the Ethiopian Orthodox community in Sweden. It offers regular services, religious education programs, and cultural events, fostering a sense of community and preserving Ethiopian traditions in a foreign land.

5. **Kidist Selassie Ethiopian Orthodox Tewahedo Church (Melbourne, Australia):** This church, located in the multicultural city of Melbourne, is a testament to the growing Ethiopian Orthodox community in Australia. It offers regular services, religious education programs, and cultural events, providing a space for worship, community gatherings, and the preservation of Ethiopian heritage.

These are just a few examples of the many Ethiopian Orthodox churches that have been established in the diaspora. These churches, with their unique blend of spiritual devotion, cultural preservation, and community building, play a vital role in the lives of Ethiopian Orthodox Christians living abroad. They offer a place of refuge, a source of identity, and a connection to their homeland.

Activities and Services Provided:

These Ethiopian Orthodox churches in the diaspora, while diverse in their specific locations and congregations, share a common mission: to provide a spiritual home for Ethiopians living abroad, preserve their rich cultural heritage, and foster a sense of community and belonging. Their activities and services reflect this multifaceted mission, catering to the diverse needs of their members.

1. **Religious Services and Liturgical Practices:** The cornerstone of these churches is the celebration of the Divine Liturgy and other liturgical services, conducted in the Ge'ez language and following the ancient traditions of the Ethiopian Orthodox Tewahedo Church. These services provide a spiritual anchor for the diaspora community, connecting them to their roots and fostering a sense of continuity with their homeland.

2. **Religious Education:** Recognizing the importance of passing on the faith to future generations, these churches offer a variety of religious education programs for children, youth, and adults. These programs include Sunday school classes, Bible study groups, and seminars on Ethiopian Orthodox theology and history. They aim to instill a deep understanding of the faith and its traditions, ensuring its continuity in the diaspora.

3. **Cultural Events and Celebrations:** The churches also organize cultural events and celebrations, such as Timkat, Meskel, and Genna, to foster a sense of community and cultural identity among the diaspora. These events often include traditional music, dance, food, and other cultural expressions, providing a platform for Ethiopians to connect with their heritage and share it with others.

4. **Social Services and Community Support:** Many Ethiopian Orthodox churches in the diaspora offer a range of social services to their members, including counseling, support groups, and assistance with immigration and settlement issues. They also provide a space for community gatherings, weddings, funerals, and other life cycle events, fostering a sense of belonging and mutual support.

5. **Charitable Activities:** The churches often engage in charitable activities, both within their local communities and in Ethiopia. They raise funds for various causes, such as education, healthcare, and poverty alleviation, and support development projects in Ethiopia. This commitment to social responsibility reflects the Church's teachings on compassion, generosity, and service to others.

These activities and services, while diverse in their nature, share a common goal: to nurture the spiritual, cultural, and social well-being of the Ethiopian Orthodox diaspora community. They provide a space for worship, learning, celebration, and mutual support, fostering a sense of belonging and identity in a foreign land. The churches' commitment to both spiritual and social welfare reflects the holistic nature of Ethiopian Orthodox faith, which sees the individual as an integral part of a larger community and emphasizes the importance of both personal salvation and social responsibility.

Intergenerational Dynamics:

Interaction between different generations in diaspora communities.

Within the Ethiopian Orthodox Tewahedo Church's diaspora communities, the interaction between different generations is a dynamic and evolving process, shaped by the contrasting experiences of those born in Ethiopia and those raised abroad. This intergenerational interplay is a microcosm of the broader challenges and opportunities faced by immigrant communities, as they strive to preserve their cultural heritage while adapting to new environments.

Older generations, who often immigrated to their adopted countries, carry with them the lived experiences of Ethiopia, its traditions, and the deep-rooted values of the Orthodox faith. They are the keepers of cultural memory, the storytellers who pass down oral traditions, and the guardians of the Church's liturgical practices. Their connection to the homeland is often visceral, shaped by memories of religious festivals, communal gatherings, and the rhythms of daily life steeped in Orthodox traditions.

Younger generations, born and raised in the diaspora, often have a different perspective. They are exposed to the cultural norms and values of their adopted countries, which may sometimes clash with their Ethiopian heritage. They may struggle to reconcile their Ethiopian identity with their Western upbringing, navigating the complexities of dual identities and cultural hybridity.

This intergenerational dynamic creates both challenges and opportunities for the Ethiopian Orthodox diaspora. On the one hand, it can lead to misunderstandings and tensions, as different generations hold different expectations and interpretations of tradition. Younger generations may question or challenge certain practices, seeking to adapt them to their modern context, while older generations may resist change, fearing the erosion of their cultural identity.

On the other hand, this intergenerational interplay can also be a source of enrichment and renewal. Younger generations, with their exposure to different cultures and ideas, can bring fresh perspectives and innovative approaches to the preservation of Ethiopian Orthodox traditions. They can utilize technology to connect with other diaspora communities, create online resources for religious education, and adapt traditional practices to new contexts.

The Church plays a crucial role in fostering intergenerational dialogue and understanding. By creating spaces for open communication, encouraging mutual respect, and promoting intergenerational activities, the Church can bridge the gap between different generations and ensure the continuity of its traditions. It can also provide guidance and support to younger generations as they navigate the complexities of their dual identities, helping them to find a balance between their Ethiopian heritage and their Western upbringing.

The interaction between different generations in the Ethiopian Orthodox diaspora is a dynamic and ongoing process. It is a testament to the Church's resilience and its ability to adapt to changing circumstances. By embracing the diversity of its members and fostering intergenerational dialogue, the Church can ensure that its rich traditions continue to thrive and evolve in the diaspora, enriching both the Ethiopian community and the broader society.

Transmission of religious and cultural values.

The transmission of religious and cultural values within the Ethiopian Orthodox Tewahedo Church's diaspora communities is a dynamic process, shaped by the interplay of tradition, innovation, and the desire to maintain a connection to their heritage in a foreign land. This transmission occurs through a variety of channels, both formal and informal, ensuring that the faith and cultural identity of Ethiopia continue to thrive across generations and continents.

1. **Family as the First School of Faith:** The family unit serves as the primary transmitter of religious and cultural values. Parents and grandparents pass down their faith through storytelling, prayers, and the observance of religious rituals and traditions in the home. Children learn the Ge'ez language, the significance of fasting, the veneration of saints, and the importance of communal values through the daily practices and teachings of their elders. This intergenerational transmission of knowledge and values creates a strong foundation for the preservation of Ethiopian Orthodox identity in the diaspora.

2. **Church Schools and Religious Education:**
   Ethiopian Orthodox churches in the diaspora
   often establish Sunday schools and religious
   education programs to provide formal instruction
   in the faith and its traditions. These programs
   teach children and youth about the Bible, Church
   history, liturgical practices, and the Ge'ez
   language. They also offer opportunities for
   spiritual growth, community building, and cultural
   exchange, fostering a sense of belonging and
   identity among young people.

3. **Mentorship and Role Models:** Religious
   leaders, such as priests, deacons, and Sunday
   school teachers, play a crucial role in transmitting
   religious and cultural values. They serve as
   mentors and role models for younger generations,
   guiding them in their spiritual journey and
   providing them with a living example of the faith
   in action. Their teachings, both in formal settings
   and through informal interactions, instill a deep
   understanding of the Church's doctrines,
   traditions, and values.

4. **Cultural Events and Celebrations:** The
   celebration of Ethiopian Orthodox festivals, such
   as Timkat, Meskel, and Genna, provides a
   platform for the transmission of cultural values
   and traditions. These events, often accompanied
   by traditional music, dance, food, and storytelling,
   create a vibrant and immersive experience that

connects the diaspora community to its roots. They also provide opportunities for intergenerational interaction, where younger generations can learn from their elders and participate in the preservation of their cultural heritage.

5. **Use of Technology:** The digital age has opened up new avenues for the transmission of religious and cultural values. Websites, social media platforms, and online forums provide a virtual space for the diaspora community to connect, share information, and engage in discussions about their faith and culture. Online resources, such as videos, podcasts, and articles, offer accessible and engaging ways to learn about Ethiopian Orthodox traditions and teachings.

The transmission of religious and cultural values within the Ethiopian Orthodox Tewahedo Church's diaspora communities is a dynamic and ongoing process. It is a testament to the resilience of the Ethiopian people, their deep-rooted faith, and their commitment to preserving their heritage in a foreign land. By embracing both tradition and innovation, the Church is ensuring that its rich spiritual and cultural legacy continues to thrive across generations and continents.

Examples of interfaith collaborations.

The Ethiopian Orthodox Tewahedo Church has actively participated in various interfaith collaborations, both within Ethiopia and on the global stage. These collaborations, often focused on shared values and common goals, have fostered understanding, cooperation, and mutual respect between different faith communities.

1. **Interfaith Peacebuilding Initiatives:** The Church has been a key player in interfaith peacebuilding initiatives, working alongside Muslim, Protestant, and other religious leaders to promote dialogue, reconciliation, and peaceful coexistence. These initiatives have addressed issues such as ethnic conflict, religious intolerance, and social injustice, contributing to a more harmonious and inclusive society.

2. **Joint Humanitarian Efforts:** The Church has collaborated with other faith-based organizations on humanitarian projects, such as providing food aid, healthcare, and education to vulnerable communities. These joint efforts have leveraged the resources and expertise of different faith communities to address pressing social needs and improve the lives of Ethiopians.

3. **Theological Dialogues:** The Church has engaged in theological dialogues with other Christian denominations, such as the Catholic Church and the Oriental Orthodox Churches, to explore areas of common ground and address

theological differences. These dialogues have fostered greater understanding and appreciation of the diverse expressions of Christian faith.

4. **Environmental Stewardship:** The Church has partnered with other faith-based organizations and environmental groups to promote environmental stewardship and sustainable development. These collaborations have focused on raising awareness about environmental issues, advocating for policy changes, and implementing projects that protect Ethiopia's natural resources.

5. **Education and Cultural Exchange:** The Church has participated in educational and cultural exchange programs with other faith communities, fostering mutual understanding and appreciation of different religious traditions. These programs have included student exchanges, interfaith conferences, and cultural events that showcase the richness and diversity of Ethiopia's religious landscape.

These examples of interfaith collaborations demonstrate the Ethiopian Orthodox Tewahedo Church's commitment to dialogue, cooperation, and mutual respect. By working together with other faith communities, the Church is not only addressing pressing social and environmental challenges but also contributing to a more peaceful, just, and inclusive society.

Challenges in the Diaspora:

- Specific challenges faced by diaspora communities:

The Ethiopian Orthodox Tewahedo Church's diaspora communities, while vibrant and resilient, face a unique set of challenges as they strive to maintain their faith, cultural identity, and communal bonds in foreign lands. These challenges, often stemming from the complexities of assimilation, generational differences, and the preservation of traditions in new contexts, require the Church to adapt its ministry and support systems to meet the evolving needs of its dispersed flock.

1. **Assimilation and Cultural Preservation:** One of the primary challenges facing diaspora communities is the pressure to assimilate into the dominant culture of their adopted countries. This can lead to a gradual erosion of Ethiopian cultural identity, as younger generations, born and raised abroad, may adopt the language, customs, and values of their host societies. The Church plays a crucial role in mitigating this challenge by providing spaces for cultural expression, language preservation, and the celebration of Ethiopian traditions. However, striking a balance between integration and cultural preservation remains an ongoing struggle.

2. **Generational Differences:** The Ethiopian diaspora is not a monolithic entity but a diverse community with varying levels of acculturation and religious commitment. Older generations, who often immigrated to their adopted countries, may hold onto traditional values and practices more tightly than younger generations, who may be more influenced by Western culture. This generational divide can lead to misunderstandings, conflicts, and a potential loss of cultural continuity. The Church must find ways to bridge this gap, fostering intergenerational dialogue and understanding while respecting the diverse perspectives and experiences of its members.

3. **Leadership and Institutional Capacity:** Many diaspora communities struggle with a lack of trained clergy, religious educators, and community leaders. This shortage of qualified personnel can hinder the Church's ability to provide adequate spiritual guidance, religious education, and social services to its members. The Church must invest in leadership development programs and create opportunities for training and mentorship to ensure the continuity of its traditions and the effective functioning of its institutions.

4. **Financial Constraints:** Financial constraints can also pose a challenge for diaspora

communities, as they often lack the resources to build and maintain churches, cultural centers, and educational institutions. Fundraising efforts, community contributions, and support from the mother Church in Ethiopia are crucial for sustaining these vital institutions and ensuring their continued service to the community.

5. **Isolation and Lack of Community:** In some regions, Ethiopian Orthodox communities may be small and scattered, leading to feelings of isolation and a lack of communal support. This can make it difficult for individuals to maintain their faith and cultural identity, especially in the face of assimilation pressures. The Church must find ways to connect these isolated communities, providing them with resources, support, and a sense of belonging to the larger Ethiopian Orthodox family.

These challenges, while significant, are not insurmountable. The Ethiopian Orthodox Tewahedo Church, with its rich history of resilience and adaptability, is well-equipped to address these issues and continue to thrive in the diaspora. By fostering intergenerational dialogue, investing in leadership development, strengthening community bonds, and embracing technology, the Church can ensure that its traditions and values continue to flourish in new lands, enriching both the Ethiopian community and the broader society.

Strategies for overcoming these challenges:

The Ethiopian Orthodox Tewahedo Church, with its deep-rooted faith and resilient spirit, is actively developing strategies to overcome the challenges faced by its diaspora communities. These strategies, while rooted in tradition, also embrace innovation and adaptability, ensuring the Church's continued relevance and vibrancy in the 21st century.

1. **Strengthening Leadership and Institutional Capacity:** Recognizing the need for strong leadership and effective institutions, the Church is investing in the training and development of clergy, religious educators, and community leaders. This includes establishing seminaries and theological colleges in the diaspora, providing scholarships for students to study in Ethiopia, and organizing leadership workshops and conferences. By empowering local leaders, the Church aims to create self-sufficient and vibrant communities that can effectively address the spiritual and cultural needs of their members.

2. **Fostering Intergenerational Dialogue:** The Church is actively promoting intergenerational dialogue and understanding, recognizing the importance of bridging the gap between older and younger generations. This includes organizing

intergenerational events and activities, creating mentorship programs, and encouraging open communication and mutual respect between different age groups. By fostering dialogue and understanding, the Church aims to ensure the transmission of its traditions and values to future generations.

3. **Embracing Technology:** The Church is harnessing the power of technology to connect with the diaspora and overcome the challenges of distance and isolation. This includes utilizing social media platforms, creating online resources for religious education, and developing virtual spaces for worship and community building. By embracing technology, the Church is making its teachings and traditions more accessible to a global audience, fostering a sense of virtual community and belonging.

4. **Promoting Cultural Education:** The Church is actively promoting cultural education programs that teach the Ge'ez language, Ethiopian history, and traditional arts and crafts. These programs aim to instill a sense of cultural pride and identity in younger generations, ensuring the preservation of Ethiopian heritage in the diaspora. The Church is also partnering with cultural organizations and educational institutions to develop resources and curricula that promote Ethiopian culture and values.

5. **Financial Sustainability:** The Church is exploring innovative ways to ensure its financial sustainability in the diaspora. This includes fundraising initiatives, community contributions, and partnerships with philanthropic organizations. The Church is also encouraging diaspora communities to become self-sufficient by developing their own resources and income-generating activities.

These strategies, while not exhaustive, represent the Ethiopian Orthodox Tewahedo Church's proactive approach to addressing the challenges faced by its diaspora communities. By strengthening leadership, fostering inter-generational dialogue, embracing technology, promoting cultural education, and ensuring financial sustainability, the Church is paving the way for a vibrant and resilient future for Ethiopian Orthodoxy in the diaspora.

Global Influence:

- Influence of the diaspora on global perceptions of Ethiopian Orthodoxy.
- Contributions to global religious and cultural landscapes.

The Ethiopian Orthodox Tewahedo Church's diaspora, a vibrant tapestry of communities scattered across the globe,

has emerged as a powerful force in shaping global perceptions of Ethiopian Orthodoxy and enriching the world's
religious and cultural landscapes. Through their unwavering faith, cultural resilience, and active engagement with
their host societies, the diaspora has become a bridge
between Ethiopia and the world, fostering understanding,
appreciation, and dialogue.

Influence on Global Perceptions of Ethiopian Orthodoxy:

1. **Challenging Stereotypes and Misconceptions:** The diaspora has played a crucial role in challenging stereotypes and misconceptions about Ethiopian Orthodoxy, often portrayed in Western media as an exotic or archaic religion. Through their active presence in various fields, including academia, the arts, and business, diaspora members have showcased the richness, diversity, and contemporary relevance of their faith. They have organized conferences, exhibitions, and cultural events that highlight the Church's contributions to Ethiopian history, culture, and spirituality, fostering a more nuanced and accurate understanding of Ethiopian Orthodoxy.

2. **Promoting Interfaith Dialogue:** The diaspora has also been instrumental in promoting interfaith dialogue and understanding. By

engaging with other Christian denominations and religious traditions, diaspora communities have fostered mutual respect and cooperation, highlighting the shared values and common goals that unite people of different faiths. They have participated in interfaith conferences, dialogues, and initiatives, sharing their unique perspectives and experiences as Ethiopian Orthodox Christians.

3. **Advocacy and Awareness-Raising:** The diaspora has been a vocal advocate for the Ethiopian Orthodox Tewahedo Church, raising awareness about its rich heritage, its challenges, and its contributions to global Christianity. Through media outreach, lobbying efforts, and educational initiatives, they have brought the Church's concerns to the attention of policymakers, religious leaders, and the wider public. This advocacy has helped to raise the profile of Ethiopian Orthodoxy on the global stage and has fostered greater understanding and support for the Church.

Contributions to Global Religious and Cultural Landscapes:

1. **Establishment of Churches and Cultural Centers:** The diaspora has established numerous Ethiopian Orthodox churches and cultural centers

in various countries, providing a spiritual home for Ethiopians living abroad and a platform for cultural exchange. These institutions not only offer religious services and educational programs but also serve as community hubs, fostering a sense of belonging and preserving Ethiopian traditions in foreign lands.

2. **Academic and Intellectual Contributions:** Ethiopian Orthodox scholars and theologians in the diaspora have made significant contributions to the fields of religious studies, theology, and Ethiopian studies. Their research, publications, and teaching have enriched the academic discourse on Ethiopian Orthodoxy, shedding light on its history, doctrines, and cultural significance.

3. **Artistic and Cultural Expressions:** The diaspora has also enriched the global cultural landscape with its vibrant artistic and cultural expressions. Ethiopian Orthodox music, dance, and visual arts have gained international recognition, captivating audiences with their unique rhythms, melodies, and aesthetic sensibilities. Diaspora artists and musicians have also incorporated elements of their adopted cultures into their work, creating a fusion of Ethiopian and global artistic traditions.

4. **Social and Economic Contributions:** The Ethiopian diaspora has made significant contributions to the social and economic

development of their host countries. They have excelled in various fields, including medicine, engineering, business, and academia, contributing to the economic growth and social fabric of their adopted societies. Their entrepreneurial spirit and strong work ethic have also led to the establishment of successful businesses and community organizations that benefit both the diaspora and their host communities.

The Ethiopian Orthodox Tewahedo Church's diaspora, a vibrant and dynamic community, has played a crucial role in shaping global perceptions of Ethiopian Orthodoxy and enriching the world's religious and cultural landscapes. Through their unwavering faith, cultural resilience, and active engagement with their host societies, the diaspora has become a bridge between Ethiopia and the world, fostering understanding, appreciation, and dialogue. Their contributions, both spiritual and secular, have not only strengthened the Church's global presence but have also enriched the lives of countless individuals and communities around the world.

Support from the Mother Church:

- Role of the Ethiopian Orthodox Church in supporting diaspora communities.
- Programs and initiatives aimed at diaspora members.

The Ethiopian Orthodox Tewahedo Church, recognizing the unique challenges and opportunities presented by its diaspora communities, has taken on an active role in supporting and nurturing these far-flung branches of its spiritual family. This support, both material and spiritual, is a testament to the Church's commitment to its global flock and its understanding of the importance of maintaining a strong connection between the diaspora and the motherland.

Spiritual Guidance and Pastoral Care:

The Church plays a crucial role in providing spiritual guidance and pastoral care to diaspora communities. This includes the appointment of bishops and clergy to oversee diaspora churches, ensuring that the faithful have access to spiritual leaders who understand their unique needs and challenges. These leaders offer guidance on matters of faith, conduct religious services, administer sacraments, and provide counseling and support to individuals and families.

The Church also disseminates religious teachings and resources to the diaspora through various channels, such as websites, social media platforms, and printed materials. This ensures that diaspora members have access to the Church's teachings and can deepen their understanding of the faith, even if they are far from their homeland.

Financial and Material Support:

The Church provides financial and material support to diaspora communities, particularly those that are newly established or facing financial difficulties. This support can take various forms, such as funding the construction or renovation of churches, providing liturgical materials and supplies, and offering scholarships for theological education. The Church also supports charitable initiatives in the diaspora, such as food banks, shelters for the homeless, and programs for refugees and asylum seekers.

Educational and Cultural Programs:

The Church recognizes the importance of preserving Ethiopian culture and identity in the diaspora. It supports various educational and cultural programs aimed at teaching the Ge'ez language, Ethiopian history, and traditional arts and crafts. These programs not only help to maintain cultural continuity but also foster a sense of pride and belonging among diaspora members.

The Church also organizes conferences, seminars, and workshops on various topics related to Ethiopian Orthodoxy, providing a platform for intellectual exchange and spiritual growth. These events bring together scholars, clergy, and laity from Ethiopia and the diaspora, fostering a sense of global community and shared purpose.

Pilgrimage and Exchange Programs:

The Church encourages pilgrimage to holy sites in Ethiopia, such as the rock-hewn churches of Lalibela and the ancient monasteries of Debre Damo and Debre Libanos. These pilgrimages provide diaspora members with a unique opportunity to connect with their spiritual roots, deepen their faith, and experience the rich cultural heritage of their homeland.

The Church also facilitates exchange programs between Ethiopia and the diaspora, allowing clergy and laity to visit each other's communities, share experiences, and learn from one another. These exchanges foster mutual understanding and strengthen the bonds between the mother Church and its diaspora branches.

Specific Programs and Initiatives:

1. **Ethiopian Orthodox Tewahedo Church Development and Inter-Church Aid Commission (EOTC-DICAC):** This commission, established by the Holy Synod, is responsible for coordinating the Church's outreach and support to the diaspora. It provides financial assistance, educational resources, and pastoral guidance to Ethiopian Orthodox communities around the world.

2. **The Ethiopian Orthodox Tewahedo Church Sunday School Department:** This department develops and implements religious education programs for children and youth in the diaspora. It provides curricula, training materials, and resources to Sunday school

teachers, ensuring that the next generation is well-versed in the Church's teachings and traditions.

3. **The Ethiopian Orthodox Tewahedo Church Media and Communication Department:** This department utilizes various media platforms, including radio, television, and the internet, to reach out to the diaspora community. It produces and broadcasts religious programs, news, and cultural events, fostering a sense of connection and belonging among Ethiopians living abroad.

4. **The Ethiopian Orthodox Tewahedo Church Youth Fellowship:** This fellowship organizes youth-oriented programs and activities, such as retreats, conferences, and service projects. It aims to empower young people, strengthen their faith, and encourage their active participation in the life of the Church.

The Ethiopian Orthodox Tewahedo Church's support for its diaspora communities is a testament to its commitment to its global flock and its understanding of the challenges and opportunities presented by globalization. By providing spiritual guidance, financial support, educational resources, and opportunities for cultural exchange, the Church is ensuring that its rich traditions and values continue to thrive in the diaspora, enriching both the Ethiopian community and the broader society.

In this chapter, we have journeyed through the intricate landscape of the Ethiopian Orthodox Tewahedo Church's relationship with the Ethiopian state, a relationship that has been both symbiotic and fraught with tension throughout history. We have witnessed the Church's profound influence on political decisions, its role as a moral compass and advocate for social justice, and the dynamic interplay between church leaders and state officials. We have also explored the historical events that have shaped this relationship, from the early days of Aksum to the complexities of the modern era.

The Ethiopian Orthodox Tewahedo Church, with its deep-rooted traditions and unwavering faith, has not only shaped the spiritual lives of millions but has also played a pivotal role in the cultural tapestry of Ethiopia. In the next chapter, we will delve into the vibrant world of Ethiopian Orthodox arts, music, literature, and social customs, uncovering the intricate ways in which the Church's teachings, rituals, and values have permeated every aspect of Ethiopian life.

Chapter 10

Interfaith Relations

The Ethiopian Orthodox Tewahedo Church, despite its geographical isolation and unique theological traditions, has a long and complex history of interactions with other Christian denominations. These interactions, shaped by historical events, theological dialogues, and cultural exchanges, have played a crucial role in the Church's development and its relationship with the broader Christian world.

Historical Interactions

The Ethiopian Orthodox Tewahedo Church's earliest interactions were primarily with the Coptic Orthodox Church of Alexandria. This relationship, established in the 4th century with the consecration of St. Frumentius as the first bishop of Aksum by the Patriarch of Alexandria, laid the foundation for a close theological and liturgical bond between the two churches. For centuries, the Ethiopian Church relied on the Coptic Church for the appointment of its Abuna, or Patriarch, and the two churches maintained close ties in matters of doctrine and practice.

During the medieval period, the Ethiopian Orthodox Church encountered European Christianity through various channels, including diplomatic missions, trade relations, and the Crusades. These encounters exposed the Church to different theological perspectives and liturgical practices, leading to both intellectual exchange and occasional friction. The Ethiopian Church's adherence to Miaphysite Christology, which differed from the Chalcedonian Christology of Western churches, sometimes led to misunderstandings and disagreements. However, these encounters also fostered a sense of curiosity and openness to dialogue, as Ethiopian scholars and theologians sought to understand and engage with the broader Christian world.

The arrival of European missionaries in the 19th century, representing various Protestant denominations, marked a new chapter in the Church's interactions with other Christian traditions. These missionaries, while providing education and healthcare, also sought to convert Ethiopians to their own brand of Christianity. This led to both collaboration and competition, as the Ethiopian Orthodox Church sought to maintain its traditions and identity while also engaging with the new theological ideas and practices introduced by the missionaries.

Significant Events and Milestones

Several key events and milestones have shaped the Ethiopian Orthodox Tewahedo Church's interactions with other Christian denominations:

1. **Council of Florence (1439):** This ecumenical council, aimed at uniting the Eastern and Western churches, saw the participation of an Ethiopian delegation. While the council's efforts ultimately failed, it marked a significant moment of dialogue and exchange between the Ethiopian Orthodox Church and the broader Christian world.

2. **Arrival of Portuguese Missionaries (16th Century):** The arrival of Portuguese Jesuit missionaries in the 16th century led to a period of intense theological debate and conflict. The Jesuits, seeking to bring the Ethiopian Church under the authority of the Pope, challenged the Church's traditional beliefs and practices. This led to a period of religious persecution and ultimately the expulsion of the Jesuits from Ethiopia.

3. **Establishment of the World Council of Churches (1948):** The Ethiopian Orthodox Church joined the World Council of Churches in 1948, marking a significant step towards greater ecumenical engagement. This membership provided the Church with a platform for dialogue and cooperation with other Christian

denominations, fostering a spirit of unity and understanding.

4. **Visit of Pope John Paul II (1995):** The historic visit of Pope John Paul II to Ethiopia in 1995 was a landmark event in the Church's relationship with the Catholic Church. The Pope's visit, marked by mutual respect and a desire for reconciliation, opened a new chapter in ecumenical dialogue between the two churches.

Theological Dialogues

The Ethiopian Orthodox Tewahedo Church has actively participated in theological dialogues with other Christian denominations, seeking to address historical disagreements and find common ground on doctrinal matters. These dialogues, often facilitated by international organizations and ecumenical bodies, have focused on issues such as Christology, the nature of the Church, and the role of tradition and scripture.

One of the most significant theological dialogues has been the ongoing dialogue with the Oriental Orthodox Churches, a family of churches that share a common Miaphysite Christology. These dialogues have led to a greater understanding and appreciation of the shared theological heritage of these churches, paving the way for closer cooperation and collaboration.

The Ethiopian Orthodox Church has also engaged in dialogues with the Catholic Church, the Eastern Orthodox Churches, and various Protestant denominations. These dialogues, while acknowledging theological differences, have also highlighted areas of common ground and shared values, such as the belief in the Trinity, the authority of Scripture, and the importance of social justice.

Ecumenical Movements

- Participation in ecumenical movements.
- Impact on the Ethiopian Orthodox Church.

The Ethiopian Orthodox Tewahedo Church's engagement with the ecumenical movement, a global endeavor aimed at promoting Christian unity and cooperation, has been a journey marked by both cautious exploration and a steadfast commitment to its unique theological and liturgical heritage. This engagement, while navigating the complexities of interdenominational dialogue, has enriched the Church's understanding of the broader Christian landscape and opened new avenues for collaboration and mutual respect.

Participation in Ecumenical Movements:

The Ethiopian Orthodox Tewahedo Church's participation in the ecumenical movement began in the mid-20th century, a time of heightened global awareness and a growing desire for interfaith dialogue. In 1948, the Church joined the World Council of Churches (WCC), a fellowship of churches from diverse traditions that seeks to promote Christian unity and address global challenges. This membership provided the Church with a platform to engage with other Christian denominations, share its unique perspectives, and learn from the experiences of others.

The Church has also participated in various regional and international ecumenical organizations, such as the All Africa Conference of Churches (AACC) and the Middle East Council of Churches (MECC). These organizations provide forums for dialogue, cooperation, and joint action on issues of common concern, such as peacebuilding, social justice, and humanitarian aid.

In addition to its participation in formal ecumenical bodies, the Ethiopian Orthodox Tewahedo Church has also engaged in bilateral dialogues with other Christian denominations, such as the Catholic Church, the Oriental Orthodox Churches, and various Protestant denominations. These dialogues have focused on theological issues, historical disagreements, and the possibilities for greater understanding and cooperation.

Impact on the Ethiopian Orthodox Church:

The Church's engagement with the ecumenical movement has had a profound impact on its theological understanding, its relationship with other Christian traditions, and its role in the global religious landscape.

1. **Broadened Theological Perspectives:** The ecumenical movement has exposed the Church to a wider range of theological perspectives and interpretations, challenging its traditional understanding of scripture and doctrine. This exposure has led to a deeper engagement with theological issues, a re-examination of long-held beliefs, and a greater appreciation for the diversity of Christian traditions.

2. **Strengthened Inter-Church Relations:** The Church's participation in ecumenical dialogues has fostered greater understanding and cooperation with other Christian denominations. This has led to joint initiatives on issues such as peacebuilding, social justice, and humanitarian aid. It has also opened up new avenues for theological exchange and collaboration, enriching the Church's intellectual and spiritual life.

3. **Enhanced Global Visibility:** The Church's engagement with the ecumenical movement has raised its profile on the global stage, making it a recognized voice in international religious discourse. This has led to greater awareness and appreciation of the Church's unique traditions, its rich history, and its contributions to global Christianity.

4. **Challenges to Traditionalism:** The ecumenical movement has also posed challenges to the Church's traditionalism. Some members have expressed concerns about the potential erosion of the Church's unique identity and the dilution of its doctrines and practices. The Church has had to navigate these concerns carefully, balancing its commitment to ecumenical dialogue with its responsibility to preserve its heritage.

The Ethiopian Orthodox Tewahedo Church's participation in the ecumenical movement is a testament to its openness to dialogue, its willingness to learn from other traditions, and its commitment to Christian unity. While the journey has not been without its challenges, the Church's engagement with the ecumenical movement has enriched its theological understanding, strengthened its relationships with other Christian denominations, and enhanced its global visibility. As the Church continues to navigate the complexities of the modern world, its participation in the ecumenical movement will undoubtedly play a crucial role in shaping its future and its contribution to the broader Christian community.

Contemporary Conflicts

1. **Theological Disputes:** While the Ethiopian Orthodox Tewahedo Church maintains a strong sense of unity in its core doctrines, theological debates and disagreements continue to arise. These debates often center on the interpretation of scripture, the role of tradition, and the relationship between faith and reason. The Church's leadership has sought to address these disputes through dialogue, education, and the reaffirmation of its traditional teachings.

2. **Power Struggles and Governance Issues:** The Church's hierarchical structure and its relationship with the state have also been sources of tension and conflict. Disputes over the appointment of bishops, the management of Church finances, and the extent of the Church's autonomy have sometimes led to internal divisions and power struggles. The Church has sought to address these issues through reforms, greater transparency, and a renewed emphasis on accountability.

3. **Challenges from Other Religious Groups:** The rise of Pentecostalism and other evangelical movements in Ethiopia has posed a challenge to the Church's traditional dominance. These movements, with their emphasis on personal

salvation, emotional expression, and charismatic leadership, have attracted a growing number of followers, particularly among the youth. The Church has responded by strengthening its outreach programs, engaging in interfaith dialogue, and adapting its message to resonate with the needs and aspirations of a changing society.

Resolution Strategies and Outcomes:

The Ethiopian Orthodox Tewahedo Church has a long-standing tradition of resolving conflicts through dialogue, compromise, and reconciliation. This tradition, rooted in the teachings of Christ and the wisdom of the Church Fathers, has enabled the Church to navigate through turbulent times and emerge stronger and more united.

1. **Church Councils and Synods:** Throughout history, the Church has convened councils and synods to address theological disputes and resolve internal conflicts. These gatherings, bringing together clergy and laity from across the country, provide a platform for open dialogue, debate, and consensus-building. The decisions reached at these councils have often shaped the Church's doctrinal and liturgical practices, ensuring its unity and continuity.

2. **Mediation and Reconciliation:** The Church has also played a crucial role in mediating conflicts and promoting reconciliation in Ethiopian society. Religious leaders, respected for their wisdom and impartiality, have often served as mediators between warring factions, helping to de-escalate tensions and find peaceful solutions. The Church's emphasis on forgiveness, compassion, and love for one's neighbor has also been instrumental in healing the wounds of conflict and fostering reconciliation.

3. **Reforms and Renewal:** In response to internal and external challenges, the Church has undertaken various reforms aimed at strengthening its institutions, improving governance, and adapting to the changing needs of its followers. These reforms have included the establishment of theological colleges and seminaries, the development of new educational and social service programs, and the embrace of technology for outreach and communication.

The Ethiopian Orthodox Tewahedo Church's ability to navigate and resolve conflicts is a testament to its resilience, adaptability, and deep-rooted faith. By embracing dialogue, compromise, and reconciliation, the Church has not only overcome challenges but has also emerged stronger and more united. Its commitment to peace, justice, and the well-being of the Ethiopian people continues to be a guiding principle in its engagement with both internal and external conflicts.

Influence on Doctrine

- Impact of interfaith interactions on Ethiopian Orthodox doctrines.
- Changes and continuities in theological perspectives.

The Ethiopian Orthodox Tewahedo Church, while steadfast in its core doctrines, has not been immune to the winds of change brought about by interfaith interactions. Throughout its history, encounters with other Christian denominations and religious traditions have sparked theological dialogues, challenged traditional interpretations, and led to subtle shifts in perspectives. However, the Church has also demonstrated a remarkable ability to assimilate new ideas while preserving its unique theological identity.

Historical Influences:

The Church's early interactions with the Coptic Orthodox Church of Alexandria, its mother church, laid the foundation for its theological framework. The Coptic Church's influence is evident in the Ethiopian Orthodox Church's adoption of Miaphysite Christology, its liturgical practices, and its monastic traditions. However, the Ethiopian

Church also developed its own unique interpretations and practices, incorporating elements of local culture and tradition.

The arrival of European missionaries in the 16th century, particularly the Jesuits, presented a significant challenge to the Church's traditional doctrines. The Jesuits, with their emphasis on papal authority and scholastic theology, sought to bring the Ethiopian Church under the Roman Catholic fold. This led to intense theological debates and ultimately the expulsion of the Jesuits from Ethiopia. However, the encounter with Western Christianity also exposed the Ethiopian Church to new ideas and perspectives, prompting a period of theological reflection and reaffirmation of its own unique traditions.

Modern Era Dialogues:

In the 20th century, the Ethiopian Orthodox Tewahedo Church engaged in ecumenical dialogues with other Christian denominations, including the Oriental Orthodox Churches, the Catholic Church, and various Protestant denominations. These dialogues, while acknowledging theological differences, have also fostered mutual understanding and respect. They have led to a greater appreciation of the diversity of Christian traditions and have opened up new avenues for cooperation and collaboration.

Changes and Continuities:

The impact of interfaith interactions on Ethiopian Orthodox doctrines has been a complex and nuanced process. While the Church has remained steadfast in its core beliefs, such as Miaphysite Christology and the authority of scripture and tradition, there have been subtle shifts in theological perspectives.

One notable change has been a greater openness to dialogue and engagement with other Christian traditions. The Church has recognized the importance of ecumenical dialogue in promoting Christian unity and addressing global challenges. This openness has led to a more nuanced understanding of theological differences and a greater willingness to find common ground on issues of shared concern.

Another change has been a growing emphasis on contextual theology, which seeks to interpret and apply Christian teachings in the Ethiopian context. This approach recognizes the importance of cultural and historical factors in shaping theological understanding and seeks to make the faith relevant to the lived experiences of the Ethiopian people.

However, despite these changes, the Ethiopian Orthodox Tewahedo Church has maintained a strong sense of continuity with its ancient traditions. The Church's liturgical practices, its veneration of saints and angels, and its emphasis on communal worship remain deeply rooted in its historical and cultural heritage. The Ge'ez language, the liturgical language of the Church, continues to be a powerful symbol of its identity and a link to its ancient past.

The Ethiopian Orthodox Tewahedo Church's engagement with other Christian denominations has been a journey of both challenge and opportunity. It has led to a deeper understanding of the diversity of Christian traditions, a renewed appreciation for the Church's own unique heritage, and a greater commitment to dialogue and cooperation. As the Church continues to navigate the complexities of the modern world, its ability to adapt and evolve while remaining true to its core values will be crucial for its continued vitality and relevance.

Community Relations

- Local-level interfaith relations.
- Examples of successful interfaith cooperation.

At the grassroots level, the Ethiopian Orthodox Tewahedo Church has a long and rich history of coexistence and cooperation with other faith communities, particularly Muslims. This interfaith harmony, fostered by shared values, cultural understanding, and mutual respect, is a testament to the Ethiopian people's spirit of tolerance and their ability to find common ground despite religious differences.

Examples of Successful Interfaith Cooperation:

1. **Shared Religious Sites:** In many parts of Ethiopia, Christians and Muslims share religious sites, such as the rock-hewn churches of Lalibela, which are revered by both communities. This shared reverence for sacred spaces fosters a sense of mutual respect and understanding, transcending religious boundaries.

2. **Joint Celebrations and Festivals:** Religious festivals, such as Timkat and Eid al-Fitr, are often celebrated jointly by Christians and Muslims, with members of both communities participating in each other's festivities. This shared celebration of religious events strengthens social bonds and promotes interfaith harmony.

3. **Intermarriage and Family Ties:** Intermarriage between Christians and Muslims is not uncommon in Ethiopia, creating families with diverse religious backgrounds. These families often celebrate both Christian and Muslim holidays, respecting each other's beliefs and practices. This intermingling of faiths within families fosters tolerance and understanding from a young age.

4. **Community Initiatives:** Ethiopian Orthodox and Muslim communities often collaborate on community initiatives, such as building schools, hospitals, and wells. These joint efforts address

common needs and promote social development, transcending religious differences and fostering a sense of shared responsibility for the well-being of the community.

5. **Conflict Resolution and Peacebuilding:** Religious leaders from both communities often play a crucial role in resolving conflicts and promoting peace. They act as mediators, facilitators of dialogue, and advocates for reconciliation, drawing upon their spiritual authority and moral influence to bridge divides and foster understanding.

Factors Contributing to Interfaith Harmony:

Several factors have contributed to the harmonious relationship between the Ethiopian Orthodox Tewahedo Church and other faith communities:

1. **Shared History and Culture:** Ethiopia's long history of religious diversity and cultural exchange has fostered a climate of tolerance and mutual respect. The Church's willingness to adapt to local customs and incorporate elements of indigenous beliefs has also contributed to its acceptance by other faith communities.

2. **Emphasis on Communal Values:** Both the Ethiopian Orthodox Church and Islam emphasize communal values, such as hospitality, generosity,

and respect for elders. These shared values create a common ground for understanding and cooperation, transcending religious differences.

3. **Role of Religious Leaders:** Religious leaders from both communities play a crucial role in promoting interfaith dialogue and understanding. Their teachings emphasize tolerance, respect for diversity, and the importance of peaceful coexistence. They also actively participate in interfaith initiatives, setting an example for their followers.

4. **Government Policies:** The Ethiopian government has also played a role in promoting religious tolerance and interfaith harmony. The constitution guarantees freedom of religion, and the government has implemented policies aimed at protecting religious minorities and promoting interfaith dialogue.

The Ethiopian Orthodox Tewahedo Church's relationship with other faith communities, particularly Muslims, is a testament to the power of dialogue, understanding, and mutual respect. This interfaith harmony, nurtured by shared values, cultural understanding, and the leadership of religious figures, is a beacon of hope in a world often marred by religious conflict. As Ethiopia continues to evolve and face new challenges, the Church's commitment to interfaith cooperation will be crucial for building a more inclusive, peaceful, and prosperous society.

In this chapter, we have explored the Ethiopian Orthodox Tewahedo Church's complex and multifaceted relationship with other Christian denominations and faith communities. We have traced the historical interactions, theological dialogues, and ecumenical movements that have shaped the Church's engagement with the broader Christian world. We have also examined the challenges and conflicts that have arisen, as well as the Church's efforts to promote dialogue, understanding, and cooperation.

As we move forward, we will shift our focus to the Ethiopian Orthodox diaspora, a vibrant and dynamic community that has carried the flame of Ethiopian Orthodoxy to new lands. We will explore the history, challenges, and triumphs of these communities, their efforts to preserve their faith and cultural heritage, and their contributions to the global religious and cultural landscapes. Join us as we embark on this journey to discover the rich tapestry of the Ethiopian Orthodox diaspora and its enduring impact on the world.

Chapter 11

Future Perspectives

Preservation of Tradition Amidst Modernity

The Ethiopian Orthodox Tewahedo Church, one of the oldest Christian institutions in the world, has preserved its rich heritage and ancient traditions for centuries. Rooted in the teachings of the early Church and shaped by Ethiopia's unique culture, it faces the challenge of maintaining its identity while adapting to the demands of modernity. presented by technological, cultural, and societal advancements.

Historical Context of Tradition

The Ethiopian Orthodox Church has been the custodian of Ethiopia's spiritual and cultural identity since its introduction in the 4th century. The Church's traditions are deeply intertwined with Ethiopian life, from the sacred Ge'ez language used in liturgy to the elaborate church music (Zema), fasting practices, and intricate iconography. These elements are not only religious expressions but also cultural treasures that have withstood the test of time.

However, modernity presents both opportunities and challenges. Rapid technological advancements, globalization, and changing cultural dynamics compel the Church to find innovative ways to engage its followers without compromising its core values.

Opportunities in Technology

1. Digitalizing Ancient Manuscripts: The Ethiopian Orthodox Church possesses an unparalleled collection of ancient manuscripts, including the Ethiopian Bible, hymns, and theological treatises. Many of these texts are written in Ge'ez and housed in monasteries like Debre Libanos and Lalibela.

Digitalization of these manuscripts offers multiple benefits:

- **Preservation**: Safeguarding these irreplaceable texts from damage, theft, or loss.
- **Accessibility**: Providing global access to scholars, students, and faithful worldwide, thereby fostering greater understanding of the Church's theological and cultural contributions.

- **Education**: Allowing young Ethiopians and diaspora members to learn about their heritage through interactive platforms.

Collaborating with international institutions like UNESCO or establishing dedicated Church-funded digital libraries can make these treasures available to future generations.

2. Online Platforms for Preaching and Teaching

In an increasingly digital world, online platforms offer unprecedented opportunities for the Church to reach its followers.

- **Social Media and Streaming Services**: Platforms like YouTube, Facebook, and Instagram can be used to live-stream liturgies, provide teachings, and share messages from Church leaders.
- **Online Sunday School**: Virtual classes can help Ethiopian Orthodox communities in the diaspora preserve their faith and culture. Platforms like Zoom can host lessons on liturgy, Bible study, and traditional hymns, making them accessible even to those far from Ethiopian Orthodox centers.

An example of this is the use of YouTube channels by clergy to provide daily prayers, explanations of fasting rules, and discussions on Ethiopian Orthodox theology.

Such outreach efforts foster a sense of connection among the faithful, bridging geographic divides.

3. Developing Mobile Applications

Mobile technology is ubiquitous, and developing apps tailored to the Ethiopian Orthodox Church can provide followers with essential tools:

- **Ethiopian Orthodox Calendar App**: Incorporating saint days, fasting periods, and liturgical schedules can help the faithful navigate the Church year more effectively.
- **Prayer and Hymn Apps**: Providing access to daily prayers, Psalms, and traditional hymns in both Ge'ez and translated languages.
- **Educational Apps**: Apps that teach the Ge'ez language, Zema chants, or Orthodox theology can ensure that these traditions remain accessible to younger generations.

An example is the emergence of apps like "Tewahedo Calendar," which provides detailed information on fasting and saint commemorations, making Church practices easier to follow in busy, modern lives.

Cultural Adaptation Without Compromise

As Ethiopia undergoes social and economic changes, the Church faces the challenge of adapting to shifting cultural norms:

- **Youth Engagement**: Youth, particularly in urban areas and the diaspora, are increasingly exposed to secular ideologies. The Church must address their spiritual needs in a way that resonates with their realities. Organizing conferences, youth retreats, and cultural events can keep young people connected to their faith.

- **Modern Aesthetic in Churches**: While maintaining traditional architectural styles, new churches can integrate modern functionality, such as accessibility features and audio-visual equipment for sermons and hymns.

- **Engaging Women and Marginalized Groups**: Expanding roles for women in non-clerical areas, such as Sunday school teaching, choir leadership, or community outreach, can enhance inclusivity while upholding doctrinal principles.

Overcoming Challenges

The Church's efforts to modernize face significant hurdles:

1. **Resistance to Change**: Traditionalists may view modernization as a threat to the Church's authenticity. Effective communication emphasizing that new tools preserve rather than replace traditions is essential.

2. **Financial and Technical Limitations**: Digitalizing manuscripts, developing apps, and maintaining online platforms require expertise and resources. Partnerships with tech-savvy diaspora members or international organizations can alleviate these challenges.

3. **Language Barriers**: Many young Ethiopians in the diaspora may not understand Amharic or Ge'ez. Offering multilingual resources ensures broader accessibility.

A Vision for the Future

To preserve its traditions amidst modernity, the Ethiopian Orthodox Church must embrace innovation while remaining steadfast in its core beliefs. By leveraging technology, fostering inclusivity, and engaging youth, the Church can continue to serve as a pillar of Ethiopian identity. The path forward is one of balance—honoring the past while embracing the future.

This vision not only ensures the survival of Ethiopian Orthodoxy but also strengthens its role as a beacon of faith and culture in an ever-changing world.

Youth Engagement

Highlight the importance of reaching out to the younger generation in Ethiopia and the diaspora.

Example: Encouraging participation in Sunday schools, organizing youth retreats, and using social media to spread Orthodox teachings.

2. Challenges and Resilience

The Ethiopian Orthodox Tewahedo Church (EOTC) has endured centuries of trials, from external invasions and ideological challenges to modern threats such as religious persecution and secularism. Despite these hardships, the Church has demonstrated remarkable resilience, adapting to evolving contexts while preserving its spiritual and cultural essence. This section explores how the Church can address two key issues: **Religious Persecution and Unity** and **Secularism and Globalization**.

Religious Persecution and Unity

1. **Historical and Recent Challenges**: The EOTC has faced persecution since its inception. From the time of the early Christian martyrs under Roman rule to the pressures of Islam's spread in the region, the Church has stood firm in its faith.
   - **Medieval Era**: During periods of Islamic expansion, Ethiopian Christians often found themselves isolated, relying on their mountains and monasteries as safe havens.

- **20th and 21st Centuries**: More recently, the Church has faced challenges from political ideologies and inter-religious tensions.
- **Under the Derg Regime (1974-1991)**: The Marxist government sought to suppress religious institutions, confiscating Church lands and imprisoning clergy.
- **Post-1991 Era**: The political landscape brought new challenges. Rising ethnic nationalism and sectarian violence have led to targeted attacks on Orthodox Christians, including church burnings, the destruction of religious artifacts, and even loss of life.

2. **The Importance of Unity:** Religious persecution has underscored the need for unity—both within the Church and with other Christian denominations or faiths.

   - **Inter-Orthodox Solidarity**: Ethiopian Orthodox Christians can strengthen bonds with other Oriental Orthodox Churches (such as the Coptic, Armenian, and Syriac Churches) through theological dialogue, shared liturgical practices, and cooperative humanitarian efforts.
   - **Ecumenical and Interfaith Dialogues**: Building bridges with other Christian denominations and Islamic communities in Ethiopia is essential to promote peace. Collaborative efforts to address common

societal issues—such as poverty, education, and health care—can help mitigate religious tensions.

- **Lessons from History**: The Church's historical resilience in the face of invasions and ideological suppression demonstrates that faith communities thrive when they prioritize unity and forgiveness over division.

Addressing Secularism and Globalization

1. **The Challenge of Secularism**: The rise of secular ideologies in Ethiopia and the diaspora poses significant challenges:
   - **Erosion of Faith**: Younger generations, exposed to secular philosophies through education, media, and globalization, may become detached from their faith.
   - **Moral Relativism**: Secularism often promotes values that conflict with Orthodox teachings, such as relativism and materialism.
   - **Marginalization**: Faith-based voices may be sidelined in public discourse, diminishing the Church's influence on national and cultural identity.
2. **Globalization's Dual Edge**: While globalization connects people and cultures, it also poses risks to the unique identity of the Ethiopian Orthodox Church:

- **Cultural Homogenization**: The dominance of Western culture through media and technology can dilute traditional Ethiopian values and practices.
- **Opportunities for Outreach**: Conversely, globalization allows the Church to share its unique heritage with the world. Ethiopian Orthodox Christianity has the potential to inspire faith and cultural appreciation on a global scale.

3. **Strategies for Maintaining Identity:** The EOTC can address these challenges through proactive engagement and adaptation:
   - **Youth Outreach**:
     - Educating young people about the Church's rich history, theology, and liturgical practices can foster a sense of pride and belonging.
     - Organizing retreats, cultural events, and discussion forums that blend modern formats with Orthodox teachings can make faith accessible to the next generation.
   - **Education and Scholarship:**
     - Establishing theological schools and research institutions that explore the intersection of faith and contemporary issues can prepare clergy and lay leaders to address modern challenges.

- Publishing works in multiple languages ensures that the Church's teachings reach diverse audiences, both in Ethiopia and abroad.
- **Digital Presence**:
  - Using social media and digital platforms to share sermons, liturgical music, and Bible study materials can reach the diaspora and tech-savvy youth.
  - Developing online courses and apps dedicated to Ge'ez language, Orthodox theology, and Ethiopian Church history can deepen engagement.

4. **The Church as a Moral Voice**: In a rapidly changing world, the Church can serve as a moral compass:
   - **Promoting Ethical Leadership**: By encouraging integrity and accountability among Ethiopia's leaders, the Church can contribute to national development while staying true to its spiritual mission.
   - **Environmental Stewardship**: The Church can draw on Biblical principles to advocate for the preservation of Ethiopia's environment, emphasizing the moral responsibility to care for creation.

3. Opportunities for Growth

The Ethiopian Orthodox Tewahedo Church (EOTC) is facing a dynamic and rapidly changing world, but it also has abundant opportunities for growth, both in the homeland and within the global diaspora. As the Church navigates challenges in the modern era, it has the potential to expand its influence through both financial and spiritual contributions, as well as social and educational outreach. These opportunities can help the Church strengthen its mission and ensure its relevance and sustainability for generations to come.

1. Diaspora Contributions

a. **Financial and Spiritual Support**: The Ethiopian diaspora, estimated to number several million people across the globe, holds a significant position in helping sustain the Church financially and spiritually. Many members of the diaspora maintain deep ties to the Church, whether through religious practices, cultural preservation, or philanthropy.

   o **Financial Contributions**: The diaspora community, especially in North America, Europe, and the Middle East, can play a pivotal role in funding the Church's activities in Ethiopia and abroad.

- **Building Churches and Monasteries**: With the financial support of the diaspora, the Church can build more churches and monasteries both within Ethiopia and in diaspora communities, ensuring the continuity of religious practices.
- **Sustaining Clergy and Ministries**: Contributions can be used to support the training and employment of clergy, as well as help sustain social welfare programs run by the Church in Ethiopia and abroad.
- **Spiritual Engagement**: The diaspora offers an opportunity to deepen spiritual engagement by creating spaces for Orthodox Christian practices in diverse cultural contexts.
  - **Mentorship Programs**: The diaspora can offer mentorship programs for young deacons and priests, fostering the next generation of Church leaders. By sharing their experiences and knowledge of living the faith in a multicultural world, diaspora members can guide young clergy in their spiritual and professional development.
  - **Strengthening Church Communities**: Diaspora communities can also serve as spiritual centers for local populations, providing a place for Ethiopians abroad to stay connected to their heritage and faith. Regular services,

cultural events, and community gatherings offer a space to nurture spiritual lives while combating the alienation many immigrants face.

b. **Establishing Ethiopian Orthodox Centers Worldwide**
   - **Creating Centers of Faith**: The establishment of Ethiopian Orthodox centers in key cities around the world can strengthen the visibility of the Church. These centers can serve as focal points for both spiritual and cultural preservation.
   - **Cultural Promotion**: These centers can promote Ethiopian arts, music, language, and culture, which are important elements of the Orthodox faith. They can serve as hubs where members of the diaspora reconnect with their roots, while also providing spaces for non-Ethiopian Orthodox Christians to learn about the Church's traditions.
   - **Unity Between Diaspora and Homeland**: Establishing stronger connections between the diaspora and communities back home is crucial. Diaspora-driven initiatives, such as educational programs, health services, and charitable projects, can directly support the Ethiopian Orthodox community in Ethiopia.

- o **Networking and Global Presence**: Through these global centers, the Church can network with other Christian denominations, religious organizations, and humanitarian groups, facilitating interfaith dialogue, cooperation on social issues, and mutual support.

2. Social and Educational Outreach

- A. **Expanding Social Services:** The Ethiopian Orthodox Church has a long history of community service and charitable work, which can be further expanded in the modern era. By focusing on social services, the Church can remain deeply integrated into the social fabric of both Ethiopia and the global community, demonstrating the connection between faith and practical action.
  - o **Building Schools and Educational Institutions**:
    - The EOTC has historically placed a significant emphasis on education, with monasteries and churches often serving as centers of learning. The Church can expand this legacy by building more schools, particularly in rural and underserved areas of Ethiopia. These

institutions can offer high-quality education while also integrating Orthodox Christian values and teachings into the curriculum.

- Establishing Orthodox schools in diaspora communities can provide children with a strong sense of identity and continuity. These schools can serve as centers for learning, cultural exchange, and the development of strong Orthodox Christian communities among younger generations.

- **Establishing Hospitals and Health Clinics**:
  - Building hospitals and health clinics in Ethiopia, particularly in remote regions, can address the nation's pressing health care needs. Many Ethiopian Orthodox monasteries and Church-affiliated organizations already run health programs; expanding these services will enhance the Church's role in improving the quality of life for many Ethiopians.
  - Hospitals can focus not only on providing medical services but also on promoting wellness, preventative care, and public health initiatives rooted in Orthodox Christian teachings about the sanctity of life and care for the poor.

- **Charitable Organizations and Social Welfare**:
  - The Church has always been at the forefront of helping the less fortunate, and it can expand these efforts to address the growing needs of displaced people, refugees, and the marginalized.
  - Through food distribution, clean water initiatives, orphanages, and shelters for the homeless, the Church can continue to be a force for good in Ethiopia and beyond. These initiatives help to embody Christ's teachings of love and charity, acting as a visible demonstration of faith in action.

B. **Partnerships for Community Development**
  - **Collaborating with Government and NGOs**: While the Church can independently run programs, partnerships with governmental bodies, international NGOs, and other faith-based organizations can increase the reach and effectiveness of these social services. By collaborating, the Church can provide more comprehensive support to the people it serves.
  - **Rural Development**: The Church's social outreach programs could also focus on rural development projects, helping to provide access to clean water, sanitation, and agriculture, supporting sustainable livelihoods

in areas where the government and other organizations may not have strong reach.
- o **Promoting Gender Equality**: The Church can also strengthen its role in advocating for gender equality and women's empowerment, ensuring that women in Ethiopian Orthodox communities have access to education, healthcare, and economic opportunities. This outreach can help the Church align with international goals for social justice while preserving its cultural identity.

4. Theology and Innovation

1. Engaging with Theological Debates

A. Maintaining Theological Foundations
- o The Ethiopian Orthodox Tewahedo Church (EOTC) is deeply rooted in its ancient theological traditions, such as the Nicene Creed, the teachings of the Church Fathers, and its interpretation of the Scriptures.
- o While engaging with contemporary debates, the Church must ensure its theological integrity remains intact, serving as a foundation for dialogue rather than compromise.

B. Addressing Environmental Stewardship

- **Theological Basis**: Highlight biblical principles such as stewardship of creation (Genesis 2:15) and the sanctity of God's creation.
- **Practical Action**: The Church can take a leadership role in promoting environmental conservation by planting trees, reducing pollution, and educating communities on sustainable living.
- **Global Advocacy**: EOTC can contribute to international discussions on climate change by emphasizing its theological perspective on humanity's responsibility to care for the Earth.

C. **Exploring Gender Roles**
- **Balancing Tradition and Progress**: The Church must navigate the sensitive topic of gender roles while maintaining its traditional values.
  - For example, it can encourage greater participation of women in non-sacramental roles, such as teaching, charity work, and church administration.
- **Women in Leadership**: Recognize and elevate the historical contributions of women in Ethiopian Orthodox history, such as Saint Walatta Petros, as a way to inspire contemporary involvement.

D. **Promoting Human Rights**

- **Orthodox Teaching and Human Dignity**: Reinforce the Church's teachings that all human beings are created in the image of God (Genesis 1:27), which forms the foundation for defending human rights.
- **Advocacy Against Injustice**:
  - The Church can engage in addressing human rights violations, such as ethnic violence, displacement, and religious persecution.
  - Develop a theology of reconciliation and peace to guide both internal Church practices and its interaction with society.

2. Training and Education for Clergy

A. **Importance of Advanced Theological Training**
  - **Contemporary Challenges**: Clergy need advanced training to address modern issues like mental health, interfaith dialogue, and technology's impact on spirituality.
  - **Modern Theology Schools**: Strengthening seminaries and theological institutions with updated curricula, including courses on pastoral counseling, social justice, and bioethics.

B. **Continuous Education Programs**
  - **Workshops and Seminars**: Regular workshops for priests, deacons, and Sunday

School teachers on emerging topics such as artificial intelligence, globalization, and cultural shifts.

- **Online Learning Platforms**: Develop virtual platforms for clergy to access training materials, theological resources, and live instruction.
- **International Exchange**: Facilitate exchange programs with other Orthodox or Christian seminaries to broaden perspectives and learn new methodologies.

C. **Enhancing Pastoral Skills**

- **Empathy and Communication**: Equip clergy with skills to handle complex pastoral cases, such as counseling individuals facing mental health crises or marital conflicts.
- **Engaging Youth and the Diaspora**: Create training modules that teach clergy how to connect with younger generations, especially those living in the diaspora, who may struggle to reconcile their Ethiopian Orthodox heritage with modern secular environments.

D. **Technology Integration in Clergy Education**

- **Digital Literacy**: Train clergy in using digital tools to preach, teach, and manage Church operations effectively.

- **Digital Outreach**: Encourage the use of apps, social media, and video platforms to reach wider audiences, including those who cannot attend services in person.

The Path Forward

By thoughtfully engaging with contemporary theological debates and investing in advanced training and education for clergy, the Ethiopian Orthodox Tewahedo Church can maintain its theological integrity while addressing the needs of the modern world. This dual approach ensures the Church remains a beacon of spiritual wisdom, a guardian of tradition, and an advocate for justice in a rapidly changing global landscape.

5. Vision for Unity and Global Orthodoxy

1. Strengthening Global Orthodoxy

A. **Historical Roots of Unity**
- The Ethiopian Orthodox Tewahedo Church (EOTC) shares a rich history with other Orthodox and Oriental Orthodox Churches, rooted in early Christian councils and theological debates.
- The 451 AD Council of Chalcedon marked a division, but today there are ongoing efforts to foster unity and theological understanding

between the Oriental Orthodox Churches (including EOTC) and Eastern Orthodox Churches.

B. **Pan-Orthodox Councils and Conferences**
   - **Participating in Global Orthodox Dialogues**:
     - The EOTC has a unique opportunity to bring its ancient liturgical traditions, biblical interpretations, and cultural contributions to pan-Orthodox gatherings.
     - Highlight Ethiopia's rich theological heritage, such as its ancient scriptural translations and hymnal compositions.
   - **Advancing Shared Goals**:
     - Collaborating with other Orthodox Churches on global issues such as religious persecution, migration, and the preservation of Christian holy sites.
     - Engaging in theological dialogues to bridge doctrinal differences and enhance mutual respect.

C. **Sharing Ethiopia's Unique Traditions**
   - **Liturgical Music and Chant**: Introduce the spiritual depth of the *Zema* chants and their role in Ethiopian worship.
   - **Fasting Practices**: Highlight Ethiopia's distinct fasting traditions as a model for spiritual discipline.

- o **Cultural Integration**: Emphasize Ethiopia's ability to merge Christian teachings with local culture, serving as an example for other Orthodox communities.

D. **Emphasizing Unity in Diversity**
  - o Promote the idea that diversity in tradition, liturgy, and cultural expression enriches Orthodoxy rather than divides it.
  - o Encourage regular inter-Orthodox visits and pilgrimages to build connections and mutual appreciation.

2. Role in African Christianity

A. **Leadership in African Christian Unity**
  - o The EOTC, as one of the oldest Christian institutions in Africa, has a responsibility to lead the movement for unity among African churches.
    - Host pan-African Christian forums focusing on theological, social, and cultural issues.
    - Advocate for a unified Christian voice in addressing challenges such as religious extremism and interfaith conflicts.

B. **Addressing Poverty and Social Injustice**
   - **Spiritual and Practical Solutions**:
     - The Church can offer moral guidance while partnering with organizations to provide tangible solutions to poverty, education gaps, and healthcare crises.
     - Examples: Building schools, providing scholarships, and supporting microfinance projects in underserved communities.
   - **Advocacy for Justice**: Use the Church's influence to champion human rights, fight corruption, and promote peace in conflict zones across Africa.

C. **Reviving African Identity through Christianity**
   - Encourage African Christians to take pride in their unique heritage, countering the narrative that Christianity is a foreign religion in Africa.
   - Collaborate with other African churches to rediscover and preserve indigenous Christian traditions and historical contributions.

D. **Training and Empowering Leaders**
   - **Education for Clergy and Lay Leaders**: Establish theological training centers and leadership programs across Africa.
   - **Youth Engagement**: Create programs that inspire young Africans to take active roles in the Church, emphasizing their potential to

lead Africa's future spiritual and social renewal.

3. Envisioning a Global Role

A. **Expanding the Church's Reach**
- Establish Ethiopian Orthodox churches and cultural centers in major African cities and diaspora communities worldwide.
- Promote Ethiopian Orthodox Christianity as a bridge between African spirituality and global Christianity.

B. **Collaborative Projects with Other Churches**
- Partner with African Protestant, Catholic, and Pentecostal churches to tackle common challenges such as famine, epidemics, and political instability.
- Lead ecumenical efforts to craft a unified Christian response to global issues like climate change and human trafficking.

Conclusion: A Global Church with African Roots

The Ethiopian Orthodox Tewahedo Church stands as a testament to the endurance of faith amidst trials. By strengthening ties with global Orthodoxy and embracing its leadership role in African Christianity, the EOTC can inspire unity, address pressing societal challenges, and solidify its place as a guiding light for Christians worldwide. In doing so, it will continue to honor its ancient legacy while shaping the future of Christianity on a global stage.

Bibliography

The richness and depth of the Ethiopian Orthodox Tewahedo Church, one of the oldest Christian traditions in the world, are thoroughly documented through various sources that provide historical, theological, and cultural insights. The references listed below are integral to understanding the multifaceted aspects of the Church as presented in this book. These sources include scholarly articles, historical texts, and contemporary analyses, offering a comprehensive view of the Ethiopian Orthodox faith and its significant role in shaping Ethiopian society and culture.

1. **Encyclopedia Britannica.** (n.d.). Ethiopian Orthodox Tewahedo Church. In Encyclopedia Britannica online. Retrieved from https://www.britannica.com/topic/Ethiopian-Orthodox-Tewahedo-Church

2. **Ethiopian Orthodox Church.** (n.d.). The Ethiopian Orthodox Tewahedo Church. Retrieved from https://ethiopianorthodox.org/

3. **Wikipedia.** (n.d.). Ethiopian Orthodox Tewahedo Church. In Wikipedia. Retrieved from https://en.wikipedia.org/wiki/Ethiopian_Orthodox_Tewahedo_Church

4. **Wikipedia.** (n.d.). Miaphysitism. In Wikipedia. Retrieved from https://en.wikipedia.org/wiki/Miaphysitism

5. **Pankhurst, R.** (1998). The Ethiopians: A History. Oxford: Blackwell Publishing.

6. **Sergew Hable Sellassie.** (1972). Ancient and Medieval Ethiopian History to 1270. Addis Ababa: United Printers.

7. **Tamrat, T.** (1972). Church and State in Ethiopia, 1270-1527. Oxford: Clarendon Press.

8. **Binns, J.** (2016). The Orthodox Church of Ethiopia: A History. London: I.B. Tauris.

9. **Erlich, H.** (1996). The Cross and Its Shadow: Explorations in Ethiopian Art and Culture. Washington, D.C.: The National Gallery of Art.

10. **Kaplan, S.** (1984). The Monastic Holy Man and the Christianization of Early Solomonic Ethiopia. Wiesbaden: Harrassowitz Verlag.

11. **Munro-Hay, S. C.** (1991). Aksum: An African Civilization of Late Antiquity. Edinburgh: Edinburgh University Press.

12. **Phillipson, D. W.** (2009). Ancient Churches of Ethiopia: Fourth-Fourteenth Centuries. New Haven: Yale University Press.

13. **Buxton, D.** (1970). The Abyssinians. New York: Praeger Publishers.

14. **Budge, E. A. Wallis.** (1928). A History of Ethiopia: Nubia and Abyssinia. London: Methuen & Co. Ltd.

15. **Taddesse Tamrat.** (2009). Kebra Nagast (The Glory of Kings). Translated by Miguel F. Brooks. Lawrenceville: Red Sea Press.

16. **Henze, P. B.** (2000). Layers of Time: A History of Ethiopia. New York: Palgrave.

17. **Marcus, H. G.** (1994). A History of Ethiopia. Berkeley: University of California Press.

18. **Beyene, T.** (2006). Ethiopian Orthodox Church: Faith and Culture. Addis Ababa: Shama Books.

19. **Haile Gebriel Dagne.** (2009). The Ethiopian Orthodox Church: Its History, Dogma, and Spiritual Life. New Jersey: Gorgias Press.

20. **Cowley, R. W.** (1974). The Traditional Interpretation of the Apocalypse of St. John in the Ethiopian Orthodox Church. Cambridge: Harvard University Press.

21. **Pankhurst, R.** (2001). The Ethiopian Borderlands: Essays in Regional History from Ancient Times to the End of the 18th Century. Lawrenceville: Red Sea Press.

22. **Chojnacki, S.** (1983). Major Themes in Ethiopian Painting: Indigenous Tradition, the Influence of Foreign Models, and Their Adaptation. Wiesbaden: Franz Steiner Verlag.

23. **Gerster, G.** (1972). Churches in Rock: Early Christian Art in Ethiopia. London: Phaidon Press.

24. **Grierson, R. & Munro-Hay, S.** (1999). The Ark of the Covenant. London: Weidenfeld & Nicolson.

25. **Hahn, M.** (2007). The Ethiopian Orthodox Tewahedo Church: Its History, Life and Spiritual Culture. New York: Orthodox Research Institute.

26. **Pankhurst, R.** (2005). Historic Images of Ethiopia. Addis Ababa: Shama Books.

27. **Pankhurst, R.** (1955). Ethiopia: A Cultural History. Essex: Lalibela House.

28. **Ullendorff, E.** (1988). The Ethiopians: An Introduction to Country and People. London: Oxford University Press.

29. **Heldman, M.** (1994). The Marian Icons of the Painter Fré Seyoum of Gunda Gunde. Wiesbaden: Harrassowitz Verlag.

30. **Pankhurst, R.** (1997). The Ethiopian Royal Chronicles. Addis Ababa: Oxford University Press.

31. **Mercier, J.** (1979). Ethiopian Magic Scrolls. New York: George Braziller, Inc.

32. **Anderson, A.** (2021). The Ethiopian Orthodox Church: An Overview. University of Sherbrooke. Retrieved from University of Sherbrooke

33. **Afework, H.** (2003). Ethiopian Christianity: The Origins and Development of the Ethiopian Orthodox Church. Nairobi: East African Educational Publishers.

34. **Crummey, D.** (2000). Land and Society in the Christian Kingdom of Ethiopia: From the Thirteenth to the Twentieth Century. Urbana: University of Illinois Press.

35. **Shelemay, K.** (1986). Music, Ritual, and Falasha History. Ann Arbor: University of Michigan Press.

36. **Fiaccadori, G.** (1996). Christianity in Aksum. In Africa: The Journal of the International African Institute. Edinburgh: Edinburgh University Press.

37. **Getatchew, H.** (1998). The African Ark: Peoples and Ancient Cultures of Ethiopia and Eritrea. New York: Abbeville Press.

38. **Levine, D.** (1965). Wax and Gold: Tradition and Innovation in Ethiopian Culture. Chicago: University of Chicago Press.

39. **Rassam, M.** (2010). The Legacy of Axum: Continuity and Change in Northeast Africa. Oxford: Oxford University Press.

40. **Isaac, E.** (1972). The Ethiopian Orthodox Tewahedo Church: The Evolution of the Ethos of a Traditional Christian Society. Washington, D.C.: The Catholic University of America Press.

41. **Kaplan, S.** (1992). The Beta Israel: Falasha in Ethiopia. New York: Routledge.

42. **Tsega, E.** (2001). The Ethiopian Monastic Tradition: Its Role and Impact on the Socio-cultural Fabric of Ethiopia. Addis Ababa: Addis Ababa University Press.

43. **Selassie, S.** (1989). Ancient and Medieval Ethiopian History to 1270. Lawrenceville: Red Sea Press.

44. **Monneret de Villard, U.** (1938). Le Chiese Monolitiche Dell'Etiopia. Rome: Instituto di Studi Orientale.

45. **Kefyalew, B.** (2002). Pilgrimage to the Holy Land: The Ethiopian Perspective. Jerusalem: Jerusalem Publishing.

46. **Peacock, A.** (2012). Early Islamic and Christian Societies in Northeast Africa: History, Culture, and Trade. London: I.B. Tauris.

47. **Pankhurst, R.** (1982). The History of Famine and Epidemics in Ethiopia Prior to the Twentieth Century. Addis Ababa: Addis Ababa University Press.

48. **Cerulli, E.** (1943). Etiopi in Palestina: Storia della Comunita Etiopica di Gerusalemme. Rome: Societa' Italiana per l'Organizzazione Internazionale.

49. **Carmichael, J.** (1992). The Eastern Christian Traditions: Ethiopian Christianity. New York: Columbia University Press.

50. **Johnson, S.** (2008). The Role of Women in the Ethiopian Orthodox Church. Nairobi: East African Educational Publishers.

375

These references serve as a robust foundation for the information presented in this book. They provide invaluable insights into the historical evolution, theological doctrines, and cultural significance of the Ethiopian Orthodox Tewahedo Church, ensuring a comprehensive understanding of its profound impact on Ethiopia and beyond.

Some last words

In the tapestry of faith, few threads are as vibrant and enduring as those woven by the Ethiopian Orthodox Tewahedo Church. This ancient institution, with its roots tracing back to the earliest days of Christianity, has not only shaped the spiritual landscape of Ethiopia but has also left an indelible mark on its culture, society, and national identity.

Throughout this book, we have embarked on a captivating journey through the rich tapestry of Ethiopian Orthodoxy. We have traced its historical roots, from the legendary arrival of the Apostle Matthew to the establishment of the Church under the guidance of St. Frumentius. We have witnessed its evolution through the ages, from the glory days of the Aksumite Empire to the challenges and triumphs of the modern era.

We have delved into the depths of its unique doctrines and beliefs, exploring the mysteries of the Holy Trinity, the profound significance of Miaphysite Christology, and the vibrant role of the Holy Spirit in the life of the Church. We have witnessed the beauty and power of its liturgical traditions, the rhythmic chants and hymns that transport the faithful into the heart of divine mystery, and the intricate rituals that mark the passage of time and the seasons of the soul.

We have explored the Church's profound impact on Ethiopian culture, from its influence on art, music, and literature to its shaping of social customs, values, and daily life. We have witnessed the enduring power of its oral traditions, the architectural marvels of its churches and monasteries, and the vibrant celebrations of its festivals.

We have also confronted the challenges and opportunities that the Church faces in the modern world. We have examined the impact of globalization, modernization, and internal conflicts on its traditions and practices. We have also explored the Church's responses to these challenges, its efforts to adapt and evolve while remaining true to its core values and teachings.

As we conclude this journey, we are left with a profound appreciation for the Ethiopian Orthodox Tewahedo Church's enduring legacy and its continued relevance in the 21st century. It is a Church that has weathered the storms of history, emerging stronger and more resilient with each passing generation. It is a Church that has embraced change while remaining steadfast in its faith, a Church that has adapted to the modern world while preserving its ancient traditions.

The Ethiopian Orthodox Tewahedo Church is not merely a religious institution; it is a living testament to the power of faith, the richness of cultural heritage, and the resilience of the human spirit. It is a beacon of hope and inspiration for millions of Ethiopians, both at home and in the diaspora, guiding them on their spiritual journey and shaping their understanding of the world.

As we bid farewell to this exploration of the Ethiopian Orthodox Tewahedo Church, we invite you to continue your own journey of discovery. May the insights and reflections shared in this book inspire you to delve deeper into the rich tapestry of this ancient faith, to appreciate its unique contributions to global Christianity, and to embrace the diversity and beauty of human spiritual expression.